I0760123

The Crimes that Inspired Agatha Christie

This book is dedicated to Renate Ruth

THE CRIMES THAT INSPIRED AGATHA CHRISTIE

THE FACTS BEHIND THE FICTION

JONATHAN OATES
AND
ANNA-LENA BERG

First published in Great Britain in 2025 by
PEN AND SWORD TRUE CRIME
An imprint of
Pen & Sword Books Limited
Yorkshire – Philadelphia

ISBN 978 1 03612 654 4

A CIP catalogue record for this book is available from the British Library.

Typeset in Times New Roman 11/14 by SJmagic DESIGN SERVICES, India.
Printed and bound in the UK by CPI Group (UK) Ltd.

The Publisher's authorised representative in the EU for product safety is Authorised Rep Compliance Ltd., Ground Floor, 71 Lower Baggot Street,
Dublin D02 P593, Ireland.
www.arccompliance.com

For a complete list of Pen & Sword titles please contact
PEN & SWORD BOOKS LIMITED
George House, Units 12 & 13, Beevor Street, Off Pontefract Road,
Barnsley, South Yorkshire, S71 1HN, England
E-mail: enquiries@pen-and-sword.co.uk
Website: www.pen-and-sword.co.uk

or

PEN AND SWORD BOOKS
1950 Lawrence Rd, Havertown, PA 19083, USA
E-mail: uspen-and-sword@casematepublishers.com
Website: www.penandswordbooks.com

Contents

Introduction

The works of Agatha Christie need no introduction. Quite apart from her phenomenal output of novels, short stories and plays, most have been televised or filmed. Sometimes twice or three times in the case of some of the most popular ones. Her best known fictional creations have been the retired Belgian sleuth Hercule Poirot and the elderly English spinster, Miss Jane Marple, though there are other detectives, mostly one offs.

The stories are mostly whodunnits; a crime occurs, usually a murder, and perhaps others follow. The detective, usually an amateur, talks to suspects and follows clues. By the end of the story the mystery will be solved, and justice is done, often after a trap is set or the suspects are brought together in a drawing room or library. The characters are almost all middle or upper middle class, independently wealthy men and women or from the ranks of the professional classes, sometimes retired. There is often a sprinkling of lawyers, doctors, actors, military men and even authors of detective fiction. Crimes are committed for good and rational reasons; money, fear of exposure, passion and revenge. The settings are often country houses or luxury forms of transport abroad. The number of suspects is usually a closed one. Methods of murder are often poison, and sadism and lust rarely feature. Violence is usually minimal. The killer is clever enough to evade initial exposure but never sufficiently so to get away with it. The stories are clever puzzles to entertain the reader: morality tales and must be judged thus.

Compare this to real life crime. Most murders are quickly solved, not due to brilliance in detection, but because the solutions are obvious. Killers confess or commit suicide. They leave behind clues or are witnessed. Their killings are not meticulously planned with alibis but are often on the spur of the moment as a result of anger, sometimes fuelled by drink or drugs. They may result from mental illness. Most are the result of domestic quarrels or are committed as the result of furthering another crime, often theft. In some rare cases, where strangers kill one another, they can be all but unsolvable. There is not always a neat solution as in Agatha Christie's fiction. And most criminals and victims are from the ranks of the working class and the poor. Detection is left to the professionals, not gifted amateur geniuses, with forensic science playing an increasing part in their solution.

In an article published in 1956 Christie stated, 'I never take my stories from real life' and in her autobiography, 'it is no good thinking about real people – you must create your characters for yourself'. This is not quite the case. 'Fiction is founded on fact' as Poirot tells Katherine Grey in *The Mystery of the Blue Train* (1928). She certainly often referred to real life criminals in her fiction, either explicitly or by allusion. Some of these are still relatively well known: Dr Crippen and Jack the Ripper to name but two. Others are less well known – few have heard of Elizabeth Canning, referred to in *Lord Edgware Dies* or that of Katie Whistance, alluded to in *Mrs McGinty's Dead.* They date from the Georgian era until the 1960s and most would have been well known both to Christie and to many of the readers of the time. It is certainly expected that they would have done so, whereas modern readers who are not experts on true crime will mostly fail to do so. It is also worth noting that as with much true crime until relatively recently the emphasis in these stories when it comes to true crime references is on the criminals not the victims; and the latter are very seldom referred to and never by name.

Often real criminals are explicitly named. Sometimes they are referred to implicitly, with a description of their crimes only, so making their identity clear to the informed reader. So whereas the book *Mrs McGinty's Dead* does not mention Dr Crippen, the description of the historic crime of a henpecked town clerk and his young mistress makes it clear who the characters are really talking about.

There are also instances where fiction is later mirrored by tragic fact, with some books inadvertently anticipating real crimes and criminals. There are also instances of real crimes which are not explicitly referenced, but the plots and commentary within the stories seem to have been inspired by them and this is certainly the case with some of the later novels, or so it seems to these authors.

As well as outlining the real criminals and their crimes, the book will also show how these are utilised as part of the plot of the stories. Often they are integral and the comparisons that can be made between reality and fiction are noteworthy. Other times the reference is only in passing and so these chapters are shorter. In some cases there are several stories which reference the same real life miscreant. Dr Crippen, Major Armstrong, Lizzie Borden and George Joseph Smith clearly had a fascination for Christie and are remarked upon in several books.

It will also discuss the accuracy of the references made. One character refers to Major Armstrong as a mass poisoner, though he was not, and in one book Crippen is described as an unassuming polite little man, and while this is or was a popular assumption, this is questionable.

Using real crime in fiction is not a trait unique to Agatha Christie. Other detective novelists do likewise. Sir Arthur Conan Doyle has Sherlock Holmes cite Doctors Palmer and Pritchard in *The Adventure of the Speckled Band.* Dorothy L. Sayers refers to Major Armstrong in *Unnatural Death and Strong Poison* and Colin Dexter to John Christie in *Last Bus to Woodstock.*

Several of the real-life killers here are mentioned by George Orwell in his 1946 essay, *Decline of the English Murder*:

> 'Our great period in murder, our Elizabethan period, so to speak, seems to have been between roughly 1850 and 1925, and the murderers whose reputation has stood the test of time are the following: Dr Palmer of Rugeley, Jack the Ripper, Neill Cream, Mrs Maybrick, Dr Crippen, Seddon, Joseph Smith, Armstrong and Bywaters and Thompson. In addition, in 1919, or thereabouts, there was another very celebrated case which fits into the general pattern, but which I had better not mention by name, because the accused man was acquitted'.

Of those named, seven feature in Christie's works and if we hypothesise that the unnamed case is that of Harold Greenwood then the tally is eight out of ten. The Ripper, Smith and Cream excepted, Orwell and Christie selected middle class, respectable and domestic murders.

It should be stated that Agatha Christie was not a true crime aficionado. As with Miss Marple, she would never have described herself as a criminologist. That said, she was interested in the Croydon poisoning case of 1928-1929 when three members of the same middle-class family died, and no one was ever charged with these murders. However, this case is never referred to even by allusion, in any of her stories. She also made a reference to the Lord Lucan disappearance case in 1974.

Many authors writing about Agatha Christie allude to true crime references in her books, though to a very limited fashion. However, some make a concerted effort in this direction. There have been several other recent books dealing with, after a fashion, Agatha Christie and true crime. One was by Mike Holgate, in *Stranger than Fiction: Agatha Christie's True Crime Inspirations* (2010). Then there is the book by Anne Powers, *True Crime Parallels to the Mysteries of Agatha Christie* (2019), where she examines ten instances of real-life crimes or other deaths which were fictionalised in Christie's novels and short stories.

Kathryn Harkup in *A is for Arsenic: the poisons of Agatha Christie* (2016) discusses some of the fictional cases in which poison plays a part and the true crimes which sometimes inspired them. Likewise, Carla Valentine, in *Murder isn't Easy* (2021) surveys the real-life forensics of the time and how such is portrayed in her novels. In both these instances Christie is usually shown as providing a high degree of accuracy in her fiction.

This book, written by two true crime authors who are also admirers of the works of Agatha Christie, aims to highlight all true crime references in the books, provide concise summaries of these cases and then discuss how they are used in the fictional stories. Unlike some books in this genre, spoilers have been avoided, so a reader new to the fiction can safely read this without any solutions being revealed.

We have tried to include all true crime references, both implicit and explicit, in a more comprehensive manner than before. It is, however, possible that we may have missed some references that sharp-eyed true crime historians may note. Even Poirot can be wrong (*The Chocolate Box*), so lesser mortals are even more fallible.

Possibly this book is not aimed primarily at the crime historian who knows most of these cases intimately. Given the space here only concise accounts can be given of cases which have led to full length studies, some of which are listed at the end of every chapter for readers who want to know more. Apart from the use of these studies, archival material has been consulted in many cases, as has the contemporary press.

Elizabeth Canning (1753)

Lord Edgware Dies (1933)

The first case in this book concerns what is probably the least well-known real-life crime mentioned in an Agatha Christie story; certainly, neither of this book's authors knew of it previously. It is a testimony to Christie's knowledge of historical crime that she refers to it at all in this novel. However, readers of Josephine Tey's *The Franchise Affair* and Lilian de la Torre's *Elizabeth is Missing* will know the story.

Elizabeth Canning was a young woman, baptised on 17 September 1734, the eldest of five children born in the City of London to William Canning, a carpenter of Aldermanbury. He died in 1751 and her mother carried on the business. Elizabeth had a very little schooling and worked for Edward Lyon as a servant. So far, so humdrum, but aged 18 she was about to be propelled to national attention.

On 21 February 1753 there was a trial at the Old Bailey where she was the chief witness for the prosecution against Mary Squires, widow and Susannah Wells, accused of assault and theft against her on 2 January 1753. Her story was that at 9pm on 1 January 1753 she left a house at Salt Petre Bank, having spent the day with her aunt and uncle. Her relatives went with her as far as Aldgate. She then walked alone through Houndsditch and Moorfields and came to Bedlam Wall. It was there that she said she was attacked 'by two lusty men in greatcoats'. They took half a guinea and three shillings from her.

The men then tied her hands, struck her a stunning blow to the head and took her with them. She next recalled being dragged along to a house in the early hours of the next day. She was taken inside and she later recalled, 'I saw the gypsy woman Squires, sitting in a chair' and one Susannah Wells. There were two others present there. Mary offered Elizabeth her freedom and fine clothes, but she refused and then Mary drew a knife and cut Elizabeth's stays.

Elizabeth was then pushed upstairs and into a hayloft and was only given bread and water to subsist. After four weeks she was able to escape by breaking the barrier on the window and climbing down. She was wearing only a cap and a ragged bed gown. She went to her mother's house in Aldermanbury. It was now 29 January. The house was identified soon after as being at Enfield Wash on the Hertfordshire Road and Mary and Susannah were arrested. Elizabeth gave her story to the magistrates, Daniel Chitty and later Henry Fielding.

In court her story was supported by one Virtue Hall. She was a lodger at the house that Elizabeth had been brought into. She recalled the occasion and said that one of the men who brought her was John Squires, Mary's son. She said that they wanted Elizabeth to work for them as a prostitute but when she refused, she was taken upstairs and Virtue said she could not help her for fear the same would happen to her. She said Mary and Susannah had been in the said house for a fortnight prior to Elizabeth's arrival.

Other witnesses, including an apothecary and also a former employer of Elizabeth, gave their testimonies to having seen and helped Elizabeth on her return home. They explained how they had accompanied the girl in identifying the house where she had been held and also to her poor physical condition after being held in the house.

Mary Squires did not speak in her defence but called witnesses to testify for her innocence. John Gibbon, publican of the Old Ship at Abbotbury, six miles from Dorchester, said that Mary lodged there from 1-9 January 1753. She was with her two children and they were to sell trinkets in the town. He was told in court to look at Mary and he did so, and was asked 'are you sure that it is her?' He said 'I am sure it is'. He had known her three years. He seemed a respectable man, married with children and who had once farmed the land.

William Clark(e) also attested to having seen Mary on 10 January near Abbotsbury. He was so sure that he had seen her then that he said 'If I was to die for the woman, I'll speak the truth'. He had seen her in Abbotsbury on 1 January as well. Thomas Greville, of Coombe, near Salisbury, a publican, recalled seeing her there on 14 January. Clearly if these witnesses were correct then Mary could not have been seen by Elizabeth in a house in Enfield on 2 January and was thus innocent.

On the other hand, there were people who claimed to have seen Mary rather nearer the alleged scene of the crime. One was John Iniser, a seller of fish and oysters at Waltham Cross and Theobalds. He knew Mary and recalled seeing her several times in the weeks leading to her arrest at the end of January. She was making money as a fortune teller. Susannah Wells simply stated that she had never seen Elizabeth before until now.

The court then pronounced Mary and Susannah were guilty and so they were both sentenced to death by hanging. Mary then spoke to say that the witnesses speaking for her had been right that she and her children had been a long way from London in the first two weeks of January and so she could not possibly have been guilty. The sentence on Mary was not carried out as doubts arose on the guilt of the defendants (though Susannah was branded and given six months in prison). Principally, the Lord Mayor who had presided over the trial was unconvinced of the guilt of Mary Squires and the matter was even discussed at cabinet level, leading to George II granting Mary a temporary reprieve.

On 6 September, the three witnesses for Mary were accused in court of perjury. All were found not guilty due to a lack of evidence. Counsel for the three men stated that Elizabeth's story was so improbable that it should not have been believed.

A war of words took place this year. Many pamphlets were being written to argue the case for and against. Henry Fielding, novelist, journalist and magistrate, had questioned Elizabeth and he was convinced that she was speaking the truth. He wrote a pamphlet in her defence. A Dr Hill was equally certain that she was a liar and so wrote against her. Many others did likewise on both sides.

This led to another trial at the Old Bailey, this time on 24 April 1754 and the accused was Elizabeth herself, for perjury. It was of great interest, 'As this event had long engaged the attention of the public, the court was crowded to an uncommon degree, and perhaps curiosity was never more strongly expressed on any occasion in the memory of man'. A summary of the prosecution's case in the previous hearing was given. Then there was a number of witnesses who came to speak on Mary's behalf. Esther Hopkins, of South Perrott, Dorsetshire, stated that Mary was at her house on 29 December 1752. Alice Farnham at Vine Yard's Gap said she was with her around Christmas. George Squires (her son) claimed the family did not arrive at Enfield until late January 1753, having been to the west of London in the previous month, at various locations. Many people attested to their having seen Mary at these places. Eleven people claimed she had been at Abbotsbury in the first week of January and four had seen her in Litton in late December. Others had seen her in other places than Enfield.

Others placed her in or around Enfield in December and January. Elizabeth Sherrard recalled seeing her at Christmas time. Mrs Brissett said that Mary was paid to tell her fortune on 21-22 December. Jane Dadwell saw her in the shops at Christmas time. William Smith said he had seen her in Enfield on 14-16 December. Apparently 'all declared they could not be mistaken in her person'.

In the anachronistic light of later centuries, what is curious about these witness descriptions is that they only state that they saw Mary. None seem to have described her appearance, her clothes, her face or anything else about her, which is usual for witnesses in trials in later centuries. Her ugliness was remarkable, as was said in court, 'Look at this face, and if you have seen it before, you must have remembered that God Almighty never made such another'. Another hoped that the model for Mary would have been thrown away. Perhaps this was how people identified her.

There was other evidence before the case, which was, unusually for the eighteenth century, heard over several days. One was the fact that Elizabeth's descriptions of the room in which she had apparently being held changed. The other inconsistency in her testimony was over the number of times and the occasions on which she said she had been given food and water by her alleged captors. She may have had a bad memory or have been a poor liar or both.

On 30 May Elizabeth was found guilty. What swung the jury was the incompatibility of her descriptions of the room in which she had allegedly been imprisoned. However, the jury did not think that she had been wilful in her actions and recommended her to mercy. The judge sentenced her to a month in prison and then to be transported for seven years to the American colonies. Her supporters furnished her with several hundred pounds. She sailed there in July and arrived at Wethersfield in Connecticut. On 24 November 1756 she married John Treat there and went on to have four children. In 1761 she briefly returned to England to claim £100 left to her in the will of a now deceased well-wisher. Elizabeth died, 'suddenly' on 12 June 1773 and it was recalled that she was 'the notorious Elizabeth Canning'.

The question of her veracity remained. On the one hand, if she was not guilty then many people had perjured themselves. If she was guilty as charged, then she had been responsible for trying to swear away a life in order to cover up her own disgraceful and possibly debauched actions. As *The Newgate Calendar* put it, 'this story is enveloped in mystery; and the truth of it must be left to the discovery of that important day, when all mists shall be wiped from our eyes'.

Mary Squires died in Farnham, Surrey, on 26 February 1762; her age is unknown. We learn very little about her in the contemporary sources apart from the fact that she was an elderly widow and may have been a gypsy.

From this story, Agatha Christie selects the central theme of contradictory witness statements. In chapter Seven of *Lord Edgware Dies*, Chief Inspector Japp tells Poirot and Hastings:

> 'Reminds me of the Elizabeth Canning case...You remember? How at least a score of witnesses on either side swore they had seen the gipsy, Mary Squires, in two different parts of England. Good reputable witnesses, too. And she with such a hideous face there couldn't be two like it. That mystery was never cleared up. It is much the same here. Here's a separate list of people prepared to swear a woman who was in two different places at the same time. Which of them is speaking the truth?'

The context here is that Lord Edgware has been found stabbed to death in his house at Regent Gate. Lady Edgware, otherwise Jane Wilkinson, an American actress, seems to have a motive as shortly before her husband is killed she tells Poirot 'I've just got to get rid of my husband', so that she can marry the Catholic Duke of Merton. She seems the obvious suspect.

The difficulty for the detectives is that although both Edgware's butler, Alton, and his secretary, Miss Carroll, swear that Jane arrived at their employer's house on the night of the crime, other witnesses place her elsewhere. Sir Montagu Corner was hosting a dinner party at his house in Chiswick and among the guests was Jane Wilkinson. She had arrived on time, did not leave until late. None of the witnesses there were people who would have lied for her.

One possibility is that the killer employed Carlotta Adams, an impersonator, to go to Edgware's house to give the impression that the killer was his wife, not knowing that the real Jane was in Chiswick, so had an alibi. Unfortunately Carlotta has died from an overdose of drugs. There are a number of others who would not have been averse to Lord Edgware's death; two being his impoverished heir who needed money and his daughter who hated her father.

Sources

Old Bailey online.
The Gentleman's Magazine (1753-1754)
The Newgate Calendar (1824)

Madeleine Smith (1857)

The Pale Horse (1961), Sleeping Murder (1976)

During the Victorian era, arsenic figured in many high-profile murder cases. Since it was not difficult to obtain and the symptoms of arsenic poisoning could easily be mistaken for gastritis, it became popular as a method of murder. One such *cause célèbre* – perhaps the most famous of them all – is the murder of Emile L'Angelier in Glasgow in 1857. The person accused of poisoning him with a large dose of arsenic was his secret fiancée, the 22-year-old Madeleine Smith. The case caused a sensation at the time, not only because Madeleine came from a solid middle-class family but also because it was revealed that she had been Emile's mistress. As in the Bywaters/Thompson case, letters were a central part of the evidence for the prosecution.

Madeleine Hamilton Smith was born in 1835 as the eldest child of five to the architect James Smith and his wife Janet Hamilton. Madeleine's grandfather, David Hamilton, was also an architect and had designed several buildings and monuments in Glasgow. The family lived at No 7, Blythswood Square, Glasgow, and spent the summers at their country estate Rowaleyn, near Helensburgh, designed and built by James Smith. Not much is known about Madeleine's upbringing except that she was privately tutored and in her teens was sent to a girls' boarding school in London, where she spent two or three years. The headmistress, Mrs Gorton, noted that Madeleine was 'diligent, attentive, and exceedingly bright' but at the same time could be provocative and 'given to stubborn sulks'.

Returning from the boarding school in 1853, Madeleine was 18 years old and of marriageable age. In terms of appearance, she is described as 'of short stature and slight form, with features sharp and prominent, and restless and sparkling eyes'; a photograph shows a serious looking, rather ordinary young woman. While waiting for a suitable suitor to appear, she spent her days strolling around Glasgow accompanied by her younger sister Bessie. It was presumably on Sauchiehall Street – known for its galleries and exclusive shops – that Madeleine was first noticed by Pierre Emile L'Angelier, a warehouse clerk from Jersey. L'Angelier, who was of French ancestry, had been born in 1823 and was thus twelve years older than Madeleine. He had lived partly in Scotland and in France, claiming to have been a member of the National Guard during the 1848 February Revolution.

Emile L'Angelier (he did not use the name Pierre) was considered industrious and well-behaved but also vain and boastful. He often talked about his acquaintances in high society and bragged about his success with women. Around 1852, however, he had been jilted by a wealthy lady from Fife to whom he claimed to have been engaged. This setback took a great toll on him; he even talked of killing himself, although his friends did not think he meant it seriously. L'Angelier is described as emotional and 'easily excitable'. The only known photograph of him shows a moustached and bearded man with a prominent lower lip and somewhat heavy features. Not an obvious ladies' man, for sure, but he was in the possession of a lot of Gallic charm that outweighed any flaws.

It seems that Emile L'Angelier was looking for an opportunity to better himself, via an advantageous marriage. His salary at Huggins' warehouse was very modest and insufficient for his desire to wear expensive clothes and live well. The young Madeleine Smith, daughter of a well-to-do architect, appeared to be the solution to his problem. Through an acquaintance who was on friendly terms with the Smiths, L'Angelier managed to meet Madeleine on the street in the spring of 1855. She was immediately attracted to the elegantly dressed and charming Frenchman. Before long, they had started an intensive correspondence. Madeleine wrote her very first letter to Emile on 30 April 1855 from her family's summer house: 'I often wish you were near us; we could take such charming walks. One enjoys walking with a pleasant companion, and where could we find one equal to yourself?' What had started as friendship quickly developed into love. In the summer of 1855, they got secretly engaged. Madeleine hoped that her father would give his approval; instead, he demanded that she break off all contact with L'Angelier.

Like the obedient daughter she was raised to be, Madeleine told L'Angelier goodbye; however, he refused to accept her decision. Before long, the correspondence and secret meetings started again. In the letters she addressed him as 'My own darling husband' and called herself 'Mimi L'Angelier'. The couple entertained serious wedding plans – as a last resort, they considered running away together. At the beginning of May 1856 Madeleine lost her virginity to L'Angelier, apparently without any pressure on his part. This was of course completely against the strict moral rules of the time, but Madeleine seems strangely unconcerned in a letter written shortly afterwards: 'Beloved, if we did wrong last night, it was in the excitement of our love. Yes, beloved, I did truly love you with my soul. I was happy; it was a pleasure to be with you'. In the same letter, she assures her lover that – after what has happened – she can never be anyone else's wife, she belongs only to him.

More than 200 letters were written by Madeleine Smith to Emile L'Angelier in the years 1855-1857. As in the Bywaters/Thompson case, he kept all hers while she burned his. L'Angelier's feelings must therefore be judged based on what he told his friends. A middle-aged woman, Miss Mary Perry, was a close confidante of his. To Miss Perry he expressed frustration: he wanted to see Mr Smith and ask for Madeleine's hand in marriage, but she refused to let him. Nor did she want to raise the matter with her father herself. As time went on, L'Angelier became increasingly worried that his beloved would find a more suitable husband than himself in Glasgow's high society, to which he was barred. He became controlling, telling Madeleine how she should behave and what she was allowed to do and not do. This was not to her liking and the previously passionate tone of her letters became more reserved.

During the autumn of 1856, L'Angelier's fears came true when a wealthy merchant named William Minnoch, a neighbour of the Smiths, began courting Madeleine. He was socially acceptable as well as agreeable and she encouraged his attentions. In late January 1857, Minnoch proposed and was accepted. It now became urgent for her to end the relationship with Emile L'Angelier. As recently as 23 January, Madeleine had written him a passionate letter: 'Oh sweet darling, at this moment my heart and soul burns with love for thee, my husband, my own sweet one. Emile, what would I not give at this moment to be your fond wife?' Only five days later she accepted Minnoch's proposal and shortly afterwards sent L'Angelier a farewell letter: '...as there is coolness on both sides, our engagement had better be broken...we had better, for the future, consider ourselves strangers'. She begged him as a gentleman not to reveal to anyone what had passed between them and asked him to return all her letters.

The distraught L'Angelier told a colleague what had happened, asking for advice. His friend urged him to return the letters but L'Angelier replied that 'he would never allow her to marry another man as long as he lived'. He added, 'she will be the death of me'. Furious and hurt, he wrote to Madeleine threatening to send all the letters to her father. Madeleine was terrified, pleading with him in an anguished letter: 'For God's sake, do not bring your once beloved Mimi to an open shame...Emile, do not drive me to death...for God's sake do not send my letters to Papa...I am ill. God knows what I have suffered...Do nothing till I see you'. In several desperate messages, Madeleine pleaded for forgiveness and to have her letters back: 'Emile, my father's wrath would kill me – you little know his temper... Despise me, hate me, but make me not the public scandal'. But L'Angelier stubbornly refused to return her letters. She then changed tack and reverted to a tone reminiscent of the earlier romantic one: 'Adieu, my love, my pet, my sweet Emile' – it seems she was trying to fool L'Angelier into believing that they were still lovers.

On 17 February 1857, Emile L'Angelier dined at Miss Perry's. He mentioned that he would meet Madeleine on the evening of the 19th. Whether the meeting really took place is unclear. Late in the night of 19 February, Emile suffered from severe stomach pains, which abated in the morning. A few days later, on 22 February, the stomach pains returned. This time the attack was so severe that Emile was bedridden for a week. On 9 March, he had tea with Miss Perry and told her, 'I cannot think why I was so unwell after getting that coffee and chocolate from her' – meaning Madeleine. He also spoke about his feelings for Madeleine: 'It is a perfect fascination my attachment to that girl; if she were to poison me, I would forgive her'.

On 19 March – now restored to health – L'Angelier went on holiday to the Bridge of Allan, 31 miles northeast of Glasgow. He was supposed to stay there for a week but unexpectedly returned to Glasgow on the evening of 22 March. To his landlady, Mrs Jenkins, he said that he had received a letter calling him back. He asked for the key to the front door, as he was going out and thought he might be late back. About half past two in the morning of 23 March, Mrs Jenkins was awakened by the violent ringing of the doorbell. Outside stood L'Angelier, clutching his stomach, 'I am very bad', he told her. A hastily summoned doctor gave the patient a little morphine, but his condition worsened rapidly. L'Angelier vomited a lot and grew weaker and weaker. At nine o'clock he asked Mrs Jenkins to draw the curtain, 'I feel as if I should be better if I could get a little sleep'. When the doctor returned some minutes later, he found L'Angelier lying on his side, seemingly sleeping peacefully – but it was the eternal sleep.

The autopsy revealed signs of inflammation in the upper part of the duodenum. In the stomach there was a dark, coffee-like liquid containing a very large amount of arsenic: 82 grains (2 grains is a lethal dose). According to the chemist who did the analysis, 'the quantity of arsenic found was considerably more than sufficient to destroy life'. In the dead man's waistcoat pocket a letter was found – the one that had called him back to Glasgow. It was from Madeleine: 'Sweet one, I waited and waited for you, but you came not. I shall wait again tomorrow night – same hour and arrangement...Come, beloved, and clasp me to your heart; come, and we shall be happy'. It could not be proved that the pair had met on the evening of 22 March, but a witness had seen L'Angelier walking down the street not far from Blythswood Square.

It soon emerged that Madeleine had purchased arsenic on 21 February, 6 March, and 18 March at local chemists, stating that the poison would be used to kill rats at her family's summer estate. The gardener, however, denied having received any arsenic from her for this purpose. This, together with the discovery of her letters in L'Angelier's desk, establishing a clear motive for murder, was sufficient to get her arrested on 31 March 1857. In a statement to the police, she did not deny her secret love affair with L'Angelier but claimed that she had not seen him for three weeks. Madeleine admitted that she had bought arsenic, but it had been for cosmetic purposes. She had said it was to kill rats because she did not want anyone to know that she was using arsenic to improve her skin. Three months later, on 30 June, she stood trial at the High Court in Edinburgh, charged with two counts of attempted murder (L'Angelier's attacks of stomach pains in February) and one count of murder. The distinguished Scottish lawyer, John Inglis – who later became a judge and presided at the trial of another accused poisoner, Dr Pritchard – had been engaged as the barrister for the defence.

The trial created an enormous public interest; spectators crowded into the hall and people waited outside to catch a glimpse of Madeleine arriving and leaving. The newspapers carried detailed accounts of the proceedings. When excerpts from the intimate letters were read aloud, the audience was stunned. Madeleine Smith had indeed defied all the rules and expectations of a young, unmarried woman in Victorian society. She herself behaved with great self-control and composure. A reporter wrote that she went up the stairs to the dock 'with all the buoyance with which she might have entered the box of a theatre'.

The defence won an important battle against the prosecution regarding the admissibility of a notebook belonging to Emile L'Angelier. It seems that Emile had made notes about having met Madeleine shortly before each of the attacks in February. The judge ruled that the notebook could not be used as evidence in court. If it had, the outcome might possibly have been different. As it was, it could not be established that Emile had met Madeleine before any of the attacks. On 9 July, the jury returned with a verdict of Not Guilty regarding the attack on 19 February and Not Proven regarding the attack on 22 February and the murder on 23 March. Not Proven is a unique Scottish sentence, usually taken to mean that the jury is inclined to believe that the defendant is guilty, but the prosecution has not provided sufficient evidence to convict.

Madeleine Smith left the courtroom as a free woman, but she and her family, because of the scandal, felt compelled to leave Glasgow. Her fiancé, Minnoch, had broken off the engagement. During her time in prison, Madeleine had received marriage proposals from scores of men who had read about her in the newspapers. However, it was not until 1861 that she was married; to an artist named George Wardle, a close friend of William Morris. They lived in London and had two children together, a son and a daughter, Madeleine now calling herself Lena. Many years later, it appears that the couple separated, and Madeleine moved to New York to be close to her son, who lived there. Following George's death, she married an American called Sheehy and died aged 92 in 1928, under the name Lena Wardle Sheehy.

The story of Madeleine Smith and Emile L'Angelier has been the subject of many books, articles, films, and plays. Most writers on the case believe that Madeleine was guilty. The only possible alternative appears to be suicide. L'Angelier had once talked about killing himself; he had told friends that he sometimes used arsenic (probably for cosmetic reasons), and he did not mention a word about having met Madeleine when he returned seriously ill to Mrs Jenkins' house on 23 March. If it was true that L'Angelier had made notes about falling ill twice after being served coffee or chocolate by Madeleine, should he not, this third and final time, have told his landlady about his suspicions? Why would he protect his murderer? On the other hand, he had once said, 'if she were to poison me, I would forgive her'. Maybe he did not realize that he was close to death – his last words were, after all, to the effect that he thought he would get better with a little sleep. Even if L'Angelier did suspect Madeleine of having poisoned him, he may have thought that he would be able to confront her about it the next day or so – only there was never another day for him.

In *The Pale Horse*, the retired pharmacist Zachariah Osborne (a character inspired by a somewhat strange pharmacist who Agatha Christie personally knew – see chapter on Murders and murderers anticipated/Graham Young) relates to the narrator Mark Easterbrook how he had always hoped he would be called upon to give evidence in a trial where someone bought poison from his shop:

> 'It was my great hope that someday, I too, might figure in a cause célèbre and be the instrument of bringing a murderer to justice!'
>
> 'Oh, I suppose a second Madeleine Smith'.
>
> 'Exactly. Alas,' Mr Osborne sighed, 'that has never happened. Or, if so, the person in question has never been brought to justice'.

A more in-depth reference to Madeleine Smith can be found in *Sleeping Murder*, where Miss Marple has a conversation with her physician, Dr Haydock, on the topic of historic murders that have gone undetected. If you happen to come across one such case, what should you do? Dr Haydock's advice is to let sleeping murders lie; it could be dangerous to start messing about with murder:

> 'People say a murderer always repeats his crimes. That's not true. There's a type who commits a murder, manages to get away with it, and is darned careful never to stick his neck out again. I won't say they live happily ever after – I don't believe that's true – there are many kinds of retribution. But outwardly at least all goes well. Perhaps that was so in the case of Madeleine Smith or again in the case of Lizzie Borden. It was not proven in the case of Madeleine Smith and Lizzie was acquitted – but many people believed both of these women were guilty. I could name you others. They never repeated their crimes – one crime gave them what they wanted and they were content.'

He goes on to warn against digging up the past, which might provoke the killer to strike again out of self-preservation. In this context it may be of interest to relate an anecdote about Madeleine Smith in later life when she was the wife of George Wardle in London. Many of the couple's friends knew about her background but were sensitive enough not to ask her anything about it. However, one guest at a dinner party did not know that the hostess was in fact Madeleine Smith. He started to talk about the case and suggested that if Madeleine had ever married, her husband – if he knew of her past – must always be uneasy. The guest babbled on for a while until someone kicked him under the table. Madeleine's reaction is not recorded – presumably she kept up appearances – but as far as is known the guest did not end up with arsenic in his coffee.

Sources

Trial of Miss Madeleine H. Smith for the alleged poisoning of M. Pierre Emile l'Angelier (1857)

Mary Hartman, *Victorian Murderesses* (1977)

Mark John Maguire, *They got away with murder* I (2023)

Constance Kent (1860)

Crooked House (1949), The Clocks (1963)

The case of Constance Kent has become famous for the same reason as that of Lizzie Borden: an unusually brutal crime in a respectable upper middle class family, where there is still some debate as to how it happened and who was guilty. The emergence of extreme violence in a refined and cultured setting fascinated contemporaries and continues to do so today. The tragic story unfolded in the summer of 1860, in the village of Road (now called Rode) in Wiltshire, on the Somerset border. Here lived the Kent family, seemingly dignified and genteel, but with strained relationships and dark secrets lurking behind the façade. This hidden hatred finally culminated in the murder of an innocent child.

Samuel Saville Kent (born in about 1800) was a factory inspector living in Sidmouth, Devon. Together with his first wife, Mary Ann Windus, he had ten children, half of whom died in infancy. These many pregnancies and deaths took a toll on Mrs Kent's health, both physically and mentally. Around 1840, a governess, 20-year-old Mary Drewe Pratt, was hired to tutor the two eldest daughters. She was vivacious and energetic, unlike Mrs Kent who had become increasingly listless and withdrawn. According to Samuel Kent, his wife had become insane. After the birth of William Saville in 1845, Samuel left the conjugal bedchamber and henceforth slept in a room immediately adjacent to that of the governess. Not surprisingly, it was soon rumoured that the master of the house was unfaithful to his wife. This persistent gossip caused the family to leave Sidmouth.

Mrs Kent died in 1852 and little more than a year later, Samuel Kent married Mary Drewe Pratt. Three years later the family moved to Road Hill House, an elegant mansion in Wiltshire. They still lived here in the summer of 1860, together with their children Mary Amelia (5 years old), Francis Saville (3, almost 4 years old) and Eveline (2 years old). In June

1860 Mrs Kent was pregnant with her fourth child. Four children from Samuel's first marriage still lived with them: Mary Ann Alice (aged 29), Elizabeth (aged 28), Constance (aged 16) and William Saville (aged 15). Three servants lived in the house, including a 22-year-old nanny, Elizabeth Gough, who took care of the youngest children. Other employees came a few times a week but were not resident. The turnover of servants was extremely high, about 100 over the course of four years, probably caused by Samuel Kent's arrogant manner and hot temper.

Constance Emilie Kent, born in 1844, was eight years old when her mother died. The following year she was bridesmaid when her father married Mary Drewe Pratt. Relations with her new stepmother appeared to be cordial; secretly, however, Constance loathed the young woman who had taken her mother's place. Her negative feelings increased when the half-siblings were born and Samuel Kent seemed to favour them, in particular Francis Saville. Constance was attached to her older brother Edward, who had gone to sea at an early age. Edward strongly disapproved of Samuel's second marriage, and possibly his negative attitude influenced her. Constance was also very close to her younger brother William. In July 1856, when she was 12 and he was 11, they tried to run away together. To escape detection, Constance had dressed like a boy and cut off her long hair. The children were soon captured and returned to their angry parents. While William was remorseful and tearful, Constance showed no emotion. It was she who had planned the escape; her brother followed her passively.

Constance was described by a family friend as a girl with 'a strong, obstinate and determined will'. She was physically strong and enjoyed taking part in wrestling matches with school friends. In June 1860, she was back at home for the summer holidays, having spent about six months at a boarding school. She slept in her own room in the big house, as did William. The nanny, Elizabeth Gough, slept in the nursery on the first floor, together with Francis Saville – who would be aged four in August – and little Eveline. Mr and Mrs Kent slept in a room across the landing with 5-year-old Mary Amelia.

At 5 o'clock in the morning of 30 June, Elizabeth Gough awoke and went to check on baby Eveline. She then looked into the cot where Francis slept and found it empty. Thinking that Mrs Kent probably had taken him, she went back to bed for another hour and a half. At about 6.45 am, when Elizabeth went in to see Mrs. Kent, it became clear that Francis was not with his mother. A frantic search of the house began, but he was not to be found. In the drawing room, a window was slightly open, suggesting that an intruder had taken the little boy. No one had heard any sounds during the night. The family's Newfoundland dog, which always barked at strangers, had been quiet.

While Samuel Kent hurried off to Trowbridge police station, the villagers searched the garden. Before long, Francis' dead body was discovered in an outhouse (a privy). His throat had been cut by a sharp knife, almost severing the head. There was also a deep cut in the chest. Despite the ferocious wounds, not much bleeding had occurred. Due to the relative lack of blood, one of the surgeons who examined the body believed that the cuts could have been inflicted after death, the real cause of death being suffocation. An inquest returned a verdict of murder by some person, or persons unknown. The local superintendent of police, John Foley, was at first suspicious about Elizabeth Gough, believing it impossible for the boy to have been abducted without her knowledge. She was arrested but soon released. Shortly afterwards, in mid-July, the magistrates asked the Home Office for assistance from Scotland Yard.

Inspector Jonathan Whicher, a highly regarded and experienced detective, was sent to investigate the case. He quickly became convinced that Constance Kent was the murderer: 'I cannot find the least motive that anyone else could have had for the act except Miss Constance and her brother William, arising from jealousy or spite entertained by them towards the youngest branches of the family'. He thought that insanity was behind it: 'It appears that her mother, uncle and grandmother were of unsound mind and the present medical adviser of the family and another medical gentleman well acquainted with Miss Constance are of opinion that she is affected with homicidal madness, and the former gentleman stated to me that he would not sleep in a house where Miss Constance was without having his door secured'.

However, Whicher failed to find any concrete evidence, except for the fact that one of Constance's nightgowns, which should have been in the weekly laundry, seemed to have disappeared. He suspected that it had been bloodstained. Despite the lack of evidence, he arrested her on 16 July, probably hoping she would break down and confess. Many in the local community were upset about a young girl from a respectable family being arrested on such flimsy grounds. At the hearing before the magistrates on 27 July, some of Constance's school friends testified that she had been unhappy about her father favouring the younger half-siblings. As the summer holidays approached one of the girls exclaimed, 'Won't it be nice to go home shortly?' Constance replied, 'It may be to your home, but mine is different'.

That was pretty much it and the solicitor representing Constance was scathing in his critique of Inspector Whicher's scenario, pointing out how unlikely, if not impossible, it would have been for a teenage girl to carry the heavy burden of a sleeping child through the house and out to the privy in the garden. The violent nature of the crime was also inconsistent with Constance as the perpetrator: 'Is it likely that hers was the arm which nearly severed the head from the body? It is perfectly incredible!' The magistrates agreed and Constance was released on bail, the case against her later being dropped. A disappointed Inspector Whicher returned to London, having been the subject of much criticism for his handling of the case. This seemed to be the end of the tragic affair. The Kent family moved to Wales and Constance was sent to a convent school in France, returning to England three years later to stay at St Mary's home in Brighton, a convent of Anglican nuns.

In April 1865, there was a sensational development when the now 21 year-old Constance Kent appeared before the Bow Street magistrate in London, confessing to the murder of her half-brother. She had first confided in a clergyman, the Rev. Arthur Wagner, who also appeared before the magistrate. However, he refused to give any details about what Constance had told him, because the information had been received during 'sacramental confession'. There was later some debate over this. Constance herself only gave a brief account of the murder: she had waited until everyone in the house was asleep, sneaked into the nursery and carried the sleeping Francis in a blanket to the privy, where she had killed him with a razor belonging to her father. The deed was obviously planned – she had hidden matches in the privy to be able to see what she was doing – and she claimed to have acted alone.

Constance Kent was brought to trial on 21 July 1865, at Salisbury Assizes, and pleaded guilty. The trial lasted only a few minutes. She was sentenced to death, but because of her youth at the time of the crime and the fact that she was convicted only on her own confession, her sentence was commuted to penal servitude for life. She was released in 1885, after serving 20 years, and emigrated to Australia the year after. Changing her name to Ruth Emilie Kaye she worked as a nurse for many years, dying in Sydney in 1944 at the age of 100. Her brother William – who changed his surname to Saville-Kent – as well as the surviving half siblings Mary

Amelia, Eveline and Acland (born one month after Francis' death) also emigrated to Australia. William became a successful marine biologist, travelling widely to collect specimens for his work. He died in 1908.

The motive for the murder did not come to light until 1878, when a physician named John Charles Bucknill, an authority on lunacy, broke his silence. Bucknill had been assigned to examine Constance Kent after she made her confession, to find out if a plea of not guilty on the ground of insanity could be justified. He concluded that she was sane. Constance told Dr Bucknill that she wanted to avenge her mother, who had been 'relegated' to a few rooms in the house while the governess took charge of the entire household. When Mary Drewe Pratt made some condescending remarks about Constance's mother, her fate was sealed. From that moment on, Constance hated her stepmother-to-be and thought of nothing but revenge. At first, she considered poisoning Mary but felt that this was too lenient a punishment. Instead, she decided to kill Mary's beloved little son, to cause her stepmother the greatest possible pain and grief. Out of consideration for the family, Dr Bucknill had kept quiet until both Samuel and Mary Kent were dead. Mary had died in 1865, a few months after Constance's confession, and Samuel had followed her to the grave in 1872.

In 1945, the Constance Kent case was referenced in the British horror film *Dead of Night*, produced by Ealing Studios. The case has been the subject of numerous articles and books. In 2008, *The Suspicions of Mr Whicher or The Murder at Road Hill House* by Kate Summerscale received much praise and was later adapted to a television film. Doubts have been cast on Constance's confession, some authors believing that she sacrificed herself to protect the real murderer – that is, her father, or her brother William. It has also been suggested that she may have acted in collusion with William. If William was involved in any way – and there is no evidence for this – he surely followed Constance's lead. She had always been the stronger of the two. All this is mere speculation, and it may be worth emphasizing that Constance herself never retracted her confession, not even after her father and brother were long gone. Why would she voluntarily take the blame for a crime she had not committed, five years after it happened, thereby risking her own neck?

For the public, victims of murder are rarely remembered to the same extent as their murderers. It is easy to forget the most important aspect of this tragic story, that an innocent little boy was never given the opportunity to grow up and live a full life. Francis' nanny describes him as 'a very good-tempered child, not troublesome' According to his mother, Mrs Mary Kent, he was 'a nice little, playful, good-tempered, chatty boy, and a general favourite'. Not even his murderer had anything bad to say about him; she played with him the day before the terrible act. The inscription on his tombstone reads:

> Francis Savill Kent
> The dearly loved son of
> Samuel Savill and Mary
> Drewe Kent who was
> cruelly murdered at Road
> June 30th 1860
> Aged 3 years and 10 months
> Shall not God search this out for he
> knoweth the secrets of the heart

In *The Clocks*, the case of Constance Kent is one of the classic crimes occupying Hercule Poirot's thoughts while he waits for a new murder mystery to challenge his little grey cells. He tells visitor Colin Lamb, 'Then there was that unfortunate adolescent, Constance Kent. The true motive that lay behind her strangling [sic] of the small brother whom she undoubtedly loved has always been a puzzle. But not to me. It was clear as soon as I read about the case'. To the reader's chagrin, this is all we learn. There is, however, an illuminating discussion along the same lines in *Crooked House*. Here we find Sir Arthur Hayward, Assistant Commissioner of Scotland Yard, venting his opinion on the nature of murderers. He reminds his son Charles – the book's narrator – that there are different forms of hate:

> 'When you say hate, I presume you mean dislike carried to excess. A jealous hate is different – that rises out of affection and frustration. Constance Kent, everybody said, was very fond of the baby brother she killed. But she wanted, one supposes, the attention and the love that was bestowed on him. I think people more often kill those they love, than those they hate. Possibly because only the people you love can really make life unendurable to you'.

From this it can be inferred that Agatha Christie accepted the confession of Constance Kent as being genuine and believed her to be guilty. The motive for the murder as given here differs from what Dr Bucknill relates about Constance's obsessive hatred for her stepmother and the strong wish to hurt her. This appears to have been the main motive, although Constance's jealousy of Francis and the other half siblings no doubt must have been a contributing factor.

The reference to Constance Kent in *Crooked House* is hardly coincidental. The plot centres around a large and somewhat dysfunctional family, whose head – the wealthy patriarch Aristide Leonides – is poisoned by someone close to him. Among the members of the family are Aristide's grandchildren, Sophia (the fiancée of Charles Hayward), 16-year-old Eustace and 12-year-old Josephine. The latter two are vaguely reminiscent of William and Constance Kent, although William was one year younger than his sister. Eustace is described as handsome but affected by a mild case of polio – William is said to have been in delicate health as a child. Josephine is portrayed as unattractive but intelligent and strong willed – Constance was plain but resourceful and determined. Although there are no parallels between the murder at Road Hill House and the two murders at Three Gables, the oddly built house in the novel, it is possible that Christie to some extent may have been inspired by the Constance Kent case in the creation of these two youngest members of the household.

Sources

National Archives file, Murder of Francis Saville Kent, MEPO3/61

Mary Hartman, *Victorian Murderesses* (1977)

Noeline Kyle, *A greater guilt: Constance Emilie Kent and the Road murder* (2009)

JW Stapleton, *The great crime of 1860, being a summary of the facts relating to the murder committed at Road* (1861)

Kate Summerscale, *The Suspicions of Mr Whicher or The Murder at Road Hill House* (2008)

Charles Bravo case (1876)

Ordeal by Innocence (1958), The Clocks (1963), Elephants Can Remember (1972)

This is a classic of the genre, an upper middle-class household with servants, a mysterious death by poisoning, and several suspects. It was a famous unsolved mystery and Christie was clearly very interested in it.

The setting was the detached house, The Priory, on Bedford Hill Road in Balham, Surrey, and close to London. It was built in 1812 in the Gothic revival style. Charles Delauney Turner Bravo had been born in London in 1836. In 1871 he was still a bachelor, living with his family in Kensington. By profession he was a barrister and was employed in the City. On 7 December 1875 he married Florence Ricardo, a rich woman and widow of a Guards officer, Alexander Louis Ricardo who had died in 1871 after seven years of marriage. They were 'said to have lived very happily together'. She had been born on 5 September 1845 in Australia. Until her second marriage she had been intimate with a married man, called Dr James Manby Gully and they had toured the Continent of Europe together. Dr Gully had been born in Jamaica in 1808 and qualified as a doctor in Edinburgh in 1829. He was a widower and had lived in Great Malvern in 1861, working as a hydropath, but by 1875 was living in Orwell Lodge, Bedford Hill Road. He had not seen Mrs Bravo since two months before her second marriage, which he had advised against because the two had only a very short engagement. He was retired from an active and a very lucrative practice.

Also in the household was Mrs Jane Cannon Cox, a widow with three children, who acted as companion to Mrs Bravo, but the two seemed to treat each other as friends. She had once resided in Jamaica and there knew Robert Campbell, Florence's father, and was on good terms with him. There were the servants: Miss French, the cook, Mary Ann Keeber and Elizabeth Evans, the two housemaids, Edward Smith, the footman and Rowe, the butler.

On Tuesday 18 April 1876, Bravo returned home in the afternoon after working in the City. He then went for a ride on one of his horses and returned between 6 and 7pm, complaining of being shaken as the pony he had been riding ran away with him. He had a hot bath and dressed for dinner, which was at about 7.30pm. The meal consisted of soup, followed by fillet of sole, roast lamb and poached eggs on toast. Bravo only ate the lamb and eggs; he drank four glasses of Burgundy, whereas the two ladies did not drink the wine, but took sherry instead. Bravo, it was later recalled, had talked pleasantly to them.

At 8.30 the three went to the morning room and were there for the next half hour. They left just before nine, Mrs Cox went with her mistress to her bedroom and Bravo went to his at 9.15 (they slept separately because Mrs Bravo recently had a miscarriage and Bravo was pressing her to have sex again). He then called urgently for a housemaid to bring him hot water. When Mary Keeber arrived, he complained that he felt unwell and she recalled him saying 'Florence, Florence, hot water, hot water'. His wife did not come, however. She reported this to Mrs Cox, who had mustard brought to him. His feet and hands were placed in a mix of mustard and water, and he was very sick.

It was then that Mrs Cox sent messages to Dr Moore of Balham and Dr Harrison of Streatham, both of whom were local. They arrived at 10.30pm. By this time Bravo was unconscious. Mrs Bravo additionally called for Dr Royes Bell, a cousin of Bravo's and he arrived at 2.30 the next morning with a Dr Johnson. Mrs Cox told the two newly arrived doctors that at 10pm Bravo had told her that he had taken poison but not to tell his wife.

The doctors asked him about the information that Mrs Cox had told them. Dr Johnson said to him, 'If you die without telling us more then we know at present, some one may be accused or suspected of having poisoned you'. He replied, 'I can tell you nothing more. I have told you the truth'. He admitted to having taken rubbed laudanum on his gums for neuralgia of the lower jaw which he was suffering from.

Although mentally lucid, Bravo was physically very unwell. He vomited blood on several occasions and was very thirsty. Arsenic poisoning was tested for without positive result. He was given a little morphia for the pain and was given iced milk and champagne. The doctors asked about what poisons were in the house and it was found that there was laudanum and chloroform and some rat poison, the latter being in the stables.

The doctors revived Bravo and he regained consciousness at 4.30 am. It was now Wednesday 19 April. Bravo then dictated his will to Dr Bell and it was witnessed by Rowe. All of his assets were to go to his wife. On Thursday his condition worsened. It was then that Sir William Withey Gull, a physician to Queen Victoria and very highly esteemed, arrived. He spent between two and three hours in consultation with Drs Bell and Johnson. Gull ordered samples of vomit from Charles to be collected and sent for analysis.

Mrs Cox visited Dr Gully, at Mrs Bravo's request, to ask what they could do for Bravo. He suggested that they place a 'mustard poultice on his back and cold bandage on the belly and a mild dose of arsenicum'.

That evening, William Henry Campbell, Mrs Bravo's brother, who lived at Buscot in Berkshire, arrived. They talked of Gull's recent visit. Bravo said, 'Willam old fellow, kiss me. I have told Sir William I have taken laudanum, but he didn't believe it: I have told him the truth'. Campbell thought, however, that his brother-in-law had taken some other poison himself.

Bravo died at 5.30 in the morning of Friday 21 April. He had been conscious to the last and died of exhaustion. Mrs Cox thought it was suicide. Dr Payne carried out a post mortem at St. Thomas' Hospital, with Drs Bell, Moore and Harrison in attendance and which revealed that there were 140 grams of the poison antimony in his stomach. The inquest would normally have been held at the Bedford Hotel, about five minutes from the house, but at Mrs Bravo's insistence it was held at the Priory. It was held on 25 April and adjourned to the 28th. It was concluded that he died of poisoning but by what means it was administered – suicide, murder or accident – was left open. Bravo was buried at Norwood Cemetery on the 26th.

In some ways, the inquest was rather odd. Some witnesses were not called; for example Dr Moore was not called, nor was Sir William, nor were the servants. There was a question whether Bravo made a dying declaration to Sir William. The jurors thought it was curious that Mrs Bravo had not come to see her husband when he became unwell and why Mrs Cox had not told the doctors about Bravo's alleged comment about self-poisoning until hours after they had first arrived. Indeed, Mrs Cox was a very vague and forgetful witness when it came to describing who ate and drank what at the dinner.

The poison may have been in the wine which only Bravo had drunk. Rowe recalled that he had taken it from the cellar some hours before the dinner and left it in the dining room therefore for some hours. As there was no immediate police investigation, the bottle and any remaining content was long gone beforehand. No one claimed to know that there was any antimony in the house. The police checked with chemists for anyone purchasing antimony but could not find any buyers.

The possibility of suicide was raised, based on what Mrs Cox said that Bravo told to her alone. It was rumoured that Bravo was being blackmailed by a former mistress of his. No evidence was found to support this conclusion and he had no known enemies. Bravo's friends did not think this was the case and they pressed for a further investigation and another inquest.

It was only then that the police became involved. Chief Inspector Frederick Williamson of Scotland Yard's detective division investigated the case. Dr Gully's previous friendship with Mrs Bravo was looked into. Although he had not apparently seen Mrs Bravo for some time before her marriage, he had met Mrs Cox on two occasions since and had asked her about Mrs Bravo. Wild rumours abounded about the possible culpability of Mrs Bravo, Mrs Cox and Dr Gully. No one seems, in the best tradition of the fictional whodunnit, to have suspected any of the servants, and Bravo was allegedly beloved by them all.

There was another inquest, held for a month, between 11 July and 11 August 1876 at the nearby Bedford Hotel (the first inquest was criticised in Parliament and in the legal profession). The corpse was exhumed for the jurors to see. This inquest was far more searching and much reported by the press. Many scandalous revelations were made, especially about the Bravos and Dr Gully. Yet it was equally futile in its results. It concluded that this was a case of murder and that the poison was tartar emetic, but that there was insufficient evidence as to who was responsible. Unusually, the police let it be known that information resulting in the killer's capture would be rewarded by £250, more than a year's wages for most people.

It was uncertain when the poison was taken and it was thought to have been after the dinner. He could have taken it with water when he was in his room, but if so, why? The wine had been left out and so it would have been easy for anyone in the household to have tampered with it, knowing who would be drinking it at dinner.

No one was ever charged with the murder of Bravo; there were no hearings at the magistrates' courts and no one was tried. Whoever poisoned him never faced any legal sanctions whatsoever. However, the shadow of potential guilt remained above all three.

None of them had happy endings. Mrs Bravo left The Priory and altered her name to Florence Turner. She took a villa in Eastney, near Southsea in March 1878 and took to drinking whisky to excess. She died there on 17 September 1878, aged but 33. Money was not her concern as her estate was worth tens of thousands of pounds. Dr Gully died on 27 March 1883 at Orwell Lodge; as with Florence he was a wealthy man on death. It is interesting to note that although he was listed in the Medical Register of 1876 his name was not listed there in 1877. It was another 30 years before Mrs Cox died, probably in Jamaica, where she went in the autumn of 1876 and where she had wealthy relatives. Their secrets were taken by them to their graves.

Agatha Christie was interested in the unsolved poisoning case. In the novel *Ordeal by Innocence*, a character says:

> 'It reminds me, you know, of the Bravo case…no one now can ever know the truth. And so Florence Bravo, abandoned by her family, died alone of drink, and Mrs Cox, ostracised, and with three little boys, lived to be an old woman with most of the people she knew believing her to be a murderess, and Dr Gully was ruined professionally and socially – Someone was guilty and got away with it. But the others were innocent – and didn't get away with anything'.

Ordeal by Innocence is a story where an elderly female philanthropist, Rachel Argyle, has adopted several children from broken homes. She gives them all the advantages that money can buy but also expects them to be grateful to her. Then she is murdered and the suspicion is that ne'er do well Jacko has killed her. Despite pleading that he has an iron clad alibi, he is tried for murder and found guilty, but is given a prison sentence rather than being hanged. He dies in prison soon afterwards.

Later Dr Arthur Calgary, just back from a Polar expedition, returns to England and hears the news. He recalls that he did indeed give Jacko a lift in his car on the night of the killing. He realises that Jacko was innocent, but given he was out of the country at the time he was unaware that he was needed to provide an alibi. He is determined to solve the mystery. The suspects are Rachel's husband, various relatives and adopted adult children.

One of them did indeed strike down the old woman, but the remainder are innocent. All, however lay under suspicion, until the real killer is found. There is another murder before the resolution is determined. In a twist, whilst Jacko was legally innocent, he was morally to blame and therefore was guilty.

So in this sense, the notion that 'it's not the guilty that matter, but the innocent' is a parallel to the Bravo case. It is assumed that either Mrs Bravo, Mrs Cox or Dr Gully was guilty, or two of them working in conjunction. The question next has to be how and why as well as who. At least one of them was innocent.

The case is mentioned in *Elephants Can Remember* too, with retired Superintendent Spence asking 'Who killed Charles Bravo and why? There are several different ideas, mostly not very well founded. But still people try to find alternative explanations'. In *The Clocks*, Poirot confidently declares, 'There is no doubt in my own mind as to who killed Charles Bravo. The companion may have been involved but she was certainly not the moving spirit in the matter'. Alas, Poirot does not reveal what his conclusion is. So this suggests that Mrs Cox was working with another. This is unlikely to have been Mrs Bravo. This would probably be Dr Gully. Possibly he provided poison for her to use and then one of them decided that she should say that Bravo told her that 'I have poisoned myself' in order to divert suspicion from the real murderer. It certainly seems that Mrs Cox was telling a lie as Bravo completely refuted her suggestion of what he had allegedly said. This ties in with Christie's own conclusion.

In 1968, in a letter to Francis Wyndham, editor of *The Sunday Times* magazine, Agatha Christie claimed that Dr Gully was her favourite suspect. She thought that as Florence 'had the money' and Mrs Cox was 'an obvious suspect at first hand but not when you look into it', they could be dismissed. As to Gully, though, 'I've always felt he was the only person who had an overwhelming motive and who was the right type: exceedingly competent, successful and always considered above suspicion'. There are many doctor murderers in her stories – though not all use poison. Yet, despite the fact that he may have had a motive of sorts and was able enough, he was not present in the house to introduce the poison, unless Christie is assuming that he might have provided it for another to use. He was a neighbour so could well have had contact with a member of the household, and we know he had at least two meetings with Mrs Cox outside the house between Florence's marriage and Charles' death. It is to be presumed that Christie thought that the doctor was motivated by his passion for Mrs Bravo or jealousy against Bravo, though the two never joined up together after Bravo's death. To do so, however, would have sealed their guilt in the eyes of contemporary society and later historians, but surely they could have foreseen this result.

There have been other theories concerning this much written about case. Most authors plump for either Florence or Mrs Cox or the two working together. Some have suggested that one of the servants was involved either as principal or as an accomplice. Could Dr Gully have been motivated by jealousy over Mrs Bravo? Could Mrs Bravo have come to hate her husband and detest his sexual advances whilst she was recovering from a miscarriage? Might Mrs Cox have been the accomplice of either of them?

As Spence says, this is a puzzle without a conclusion. The reader can take their pick of at least three suspects. Money does not seem to have been the motive for Mrs Bravo was richer than her husband and she was the only monetary gainer. Was there still passion between Mrs Bravo and Dr Gully and was this strong enough for one of them to risk their life in killing Bravo? Was there any reason for Mrs Cox to kill Bravo? Yes, because she had recently been informed by him that she was to be dismissed. Possibly she may have been assisting one or both of the others. Could a servant have been involved? Or was this a tragic accident? Could Bravo have taken poison in error and then could not bring himself to admit it? Suicide seems to be ruled out as this was a slow and painful way to die, but author Yseult Bridges believed he had administered it himself.

The house still stands, though as No. 225 Balham Hill. Like many large Victorian houses which have survived, it has been divided into flats and is a grade two listed building.

Sources

The National Archives files:

Police file: Murder of Charles Delauney Bravo at Bedford Hill, Balham, MEPO3/123

Bravo, Charles, suspicious death, inquest, HO45/9410/55336

Jan Bondeson, *Murder Houses of South London* (2014)

Swindlers

The Tichborne claimant (1874), Adolf Beck case (1896, 1904), Horatio Bottomley (1922), The Stavisky affair (1934), *Death in the Clouds (1935), They Came to Baghdad (1951), Witness for the Prosecution (1953), Third Girl (1966)*

Swindlers and imposters are referred to in at least three of Agatha Christie's novels, as well as in a play. In *Death in the Clouds*, the French moneylender, Madame Giselle, is found dead in her seat, killed by a poisoned dart. Poirot – who happens to be on board the plane, flying from Paris to London – is soon working on the case alongside Japp and his French colleague Fournier. In a discussion about potential suspects, Japp suggests that father and son Dupont – both archaeologists – might be worth considering, '…I suppose that they've knocked about the world and dug things up in a lot of queer places; they might easily have got hold of some native snake poison'. Fournier, however, is sceptical:

> 'M. Dupont lives for his profession. He is an enthusiast. He was formerly an antique dealer. He gave up a flourishing business to devote himself to excavation. Both he and his son are devoted heart and soul to their profession. It seems to me unlikely – I will not say impossible; since the ramifications of the Stavisky business, I will believe anything! – unlikely that they are mixed up in this business'.

The name Stavisky figures also in a notebook kept by Madame Giselle, where she has made discreet annotations about her customers; namely 'GF 342. French Deputy, Stavisky connection' is one of the entries.

The Stavisky affair was a financial scandal that took place in France in 1934, at the centre of which was a swindler called Serge Alexandre

Stavisky, also known as *le beau* Sasha. He was a plausible fraudster and ladies' man who tricked wealthy women into paying for his expensive tastes. Stavisky also collaborated with other criminals, forging cheques and cheating people in various scams. Apart from a few short prison stints he usually managed to escape the consequences of his crimes, mainly by using bribes and extortion.

By the late 1920s, Stavisky had climbed the social ladder, mingling with the rich and influential, and marrying a glamorous Chanel model. He now embarked on his most profitable enterprise, selling hundreds of millions of francs' worth of false bonds at the city of Bayonne's municipal pawnshop, which were purchased by life-insurance companies. In this scheme he worked in partnership with the mayor of Bayonne, who assisted him in opening the pawnshop. In December 1933, fearing arrest, he fled from Bayonne. On January 8, 1934, *le beau* Sasha was found dead in a Chamonix villa, killed by a gunshot wound to the head. The police said this was a suicide – but rumours spread that he had been murdered to cover up the involvement of highly placed people in his scams.

The snowball quickly got rolling. The opposition to the ruling left-wing coalition took advantage of the situation, accusing the government of corruption. The Prime Minister, Camille Chautemps, was forced to resign. He was succeeded by the radical socialist Édouard Daladier, who immediately dismissed the prefect of the Paris police, a man known for his right-wing sympathies. This led to a large anti-government demonstration at Place de la Concorde on 6 February 1934. The police shot at the protesters, killing a dozen, and injuring many more. Consequently, Daladier too had to resign. He was succeeded by the conservative Gaston Doumergue, who formed a coalition government. This finally restored stability.

In *They Came to Baghdad*, there is a reference to another well-known swindler, this time an Englishman. The heroine Victoria Jones has a conversation with Edward, a very handsome young man whom she has a crush on. They talk about Dr Rathbone, the director of a welfare organization called the Olive Branch. Edward reveals that Rathbone has embezzled a large part of the donations for his personal use:

> 'Do you know what he's been doing all these years? Cleverly appropriating about three-quarters of the subscriptions which pour in from all over the world to his own use. It's the cleverest swindle since the time of Horatio Bottomley'.

Horatio William Bottomley (1860-1933) was a businessman/politician who had an astonishing career. Having lost his parents as a young child, he spent several years in an orphanage, ending his formal education at the age of 14. Working his way up from errand boy to solicitor's clerk, he founded his own publishing company ten years later. In 1893 he was arraigned on fraud charges in connection with one of his enterprises, the Hansard Publishing Union Limited. Conducting his own defence, Bottomley – a skilled orator – was acquitted.

Moving on to new projects, this energetic businessman successfully promoted Australian gold mining shares. He became rich and enjoyed a lavish lifestyle, spending his money on women and racehorses. In 1906, he was elected to Parliament as the Liberal MP for Hackney South. In the same year, he launched the weekly magazine, *John Bull*, which became extremely popular. Two years later, he was again under scrutiny for dubious business practices but used his considerable oratory talent to absolve himself from responsibility.

At the outbreak of the First World War, Bottomley became an influential propagandist for the war effort, addressing hundreds of public meetings. He used strong language against the Germans, calling them 'unnatural freaks' who should be exterminated. In 1918, Bottomley was again elected to Parliament, this time as an independent member. 'I am now prepared to proceed to Westminster to run the show', he confidently told a journalist. For a while, the future looked bright – but the multi-talented MP was unable to keep within the bounds of the law.

In the summer of 1919, Bottomley announced his Victory Bonds Club, where subscribers for a minimum investment of £1 (compared with the normal price of £5 for the bonds) would get the chance to win prizes from a lottery funded by the accrued interest. Bottomley, however, used the money to finance his newspaper enterprises, as well as his expensive lifestyle. In May 1922, Bottomley was on trial at the Old Bailey, on the charge of fraudulent conversion of Victory Bond Club funds. He again defended himself, but this time to no avail. Convicted of fraud, he was sentenced to seven years in prison and expelled from Parliament. Upon his release in 1927, Bottomley tried to revive his business career but failed, spending his last years in poverty.

A very different type of fraud was involved in the famous case of Adolf Beck, the man who was innocently imprisoned for a crime committed by someone else. Beck was a Norwegian, born in 1841, who had lived most of his life elsewhere. From 1885 he lived in England, being engaged in various business schemes. In December 1895, a woman accosted him on Victoria Street in London, accusing him of having swindled her out of two watches and some rings. This was the beginning of a veritable nightmare for the unfortunate Beck. The woman was one of many – twenty-two in all – who had been defrauded in the same way, by a grey-haired man with a moustache calling himself 'Lord Wilton de Willoughby'. His modus operandi was to flatter his victims, impress them by his title and persuade them to hand over jewellery in exchange for a worthless cheque.

In a flawed line-up where Beck was the only grey-haired man with a moustache, he was identified by the women as the person who had defrauded them. It was discovered that a man named John Smith had been convicted in 1877 for swindling single women, using the name Lord Willoughby. After his release Smith had disappeared and it was now assumed that he and Beck were one and the same person. A policeman who had arrested Smith eighteen years earlier identified Beck as Smith, despite Beck's insistence that he had been in South America at that time and had witnesses to prove it.

At Beck's trial at the Old Bailey in March 1896, the defence argued that he was a victim of mistaken identity. However, the women who had been swindled by 'Lord Willoughby' swore in court that Beck was the man. He was found guilty of fraud and sentenced to seven years imprisonment. Beck's solicitor made several attempts to get the case re-opened, without any success. In 1898 an official at the Home Office had a look at John Smith's prison file and discovered that he was a Jew and had been circumcised. This meant that Beck and Smith could not possibly be the same person, which was acknowledged in a report by the judge who had presided at Beck's trial. Incredibly, nothing more was done about it. Adolf Beck remained in prison until July 1901, when he was paroled for good behaviour.

This could have been the end of the story, but worse was to come. In March 1904, Beck was again accused of fraud by a woman who had encountered a grey-haired gentleman who had given her compliments and then stolen her jewellery. Once more he was put on trial at the Old Bailey, once more he was found guilty by the jury. This time, however, the judge (not the same as in the previous trial) was not fully convinced and decided to postpone the sentencing. Shortly afterwards, a man was arrested for having swindled rings from two women. This was none other than John Smith, whose real name was Wilhelm Meyer, of Austria. He bore a certain resemblance to Adolf Beck, although the latter was younger and not so heavy in build. Meyer was a university-educated man who had fallen on hard times, turning to fraud as a means of living. He was put on trial, pleaded guilty and was sentenced to five years in prison.

Adolf Beck was given a free pardon by Edward VII and – in compensation for his false imprisonment – was awarded £2,000, which was later raised to £5,000 due to public clamour. A Committee of Inquiry was set up to investigate the case. It concluded that there were many errors made by the prosecution and judge at Beck's first trial; there was also criticism of the Home Office for not having acted in 1898 when it became clear that Beck and Smith were not the same man. As a result of the report, the Court of Criminal Appeal was created in 1907.

In the play version of *Witness for the Prosecution*, there is an interesting reference to the Beck case. Leonard Vole, worried that he is about to be arrested for the murder of an old lady, gives vent to his fears in a conversation with the solicitor, Mr Mayhew:

> Vole: '…But I suppose it will be – all right, won't it? I mean you don't get convicted for things you haven't done in this country, do you?'
>
> Mayhew: 'Our English judicial system is, in my opinion, the finest in the world'.
>
> Vole: 'Of course there was that case of – what was his name – Adolf Beck. I read about it only the other day. After he'd been in prison for years, they found out it was another chap called Smith. They gave him a free pardon then. That's a thing that seems odd to me – giving you a "pardon" for something you haven't done'.
>
> Mayhew: 'It is the necessary legal term'.
>
> Vole: 'Well, it doesn't seem right to me'.
>
> Mayhew: 'The important thing was that Beck was set at liberty'.
>
> Vole: 'Yes, it was all right for him. But if it had been murder now – if it had been murder it would have been too late. He would have been hanged'.

Witness for the Prosecution was considered by Agatha Christie to be the best play she had ever written. She wanted to get the courtroom scene as accurate as possible, preparing herself by reading several of the *Famous British Trials* volumes. The play was turned into a successful Hollywood film in 1957, starring Charles Laughton as Mayhew, Tyrone Power as Vole, and Marlene Dietrich as Romaine Vole. Adolf Beck is discussed in the film as well, although not in the short story on which both the play and film are based. The play has had a successful rerun in London in recent years.

Another reference to a famous fraud case involving false identities can be found in *Third Girl*, a novel set in London's swinging sixties. Andrew Restarick, a man who has spent many years abroad, returns to England upon the death of his brother. It turns out that he is an imposter. When Mrs Oliver reflects that it was a great risk for him to take, Poirot retorts, 'Less than you might think. He was never a claimant, you see, in the Tichborne sense'. This refers to the so-called Tichborne claimant, a man who came from Australia to England in 1866, asserting that he was the missing heir to the Tichborne baronetcy.

The Tichbornes were a distinguished Catholic family living in Hampshire. Roger Tichborne (born in 1829) was the eldest son of James Tichborne, the 10th baronet. Much of Roger's upbringing was spent in Paris together with his mother Henriette, and he spoke French fluently. After completing his education at Stonyhurst College he embarked on a military career, serving in the 6th Dragoon Guards. In 1853 he went to South America. On 20 April 1854, he boarded the ship *Bella* at Rio de Janeiro, sailing for Jamaica. Four days later, the ship's capsized longboat was found off the Brazilian coast. It was assumed that all onboard had been lost.

After the death of James Tichborne in 1862, the baronetcy passed to Alfred, Roger's younger brother. Lady Henriette, however, held on to the hope that her eldest son somehow had survived, perhaps – as rumours said – to begin a new life in Australia. She advertised for information about Roger in Australian newspapers, offering a large reward. In 1866, a butcher from Wagga Wagga known as Thomas Castro came forward, claiming to be Roger Tichborne. He bore a certain facial resemblance to the lost heir, although his build was much heavier. His story was that he and other survivors of the shipwreck had been picked up by another ship bound for Melbourne.

Lady Tichborne sent money for Castro to travel to England. Upon meeting him, she immediately accepted him as her son. It has been suggested that she may have been influenced by wishful thinking, her younger son Alfred having died in February 1866. Other relatives were more sceptical, pointing out Castro's total ignorance of the French language. After the death of Lady

Tichborne in 1868, the still sceptical relatives initiated an investigation, employing former Detective Inspector Jonathan Whicher (famous from the Constance Kent case). It now emerged that Castro might be identical with an Englishman called Arthur Orton, who had emigrated to Australia.

After the Tichborne claimant lost a civil suit against the tenant of the family manor Tichborne Park, he was arrested on charges of perjury. In the ensuing criminal trial, ending in February 1874, he was convicted and sentenced to 14 years imprisonment, being released in 1884. At that time, he still maintained that he was Sir Roger Tichborne. Eleven years later, he confessed to a newspaper that he was, after all, Arthur Orton – only to retract the confession shortly afterwards. He tried his hand at various business enterprises before dying destitute in 1898.

Back to *Third Girl*: it seems like Poirot's assertion that Andrew Restarick 'was never a claimant in the Tichborne sense' is not completely correct. In fact, there is a clear parallel between fiction and reality here. Restarick, like Orton, pretends to be the brother of a dead man. In both cases, the purpose is to obtain money fraudulently. Restarick does not face the same sort of challenge as the Tichborne claimant, though, because his only surviving relative is a half blind old uncle.

That Agatha Christie knew the Tichborne case well may be inferred from the fact that her sister Margaret Miller was the author of a play called *The Claimant*. It ran for a short time in the West End at the Queen's Theatre in 1924. Christie was very excited for her sister's sake. The play contained a fictitious character named Charles, the claimant's accomplice, who was modelled after the sisters' beloved but somewhat erratic brother Monty.

Sources

Janet Morgan, *Agatha Christie, a biography* (1984)

Tom Zaniello, *Saints and sinners in Queen Victoria's courts – ten scandalous trials* (2021)

Paul Jankowski, *Stavisky – A Confidence Man in the Republic of Virtue* (2002)

Julian Symons, *Horatio Bottomley* (2001)

Sam Poyser; Angus Nurse & Rebecca Milne, *Miscarriages of Justice: Causes, Consequences and Remedies* (2018)

Charles Osborne, *The Life and Crimes of Agatha Christie* (1982)

Adelaide Bartlett (1886)

The Clocks (1963)

During the second half of the nineteenth century, chloroform was a commonly used anaesthetic. The patient inhaled the compound via a handkerchief or mask. At lower doses it did not cause unconsciousness but merely relaxation and drowsiness. After Queen Victoria gave birth to her eighth child, Prince Leopold, under the pleasant influence of chloroform, it became almost more popular than ether. However, a series of unexplained deaths in connection with anaesthesia put a stop to that: it turned out that chloroform could cause fatal cardiac arrhythmia. Suicide by ingestion of liquid chloroform, although uncommon, has been occasionally reported. In contrast, murder by the same means is extremely rare. Perhaps the most famous case – if murder it was – is the so-called Pimlico Mystery, which took place in London on New Year's Eve 1885/1886.

On 6 April 1875, 30-year-old grocer Thomas Edwin Bartlett married 19 year old Adelaide Blanche de la Tremoille de Thouars d'Escury in Croydon, Surrey. Adelaide's portrait shows an attractive young woman with large, expressive eyes. Her mother, Clara Chamberlain, was the daughter of a Stock Exchange clerk. There is contradictory information as to the identity of Adelaide's father. The official father – married to Clara in 1853 – was a Frenchman with the unlikely name of Adolphe Collot de la Tremoille, Comte de Thouars d'Escury. Anyone looking for him in the *Almanch de Gotha* will be disappointed: the surname is a mixture of two completely different family names. Possibly Adolphe was an illegitimate descendant of one of these families, alternatively the surname was a pure figment of imagination.

Clara and Adolphe had four children, of which Adelaide (born in 1855) was the second. By 1866 both parents were dead. Five years later, the census records show Adelaide to be cared for as an adoptive daughter by a confectioner and his wife in Hampton Wick in southwest London. In early 1875 she lodged near Kingston upon Thames at the house of Charles Bartlett, who had a brother named Edwin. When Edwin Bartlett came to visit and happened to meet Adelaide, he fell in love with her at first sight. They married a few months later but did not at first live together. Instead, Adelaide spent two years at various educational institutions, including one in Belgium, reuniting with her husband during school holidays. No doubt her education was paid for by Edwin, who was a wealthy man. Together with a business partner he owned six grocery stores in Herne Hill and Dulwich in southwest London.

Between 1877 and 1883 the Bartletts lived in a flat above one of the shops in Herne Hill. Edwin's father, a widower, lived there too. The relationship between him and his daughter-in-law was strained and came to an open break in 1878, when Adelaide suddenly left home, staying away for a week. According to Bartlett the elder, she had had an affair with his younger son Frederick, who shortly afterwards emigrated to the United States. Adelaide denied this and demanded a written apology from her father-in-law, which he agreed to for the sake of domestic peace. Around Christmas 1881, Adelaide gave birth to a stillborn child. It was a difficult delivery and Adelaide told her midwife, Annie Walker, that she never intended to have another child.

Two years later, the Bartletts moved to Merton Abbey, not far from Wimbledon. Here, in January 1885, they became acquainted with the 27-year-old Reverend George Dyson, a Wesleyan minister. The acquaintance quickly developed into intimate friendship: Dyson often came to dinner and even visited Adelaide alone to give her spiritual guidance as well as lessons in geography, history, Latin and mathematics. Both the Bartletts admired the young minister for his cultured nature, referring to him as 'Georgius Rex' – King George. In September 1885, Edwin Bartlett had a will drawn up, in which he appointed Dyson as his executor. Previously, Edwin's will had stipulated that Adelaide would inherit from him only on the condition that she did not remarry. In the new version, this clause had been removed, Edwin leaving everything to Adelaide without reservation.

In early October 1885, the Bartletts moved to 85 Claverton Street, Pimlico. Here they rented two furnished rooms from a couple named Doggett. George Dyson continued to visit frequently. On one occasion, the housemaid saw how Adelaide – sitting on the floor – rested her head on Dyson's lap. The young minister later admitted to having kissed Adelaide a few times but claimed that nothing more had happened between them.

He also stated that he had told Edwin about his feelings for Adelaide and had offered to stop visiting, but that Edwin did not seem to mind, on the contrary encouraging his wife's association with the younger man.

Edwin Bartlett is described as a man of strong physique, active and constantly working. The only problem was his teeth, or rather stumps of teeth, that remained after a clumsy dentist's work. It therefore came as a surprise to George Dyson when Adelaide confided to him that her husband did not have long to live. Edwin had been suffering from 'an internal complaint' for several years, had been told by a doctor that the situation was serious, and was therefore looking for a reliable man who could protect Adelaide when he himself was gone. Later, Adelaide told Dyson that she used to give Edwin chloroform, because of the severe pains caused by his internal disease. She did this on the advice of a Dr Nichols, the same one who had told her that Edwin had only one year left to live. Adelaide asked George not to mention anything about Edwin's internal complaint to Edwin himself, as it was a sensitive matter.

In early December 1885, Edwin Bartlett fell ill with stomach pains, vomiting and diarrhoea. A local physician, Dr Leach, was called in and discovered a blue line along the margins of Edwin's gums. Leach took this as a sign of mercury poisoning and assumed that the patient had been in the habit of taking mercury for syphilis. This Edwin emphatically denied. In fact, the thin blue line – called Burton's line – is a classic symptom of chronic lead poisoning. The origin of this was never clarified. In addition to gastrointestinal symptoms, Edwin suffered from insomnia and depression. Dr Leach prescribed various medicines, including a tincture with a small amount of chloroform in it.

Over the following weeks, Edwin's general condition improved but insomnia was still a concern. On 27 December, Adelaide asked Dyson to buy some chloroform to help with her husband's insomnia. She explained that she had previously been given chloroform by her midwife Annie Walker, who had gone to the United States. The obliging Dyson went to three different chemists' shops and procured chloroform, which he stated would be used to remove stains from clothing. He poured the contents of four bottles into a larger one, which he gave to Adelaide. Edwin was by now almost restored to health. His business partner describes him as 'quite cheerful...getting on very nicely'. On New Year's Eve, the Bartletts had roast hare for dinner. Later that evening, Edwin went to the dentist to have a tooth extracted. For supper, the couple ate oysters. Edwin told the housemaid that he wanted haddock for breakfast the next morning and that he was very much looking forward to it.

At 4am on 1 January 1886, Mr Doggett was woken by Adelaide, who asked him to come downstairs quickly, as she thought Edwin was dead. The landlord found him in the drawing room, lying on the bed in the corner by the fireplace. According to Adelaide, she had been sitting in an armchair close to the bed and fallen asleep; when she awoke, Edwin was face down. She turned him on his back and tried to pour brandy into his mouth. Doggett could smell a strong odour of 'chloric ether' in the room. On the mantelpiece was a wine glass containing some liquid. According to Doggett, it smelled of brandy mixed with an ether-like substance. Dr Leach arrived a short time later. Edwin's body was cold, the doctor estimating that death had occurred about three hours earlier. As there was no obvious cause of death, it was decided to perform a post mortem examination.

Edwin Bartlett's stomach and lower part of the oesophagus showed signs of acute inflammation. In the stomach, 1 ounce (29 ml) of a liquid containing chloroform was discovered. Apart from this, nothing out of the ordinary was found. There were no signs of any internal disease. Edwin had evidently ingested a considerable quantity of chloroform, which is a local irritant, but his mouth and throat appeared perfectly normal. Several bottles and glasses found in the drawing room were analysed for the presence of chloroform, none was detected. The wine glass on the mantelpiece was never examined, however, because it had been taken away and cleaned by the housemaid.

At the end of January 1886, when all analyses were completed, Dr Leach told Adelaide that the cause of death was chloroform poisoning. To his surprise, she exclaimed: 'I wish anything but chloroform had been found'. She went on to explain that she and Edwin had agreed to have a platonic marriage and that they only had sex once, because she wished to be a mother. Edwin had encouraged Adelaide's friendship with George Dyson and had more or less 'given her' to the younger man. But suddenly, during the last few weeks, Edwin had insisted on resuming his conjugal rights. Adelaide had objected to this, and to restrain her husband's passions she had procured chloroform. The idea was to wave a handkerchief soaked in chloroform in front of his face, so that he would become sleepy. On New Year's Eve, Adelaide had confessed her plan to Edwin and handed him the bottle of chloroform.

By now George Dyson had become alarmed over his purchase of chloroform, telling Adelaide and one of her friends that he was 'a ruined man'. He went to the police and told the whole story. An inquest returned a verdict of wilful murder by Adelaide Bartlett and George Dyson on 18 February 1886, and they were both arrested the same day. The trial was held between 12 and 17 April at the Central Criminal Court (Old Bailey). The Attorney-General, Sir Charles Russell, prosecuted and Mr (later Sir) Edward Clarke led for the defence. The judge was Sir Alfred Wills, who later presided at the final trial of Oscar Wilde. The charge against Dyson was immediately dropped by the prosecution and he was formally acquitted, being called as an important witness against Adelaide Bartlett. Their friendship had come to an end in January, when she had been angry over his persistent worry over the chloroform.

At the trial, it became clear that Adelaide had lied about several things. Dr Nichols denied that he had ever been consulted by her regarding Edwin's health. Annie Walker denied having been to the United States, nor had she given any chloroform to Adelaide. Her testimony also contradicted Adelaide's story about a platonic marriage. 'The only occasion' was the only time they had sexual intercourse without protection, otherwise preventives were used – probably 'French letters' found among Edwin's belongings after his death. The bottle of chloroform that Dyson had prepared for Adelaide was never recovered. She claimed that she had put it in a drawer, later removing it and throwing it into a pond.

The prosecution suggested that Adelaide had been tired of her husband, finding him physically repulsive, and had wanted to replace him with Dyson. When Edwin fell ill in December, she took advantage of the situation to get rid of him in a cunning way. After first making him drowsy with chloroform inhaled from a handkerchief, she had somehow managed to pour liquid chloroform into his mouth, without causing local irritation. Edward Clarke brilliantly defended Adelaide, addressing the jury in an eloquent speech. He made the most of the medical uncertainties, emphasizing that murder had never been committed by the administration of liquid chloroform (there had, actually, been a case in Manchester in 1876). Clarke's version was that Edwin committed suicide by quickly swallowing a large amount of chloroform. This would explain the absence of irritation and inflammation in the mouth and throat. On the other hand, Edwin's cheerful demeanour on New Year's Eve hardly indicated that he was thinking about suicide. The judge, in his summing up, proposed an alternative: that Edwin had taken chloroform as a sleeping drug but had, in the darkness, misjudged the amount. The judge also pointed out that much of the evidence against

Adelaide consisted of George Dyson's testimony, a man who apparently acted out of self-preservation.

The jury returned a verdict of Not Guilty, adding that 'although we think grave suspicion is attached to the prisoner, we do not think there is sufficient evidence to show how or by whom the chloroform was administered'. Adelaide Bartlett left the courtroom to the applause of the audience. What became of her afterwards is shrouded in mystery. One of her brothers had emigrated to Australia; it is possible that she joined him there. George Dyson is said to have emigrated to the United States, changing his name, and becoming a journalist, even an editor of *Scientific American*. Whether there is solid evidence for this is unclear. Edward Clarke said in his speech to the jury that 'this case will be long memorable in the annals of medical jurisprudence'. He was right. The Pimlico Mystery will always be remembered, perhaps best summarized in the famous statement attributed to Sir James Paget: 'Now that she has been acquitted for murder and cannot be tried again, she should tell us in the interest of science how she did it!'

In *The Clocks*, we find Poirot sitting in his armchair, surrounded by piles of books. His valet, the always discreet and correct George, confides to visitor Colin Lamb that his master sometimes gets a little depressed. The reason for this seems to be that he longs to solve a difficult murder mystery. Waiting for one to appear, Poirot spends his time applying the little grey cells to some of the classic unsolved cases. In a dialogue with Lamb he explains:

> 'I have occupied myself of late in reading various real life unsolved mysteries. I apply to them my own solutions'.
>
> 'You mean cases like the Bravo case, Adelaide Bartlett and all the rest of them?'
>
> 'Exactly'.

Poirot goes on to discuss the murder of Charles Bravo, the Constance Kent case, and finally Lizzie Borden, but strangely he says nothing about Adelaide Bartlett. Maybe the Pimlico Mystery is too tough a nut to crack even for him? The reader is left in the dark concerning Poirot's – and Agatha Christie's – views on the case.

Chloroform does not appear as a method of murder in any of Christie's novels, although it figures as a means of incapacitating victims. In the short story 'The Plymouth Express', the murder victim – rich heiress Flossie Halliday – is first chloroformed, then stabbed in the heart on board a train. In another short story, 'The Kidnapped Prime Minister', Captain Danels is chloroformed, bound, and gagged. Further examples of characters sedated with chloroform are Lady Frances Derwent in *Why Didn't They Ask Evans?* (1934), Victoria Jones in *They Came to Baghdad* (1951) and Tommy Beresford in the short story 'The Adventure of the Sinister Stranger' in *Partners in Crime* (1929). The description of how the victim is chloroformed is similar in all cases, a handkerchief saturated with the solvent being pressed against the mouth and nose, causing almost immediate unconsciousness. This is also the impression conveyed from numerous films. In reality, it takes at least five minutes of inhalation of chloroform to render a person unconscious.

As a curiosity, it can be mentioned that Agatha Christie herself once successfully chloroformed a hedgehog that had become entangled in the tennis net and so managed to release it.

Sources

The Trial of Adelaide Bartlett for Murder, Held at the Central Criminal Court, edited by Edward Beal (1886)

Proceedings of the Old Bailey (accessed at https://www.oldbaileyonline.org/)

John Emsley, *Molecules of Murder – Criminal Molecules and Classic Cases* (2016).

Jack the Ripper (1888)

The ABC Murders (1936),
Cat Among the Pigeons (1959)

Murders of prostitutes in the London slums may seem a far cry away from the image many have of genteel poisonings in drawing rooms as depicted by some of Agatha Christie's books. Yet the killer is referenced in two books of hers as noted above. The killings by Jack the Ripper are the most notorious unsolved murders in Britain; perhaps in the world. Yet virtually nothing is known for certain about the criminal himself, despite a great deal of theorising in recent decades. All that is clear are his actions which took place in Whitechapel and Spitalfields in the autumn of 1888. From these it is evident that he was a very dangerous and disturbed individual indeed.

It is even uncertain as to how many women he killed. Some allege that his first victim was Emma Elizabeth Smith, attacked in Whitechapel on the night of 3 April 1888 and who died shortly after, but given that this was a gang attack, most do not include it in his tally. On firmer, yet still unsure ground, is the murder of Martha Tabram, in George Yard Buildings just off Wentworth Street, on 7 August 1888. She had been stabbed 39 times, but again another killer may have been to blame. No clear suspect emerged for either murder.

There are five 'canonical victims' who are usually attributed to the Ripper. The first was Mary Ann Nichols who was murdered on 31 August. Her corpse was found lying on Bucks Row in the early hours of the day. Her throat had been cut, but there was worse to come; there were deep wounds in the lower abdomen. There was no obvious motive for the crime and no one was ever charged and these features were to follow in the subsequent murders.

Only a week was to pass before the murderer struck again. This time the unfortunate woman was Annie Chapman. Her body was found in the early hours of 8 September in the backyard of 29 Hanbury Street in Spitalfields. Again, her throat had been cut. This time, however, as well as abdominal wounds, some of her internal organs had been removed by the killer; these were her uterus and her bladder. It was thought by some that this did show a degree of anatomical skill on the killer's part.

Then there was a gap of three weeks. The killer perhaps, had been briefly sated in his evil appetite or perhaps there was another reason why he did not act in the intervening weeks. This time, though, he probably killed two victims in what was known as The Double Event. On 30 September, the body of Elizabeth Stride was found in Dutfields Yard outside the entrance to the International Men's Working Club in Berner Street. Her throat had been cut but otherwise the body had not been mutilated. It is presumed that this was so because the killer was interrupted by a local man entering the Yard with his pony and cart, so hid and fled.

Soon after this discovery, the body of Catherine Eddowes was found in Mitre Square. Presumably the thwarted killer, unable to do all that he wanted to on Elizabeth, had gone in search of another victim and unfortunately found one. Her throat had been cut, but there was also severe mutilation to her body, and also organs had been removed. There were many cuts to the face and a kidney had been removed. As with the earlier victims there was discussion as to how much anatomical knowledge the killer had. It was surmised that he might have been a slaughterer or a butcher of animals.

The gap of time between this murder and what may well have been the final killing was the longest of all. It was not until the morning of 9 November, that the remains of Mary Jane Kelly were found in the room she lived in at 13 Miller's Court off Dorset Street, Spitalfields. Mary Jane was younger than all the other victims, but like them she had an addiction to alcohol and that made her desperate and vulnerable enough to go out at night to find a man or men willing to pay her for sex. Her body had almost been completely destroyed in the murderer's frenzy. The heart was missing and other portions of her anatomy had been cut off and were found in the room. Working indoors, the killer had been able to do all the damage he could without fear of interruption, a luxury previously denied to him.

This was probably the final murder but there were instances of other women being killed in the locality in the next few years: Alice Mackenzie in 1889 and Frances Coles in 1891. Both were killed in the streets at nighttime by having their throats cut. Although there were some cuts to Alice's abdomen, in neither case were organs removed and so whether this was the same killer seems unlikely. No one was ever charged with these crimes and they remain unsolved to this day. There were no real clues, the man was not caught in the act or shortly afterwards, no one witnessed the actual murders and no one made an authentic confession. There were many letters written to the police and press, some claiming to be from the murderer, discussed below, and just after the fourth murder there was a message written in chalk on the wall of a tenement building on Goulston Street, which may have been written by the killer, may have been a clue or may have been anti-Semitic graffiti in a Jewish district. It read, according to the most accepted version, 'The Juwes are the men that will not be blamed for nothing'.

It is not known why the killer stopped. Possibly he became too ill to carry on, possibly he died, though suicide is unlikely. Perhaps he was gaoled for another offence. Perhaps he was consigned to an asylum. Or maybe he moved from London, (there were lots of similar crimes reported all over the country). Possibly he feared detection and was rational enough to know that continued murders increased the chance of being hanged. Or maybe the final, terrible murder and mutilation, sated his lusts. We shall never know, but the murders ceased, probably in November 1888.

The police attempted to solve the murders but faced many handicaps. There was a lack of technological and scientific aids that became increasingly known about and used in the next century and beyond. There were no forensics as we know today. They had never dealt with such a killer before. There had been multiple murderers in the past but most were poisoners and most had obvious motives, usually monetary. And they tended to kill members of their own family and others known to them personally. There is no evidence that the killer here was acquainted with any of his victims hitherto. Yet the police and the Commissioner of the Metropolitan Police in particular were singled out for vitriolic abuse in the press for their alleged incompetence.

Who the killer was has engaged the attention of many authors in recent decades and many suspects have been added to those few posited by the police in 1888 and its aftermath. There was no one suspect favoured by the police. Different officials had different views. Aaron Kosminski, a Polish barber of Whitechapel, later committed to an asylum, was favoured by some senior officials; Montague John Druitt, a teacher/barrister who committed suicide later that year was another. Michael Ostrog, a Russian conman and thief was another, as was Dr Francis Tumblety, an American quack doctor.

Later London serial killers such as Dr Thomas Neill Cream, who preyed on prostitutes, and George Chapman who killed the women who passed as his wives, were suspected. Both were poisoners. There is, however, almost no evidence to make a strong case for any of these men.

Some witnesses did see a man with some of the victims before they were killed. Naturally, these sightings, made briefly and at night time, differ. And whether any of these men was the killer is another question. One witness thought that a man seen with Annie Chapman was a foreigner, middle aged and wearing 'shabby genteel' clothes. One witness who saw Elizabeth Stride with a man thought he seemed similar in age and perhaps occupation as that seen with Annie Chapman. Yet another witness thought a man seen with Elizabeth was rather younger and wore a peaked sailor's cap. As had the man last seen with Catherine Eddowes, although he was generally looking less smart than the others. Height was variously ascribed to being five feet three to five feet seven. Finally one George Hutchinson described a man seen with Mary Jane Kelly as being well dressed and 'Jewish' in appearance.

Modern commentators have suggested that the killer was a young man who lived locally and who had a fierce hatred of women. The motive appears to have been a wish to mutilate and remove organs from women's bodies. He was probably in a legitimate trade that allowed him access to animal or human bodies and so knew their anatomy. One historian, in a series of the worst Britons in history, has nominated the Ripper as being number one for the nineteenth century.

This notorious serial killer is referenced in two Poirot adventures. At these times (1936 and 1959), 'Ripperology' as the study of Jack the Ripper and his milieu is now known, was still in its infancy. There were then very few books on the subject. One, perhaps the most important before 1965, was by Leonard Matters, *The Mystery of Jack the Ripper* (1929), but otherwise, compared to more recent years, there was little in print or on screen on the topic. Other books after this were William Stewart's *Jack the Ripper: A New Theory* in 1939 and Donald McCormick's *Identity of Jack the Ripper* in 1959. Matters' book is largely a work of fiction and he offers as a solution a doctor who is avenging the death of his son, who died due to acquiring a sexual disease from one of these women. This is not now seen as a plausible solution. Whether Christie read this book is not known.

The ABC Murders has been widely viewed as one of Agatha Christie's masterpieces. It has been filmed once and televised twice. In this novel

Poirot receives anonymous letters informing him that there will be a murder in Andover, which there is, then Bexhill and so on, with victims whose surnames begin with A, then B etc., and an ABC Railway Guide is found at each crime scene. The letter writer, who is using a typewriter, taunts Poirot, stating that he thinks he is so much more intelligent than the police, only this killer knows better. As has been said, this is a reference to the letters sent allegedly by the killer. In one case, just before the 'Double Event' a letter was sent to the Central News Agency, titled 'Dear Boss' and, most famously, ending with the name 'Jack the Ripper'. The letter may well have been written by a journalist but its importance is that it gave the murderer a nom de plume by which he has been known thereafter. The other well-known letter was sent a week later, to George Lusk, chairman of the Whitechapel Vigilance Committee. It was stated to be 'From Hell' and included a human kidney which may or may not have been that of Catherine Eddowes, which had been removed from her body. Whether these letters were sent from the killer is a moot point; most think not, but this works well as a crucial plot device informed by an interpretation of reality.

The killer in the story seems to be choosing victims without any personal motive, such as greed, jealousy, fear, just as the Ripper did. The killer is not anyone who seems to have any animosity against those he kills. It would appear that his motivation is internalised, as was the Ripper's. Almost anyone might be his next victim. And so anyone might be the killer, whereas in most murders the number of possible suspects is a very close circle of people known to the victim. Poirot often refers to the personality of the victim being the clue to the case but here, as with the Ripper, it is the killer's personality which is the driving force against his innocent victims. There are suspects, such as the estranged husband of the Andover victim, shopkeeper Mrs Ascher, but none seem likely.

In fact the first two killings in the book place Poirot and Hastings in the, for them, unusual world of the working class. These murders and the subsequent investigations are described in an authentic manner and this gives them a more disturbing edge than is found in Christie's other books of this era. The stabbing of an unpleasant peer in *Lord Edgware Dies (1933)* is in the realm of fiction; that of an elderly female shopkeeper clubbed to death or a young waitress strangled on the beach is not.

Jack the Ripper is referred to in this book explicitly as well. Direct references are 'Remember the long continued success of Jack the Ripper'

Poirot tells Hastings, who replies, 'It's horrible'. 'It's like Jack the Ripper all over again' says a landlady. There are also references to the type of crime, 'the "chain" or "series" type of murder' as a policer officer puts it, and whether the killer is mad, or has a logic to his crimes, in this case an alphabetical complex rather than a hatred of a particular class of people – prostitutes being mentioned as one category. As Dr Thompson says, 'He removes people, policemen, clergymen or prostitutes, who he thinks should be removed'. It was once thought that the Ripper was a religious zealot who saw it as his God given mission to kill prostitutes, but this now seems unlikely. They were the victims but only because they were so vulnerable, being in the streets in the lonely early hours of the morning. In the book, there is also a realistic discussion on police tactics, especially in handling the media, whether the police feeding the press with extensive information on the murders will provoke more by stroking the killer's ego or whether it will assist in his detection is the point at stake.

It is also worth noting that the term serial killer, now a very well-known one, was not coined until the 1980s by an American detective to categorise a crime, all too common in America, where the same killer murders at least three victims leaving a gap of time between each, usually for the same reason and by the same method. This is to differentiate them from spree killers, who kill many people but all on one occasion, often using a gun. So this is an example of Christie being the first to use a term which has been modified into more common usage.

Finally, in the denouement, Poirot tells the suspects, 'Not all the crimes of Jack the Ripper were committed by Jack the Ripper', for in reality there had been (in the MacNaughton Memorandum of 1894) a list of eleven names put forward as possible victims in 1888-1891, whereas the generally agreed number of victims is five. Apart from the nine women already mentioned, in late 1888 the corpse of Rose Mylett was found in Whitechapel as was part of an unidentified woman. Ripper authors are divided over whom they include in the body count; some surmise that Elizabeth Stride was killed by another, possibly her boyfriend, Michael Kidney, and others include Martha Tabram. This is because in the first case Elizabeth's body was not mutilated, though others contend that the time between murder and possible discovery was too short to allow such. With Martha Tabram, though the modus operandi is different, this could have been because this was the first murder by the unknown killer and multiple murderers sometimes change their way of killing as they proceed.

As the novel progresses, the reader is shown glimpses of the man who appears to be the killer and so this seems to be more a thriller rather than a whodunnit. Yet this is an elaborate and clever charade. It turns out that of the ABC murders, which progress as far as D, only one is the 'real' one and the other three are camouflage to conceal the identity and motive of the criminal. The murder in question is carried out for rational reasons as we would expect in an Agatha Christie story. The apparent murderer (who shall be further discussed in the chapter called Murders and murderers anticipated) is but a dupe on whom guilt can be affixed whilst the real killer hopes to get away with their crimes. The 1990s David Suchet version of this story also makes an explicit reference to Jack the Ripper (the series rarely refers to real criminals as the books do), presumably because 1990s audiences would be certain to know who was being referenced.

In the Poirot novel *Cat Among the Pigeons*, Jack the Ripper is also mentioned alongside less well known Victorian serial poisoner Dr Thomas Neill Cream (detailed in the next chapter), but only very fleetingly. This is following the deaths of three members of female staff at Meadowfield, an exclusive girls' boarding school, and a Mrs Sutcliffe, mother to one of the girls at the said school, wonders, 'Who went about killing an unfortunate type of woman. I suppose this murderer just goes about killing schoolmistresses'. As noted, this is a fallacy; the Ripper did kill several of 'an unfortunate type of woman' but only because they were so easy to find on the streets at that hour and were only too willing to go with a strange man to a lonely place because they needed the money. Any woman would have suited the Ripper's perverted desires.

The novel's three victims are all killed on school premises, by different methods and by two different killers and for different reasons. The main plot here revolves around the quest for some precious jewels smuggled out of a Middle eastern country. As with *The ABC murders,* crimes in Christie's milieu occur for very recognisable reasons. So the comparison here with the Ripper and his victims falls rather flat.

Sources

Richard Jones, *The Jack the Ripper files* (2014)
Jonathan Oates, *London Serial Killers, 1888-1965* (2022)
Philip Sugden, *The Complete Jack the Ripper* (1995)

Dr Thomas Neill Cream (1891-1892)

Cat Among the Pigeons (1959)

Dr Thomas Neill Cream was a notorious late Victorian serial poisoner, who has been accused of being Jack the Ripper, which is perhaps why he has a higher profile than other once noted Victorian killers. As with the Ripper he seems an unlikely candidate for reference in an Agatha Christie novel. This is despite his middle class and professional status and the fact that like most medical murderers he used poison. His motives are less easy to be certain about but probably included the desire for money and a hatred of women. Another parallel with Jack the Ripper is that both murderers preyed on one of the most vulnerable classes of women, that is to say prostitutes (sex workers).

Cream was born in Glasgow in 1850 but emigrated to Quebec with his family. After working with his father, he showed an interest in medicine and took a degree in Montreal. On returning to England he subsequently studied at St. Thomas' Hospital in London and then at Edinburgh, qualifying as a doctor there. Returning to Canada in 1879 he began a medical practice there. His wife and two other women died in suspicious circumstances. Moving to Chicago one Julia Faulkner died as the result of an abortion he carried out, but he was acquitted of murder. He then (1881) went on to poison Daniel Stott, the husband of a woman he was having an affair with. Although deemed a natural death, incredibly Cream demanded an investigation and he was put on trial, found guilty and served ten years in prison. This may have been a sign of overweaning vanity or even insanity.

It was in 1891 that he arrived in London. On 13 October he was in Lambeth where he met Ellen Donworth, aged 18. He gave her 'something white to drink' in the street and she recalled he was 'a gentleman in a tall hat and a dark beard', but did not know his name. In any case, it was too late for her. Collapsing in the street, she was taken to St. Thomas' Hospital where she died later that night. In her stomach were found strychnine and morphia. These poisons had killed her.

A man was charged, but released and in any case an open verdict was returned; it being uncertain whether she was murdered or committed suicide. Meanwhile, Mr Alfred Acland received a note from a blackmailer asking him for money to avoid exposure, but the innocent Acland refused to do so. He was a wealthy and well-known man in the public eye so presumably Cream thought he could pay up and might do so to avoid adverse publicity.

On 20 October, Matilda Clover, another young woman who lived in Lambeth, received a tall, broad man wearing a silk top hat, in her rooms. He left later and early next morning Matilda was screaming in agony. She died that morning after revealing that she had been given a pill the night before. The doctor believed that she had died as a result of alcoholism (a far more common cause of death in the district than murder) and so she was buried without any further fuss. Cream wrote a blackmail letter to a Dr Seymour, but again this was rebuffed.

On the evening of the day of Matilda's death, Cream met one Louisa Harris, at a music hall, and they spent the night together in a hotel room. They met the next night and had a drink. Cream gave Louisa some pills for her health. She was told to swallow them but did not do so. Instead, smelling a rat, she concealed them from him before the two parted.

On 11 April 1892, Cream was back in London after a trip to the USA. He met two young women, Alice Marsh and Emma Elizabeth Shrivell and they ate and drank in their room. Explaining that he was a doctor, he offered the two young women a pill each and they took them. He left in the early hours but soon after his departure they were screaming in pain. On being taken to hospital, Alice died en route and Emma shortly after arrival. Both had died of strychnine poisoning. In both cases the inquest concluded that these were cases of murder.

Dr Harper received a letter asking for £15,000 or his son would be exposed as their killer. Young Harper resided at 103 Lambeth Palace Road, as did Dr Cream. During the investigation, Matilda Clover's corpse was exhumed, and strychnine found there. Cream was fascinated with the murders and discussed them with his female acquaintances.

He said that he had seen the victims, soliciting at nighttime on Waterloo Bridge. He was also engaged to a young woman from Berkhamstead, one Laura Sabbatini. Cream continued to seek victims, however. On 17 May he approached one Violet Beverley, and offered her drink and pills. She declined.

Cream talked about the case to detectives and claimed he was being followed. However, a constable had seen him with his two final victims and so his description was circulated. The handwriting on the blackmail letters was compared to his and they matched. Finally on 3 June he was arrested at his lodgings. He claimed he was innocent, but was put on trial at the Old Bailey in October for murder, attempted murder and attempted blackmail. He was found guilty and sentenced to death. His execution took place on 15 November. It is alleged by some that on the scaffold his final words were 'I'm Jack the—' but contemporary sources do not corroborate this and in any case in 1888 he was in the Joliett Prison in Illinois. A wax statue of Cream soon appeared in Madame Tussaud's Waxworks.

Cream never made any confession nor explained why and how he committed the four murders. He would seem to have been motivated by money for he had tried to levy blackmail from rich men after committing his murders. It is also possible that he delighted in the sufferings of others and knowing that he was responsible for such. On the other hand, he was not there to actually see his victims collapse with intense pain, so whether such second-hand sadism was his lot is another question.

In the Poirot novel *Cat Among the Pigeons*, Dr Cream is referenced alongside Jack the Ripper when, following the deaths of three members of staff at Meadowfield, an exclusive girls' boarding school, a Mrs Sutcliffe wonders, 'Who went about killing an unfortunate type of woman. I suppose this murderer just goes about killing schoolmistresses'. Cream, as with the Ripper, did kill prostitutes (often known in the nineteenth century as unfortunates), though, as with the Ripper, he may have done so because they were simply easier to meet and to kill. It turns out in the book that there are two murderers, working independently of one another and for different motives, which needless to say are not due to sadism and a hatred of women. Unlike some of the murderers discussed in this book, this is very much a throw away line which has very little relevance to the overall plot. Serial killers often prey on the same type of victim and so the parallel clearly presented itself to Mrs Sutcliffe. But as with most parallels, the differences outweigh the similarities.

Sources

Angus McLaren, *A Prescription for Murder: The Victorian Serial Killings of Dr Thomas Neill Cream* (1990)
Jonathan Oates, *London Serial killers, 1888-1965* (2022)
W.T. Shore, *The Trial of Neill Cream* (1922)

Lizzie Borden (1892)

And Then There Were None (1939), The Moving Finger (1943), After the Funeral (1953), Ordeal by Innocence (1958), The Clocks (1963), Elephants Can Remember (1972), Sleeping Murder (1976)

The case of Lizzie Borden, the neatly dressed Sunday school teacher who was charged – and acquitted – of the gruesome axe murders of her father and stepmother is a classic true crime mystery. Countless books, newspaper articles, plays and films have sought to find the solution to the riddle. How could a respectable young American woman commit such a horrific crime? What was the motive? Was she guilty or not? The case is still formally unsolved, a fact that has certainly contributed to keeping interest and fascination alive for 130 years. Agatha Christie mentions it directly or indirectly in several of her books and in one – *And Then There Were None* – she seems to have modelled one of the characters after Lizzie Borden. More on that soon.

Andrew Borden – Lizzie's father – was a wealthy businessman and banker in the town of Fall River in Massachusetts on the northeast coast of the United States. He had worked his way up from selling coffins to becoming a factory and real estate owner, as well as president of the Union Savings Bank. After his death, his estate was valued at $300,000, a large fortune at the time. In the summer of 1892, Borden was 70 years old but showed no signs of wanting to retire from professional life. He had a reputation for being tough – although honest and fair – in business dealings. In Fall River he was respected but hardly liked. He lived with his family, 64-year-old wife Abby and two adult daughters Emma and Lizzie, in a two-storey house at 92 Second Street, a middle-class neighbourhood. The wealthy of the city mostly preferred the more exclusive region of The Hill, but Andrew Borden was a frugal man who did not waste money on luxury and comfort.

Abby Borden, née Gray, was Andrew's second wife. He had first married Sarah Morse and together with her had three daughters, one of whom died young. Emma was born in 1851, Lizzie in 1860. Three years after Lizzie's birth, Sarah died at the age of 40. It is said that on her deathbed she asked the then 12-year-old Emma to take care of Lizzie, something the older sister devoted most of her life to. Two years after Sarah's death, Andrew Borden married Abby Gray. The relationship between the stepmother and Andrew's daughters was polite but distant. When Lizzie was later asked if she had a cordial relationship with Abby, she replied: 'It depends upon one's idea of cordiality perhaps'. It seems that Emma filled the role of mother to Lizzie and the girls never became close to Abby.

The Borden sisters were of different temperament. Emma was quiet and withdrawn while Lizzie was outgoing and active in several of Fall River's Christian associations. She also taught at Sunday school. They were not, perhaps, great beauties, but not unattractive either. Given the family's wealth, there should have been plenty of suitors. The reason why both sisters remained single is unclear. Andrew Borden is said to have been wary of fortune-seekers; however, a relative denied in a newspaper interview that this was the case. Perhaps the Borden sisters simply were not interested in marriage. Since they were wealthy, there was no pressure for them to marry. In the summer of 1892, Emma had turned 41 and Lizzie 32. They did not have to work and were free to do whatever they wanted. At home they mostly kept to themselves and rarely shared meals with their father and stepmother.

The family's maid Bridget 'Maggie' Sullivan later testified that everyone in the house behaved civilly towards each other and that she never heard any raised voices or arguments. But beneath the polished surface, a lot of frustration was brewing. In 1887, Andrew Borden had bought a house for Abby's half-sister, which upset Emma and Lizzie. They felt that he should be equally generous to them. Andrew tried to appease his daughters by selling them their grandfather's house for the token sum of $1. Five years later, just weeks before the murders, the daughters sold the property back to their father for $5,000. There was no reason for Emma and Lizzie to be dissatisfied, yet this seemingly trivial affair seems to have stirred up bad feelings, causing Lizzie to start calling Abby 'Mrs Borden' instead of 'Mother'. The frosty relationship between the two is evident from the fact that in the spring of 1892, in a conversation with her dressmaker, Lizzie referred to Abby as 'a mean good-for nothing thing'. She also had a strained relationship with her father. According to an acquaintance of the family, Lizzie wanted to live as befits a society lady and host parties in their home, something that Andrew firmly opposed.

At the beginning of August 1892, several members of the Borden family fell sick with symptoms of stomach flu. Abby became so ill that she went to see her doctor, expressing a fear of having been poisoned. Lizzie and Andrew also fell sick. Emma had gone for a visit to friends in Fairhaven, thus escaping the mysterious illness. On 3 August, John Morse, a brother of Andrew Borden's late wife Sarah, came to discuss business matters with his brother-in-law. That same evening, Lizzie met her good friend Alice Russell and expressed concern that something was going to happen. She said she wanted to sleep with one eye open half the time 'for fear somebody might burn the house down or hurt her father because he was so discourteous to people'.

At 7 o'clock on the morning of 4 August, John Morse (who had stayed in a guest room overnight) had breakfast with the Bordens. The two men then sat down to discuss business. About 9 o'clock Lizzie came down to the kitchen, Morse having left the house by then. A few minutes later, Andrew Borden set off on his usual morning walk. He brought with him some letters that Lizzie asked him to post. Abby Borden went upstairs to clean the guest room where Morse had spent the night. Bridget Sullivan went out to wash windows. At 11 o'clock Andrew Borden returned. When Bridget was about to open the door for him, she had trouble with the lock and gave an exasperated exclamation. From upstairs she heard Lizzie laughing. Andrew Borden went into the sitting room to rest. Lizzie spoke briefly with him, and Bridget heard her say that Abby had gone out after having received a message about someone being ill.

Bridget Sullivan, not feeling well, went up to her room in the attic to rest. About ten minutes later, she heard Lizzie call out, 'Maggie, come quick! Father's dead. Somebody came in and killed him'. Before long, the house was full of doctors and police officers. Andrew Borden was found slumped on the couch in the sitting room, his head covered in blood. The autopsy showed at least ten blows to the face and head, caused by an axe-like weapon. Blood was still flowing from the wounds, indicating a very recent attack. Half an hour after the discovery of Andrew's body, Abby Borden was found murdered upstairs. She was lying face down on the floor in the guest room, hacked to death in the same way as her husband. Abby appeared to have faced the killer when the attack began. She first received a blow to the side of her head, then turned around to escape but fell, the murderer raining blows on the back of her head. In the basement, police officers found several hatchets and axes, including one with a broken handle. The latter one was believed to be the murder weapon.

It was initially assumed that a malevolent stranger had somehow entered the house, attacked Abby, and then remained hidden until Andrew returned home. Abby's body was cold when discovered and the blood had coagulated, meaning that she must have been killed at least one hour before her husband. However, neither Bridget Sullivan, neighbours nor passers-by had seen any outsiders moving around the house. Slowly but surely, the police began to suspect that the murders were committed by someone within the family. The prime suspect was Lizzie. She said she had been out in a barn on the property looking for a sinker for a fishing rod at the time her father was murdered. However, there were no witnesses who could confirm this, neither could anyone confirm Lizzie's claim that Abby had gone out after having received a message about a sick friend. Bridget Sullivan had not noticed any messenger coming to the door, neither had she seen Mrs Borden leave the house. At 11 o'clock, when opening the door for Andrew Borden, Bridget had heard Lizzie's laughter from upstairs. Abby must have been dead by then and her body lay visible inside the open door to the guest room. How come Lizzie had not seen it?

When Alice Russell informed the police that Lizzie had burnt a blue dress a few days after the murders, suspicions were strengthened. Bridget Sullivan remembered Lizzie wearing a blue dress on the morning of 4 August. A drugstore clerk said that a woman he identified as Lizzie Borden had tried to buy prussic acid, a strong poison, the day before the murders. This was denied by Lizzie, but the clerk insisted it was indeed her he had seen. Had Lizzie intended to use the family's stomach illness – probably caused by mutton left on the stove over several days – as a cover to poison her parents? And had she then decided on a different method when the plan to buy prussic acid failed? At the inquest on 9 August 1892, Lizzie gave contradictory and sometimes confused answers. Two days later she was arrested and in November she was indicted by a grand jury for double murder.

The trial of Lizzie Borden began on 5 June 1893 in New Bedford. Her defence was handled by top solicitors Andrew Jennings and George Robinson (a former governor of Massachusetts). The prosecution was led by Hosea Knowlton, an able barrister. Lizzie did not testify, and her inquest testimony was not allowed to be presented to the jury. Nor was the testimony about her attempt to buy prussic acid allowed. George Robinson skilfully cast doubts on the time frame: was it really possible to kill a person, wash off all the blood, change clothes, clean and hide the murder weapon in ten minutes? Despite a compelling chain of circumstantial evidence and the absence of other suspects, the prosecutor failed to secure a conviction. Apparently, it was beyond the jury's imagination that a respectable Christian lady could commit such a heinous crime. On 20 June, after a short deliberation, they returned with a verdict of Not Guilty.

The now very wealthy Borden sisters used their inheritance to buy a luxurious villa in The Hill, employing several servants. Despite Lizzie being acquitted, society turned its back on her. Still preferring to remain in Fall River, she spent most of her time at home with her beloved dogs and cats. In 1905, something caused the two sisters to part ways. Emma moved out and never came back. Lizzie seems to have socialized a little with theatre people but was otherwise completely alone. She died of pneumonia in 1927. Nine days later Emma also died. In American folklore, the case lives on in the famous rhyme: 'Lizzie Borden took an axe, And gave her mother forty whacks, When she saw what she had done, She gave her father forty-one'.

Agatha Christie refers to Lizzie Borden in *The Moving Finger*, where the effeminate antique collector Mr Pye states, 'Such apparently unlikely people do the most fantastic things. Take the case of Lizzie Borden. There's not really a reasonable explanation of that'. He believes that the police should study people's character more and physical evidence less. In *Sleeping Murder*, Dr. Haydock discusses murders in which the killer escapes justice but never kills again and refers to Lizzie Borden as being acquitted. In *The Clocks*, Poirot is studying historical crimes, figuring out his own solutions. One of these is the Borden case: 'As for Lizzie Borden, one wishes only that one could put a few necessary questions to various people concerned. I am fairly sure in my own mind of what the answers would be. Alas, they are all dead'.

In *Elephants Can Remember*, Superintendent Garroway asks, 'Did Lizzie Borden really kill her father and mother with an axe? There are people who still don't think so'. In *Ordeal by Innocence*, the solicitor Mr Marshall draws a parallel between the current murder of a woman 'surrounded by the members of her own family and household' and the case where 'Mr Borden and his wife were struck down by blows of an axe on a

Sunday morning. Nobody in the house heard anything, nobody was known or seen to approach the house'.

In *After the Funeral*, the eccentric Cora Lansquenet is hacked to death with an axe, prompting her young relative Susan to speculate about the killer's character: 'It's definitely got to be a certain kind of person. A brutal, perhaps slightly half-witted type – a discharged soldier or a gaol bird. I mean, using a hatchet like that.' The solicitor Mr Entwhistle then recites the famous verse about 'forty whacks' to make the point that a killer using an axe does not necessarily need to be male. Susan retorts that Lizzie was actually acquitted and no one knows for sure if she killed her father and stepmother. Mr Entwhistle agrees that 'the rhyme is quite definitely libellous'.

But it is mainly in the famous thriller *And Then There Were None* that Agatha Christie highlights the Borden case, even though she does not mention the name itself (in the play version, it is written out). It is the rugged ex-Inspector Blore who, after the body of Rogers the butler has been found with axe blows to his head, remarks:

> 'There was a case in America. Old gentleman and his wife – both killed with an axe. Middle of the morning. Nobody in the house but the daughter and a maid. Maid, it was proved, couldn't have done it. Daughter was a respectable middle-aged spinster. Seemed incredible. So incredible that they acquitted her. But they never found any other explanation…I thought of that when I saw the axe'.

The reason why Blore makes an association with the Borden case is not only because of the murder weapon but also because there is a lady among the unfortunate guests on the island who reminds him of Lizzie: '…I went into the kitchen and saw her there so neat and calm. Hadn't turned a hair!' The lady in question is Emily Brent, a respectable, fanatically religious elderly spinster. Her unnatural calmness just after the occurrence of a violent murder is reminiscent of Lizzie Borden, whose cool and collected demeanour directly after the murders of her parents puzzled the police. Blore further remarks that Miss Brent has been out wandering alone on the island:

> 'If the woman was innocent she'd be too dead scared to go wandering about by herself. She'd only do that if she knew

> that she had nothing to fear. That's to say if she herself was the criminal'.

This is another parallel to Lizzie Borden, who, after the discovery of her father's bloody corpse, sent Bridget Sullivan off to fetch various people, while she herself remained alone in the house. Would it not have been more natural for her to leave the house as soon as possible? After all, the murderous intruder could still have been hiding inside.

Emily Brent is one of the most unsympathetic characters in *And Then There Were None*, being portrayed as an extremely self-righteous and judgmental Christian lady. Her background story is that a young woman in her service became pregnant and consequently was fired by her employer. The girl was later found drowned – she had taken her own life. Emily Brent does not believe that she has anything to reproach herself with: 'I have always acted in accordance with the dictates of my conscience'. If the portrait of the cold and unforgiving Miss Brent has been inspired by Lizzie Borden, which there are many indications of, it suggests that Christie perceived Lizzie to be guilty of murder. That view is shared by most who have studied the case.

Sources

Michael Burgan, *Lizzie Borden* (New York, 2018)
David Kent, *The Lizzie Borden Sourcebook* (Boston, 1992)
Mark John Maguire, *They got away with murder II* (2023)
David Rehak, *Did Lizzie Borden axe for it?* (Wilmington, Ohio, 2005)
Cara Robertson, *The trial of Lizzie Borden* (New York, 2019)
https://famous-trials.com/lizzieborden/1436-biographies (website containing excerpts from the trial of Lizzie Borden, her inquest testimony and other documents; accessed 2023-11-28).

Marguerite Steinheil (1908)

Murder on the Links (1923)

In her autobiography, Agatha Christie reveals how she got the idea for the plot in her third novel, *Murder on the Links.* She had read about a French *cause célèbre*: 'I can't remember the name of any of the participants by now. It was some tale of masked men who had broken into a house, killed the owner, tied up and gagged the wife – the mother-in-law had also died, but only apparently because she had choked on her false teeth. Anyway, the wife's story was disproved, and there was a suggestion that it was the wife who had killed her husband…It struck me as a good plot on which to weave my own story…'

When Agatha Christie wrote her autobiography, many years had passed since the publication of *Murder on the Links*. That she no longer could recall the names of the people involved in the real-life story is thus understandable. Her description of the case, however, is detailed enough to enable an immediate identification: this was the famous *l'affaire Steinheil*, or *l'affaire de l'Impasse Ronsin*, which caused a huge scandal in Paris high society in 1908. At the centre of it all was a charming and attractive woman – a true *femme fatale* – who had once been the mistress of the French president, Félix Faure.

Marguerite-Jeanne Japy, usually called Meg, was born in 1869, the third child of four to wealthy industrialist Édouard Japy and his wife Émilie Rau. She grew up in Beaucourt, a small town in eastern France, where the family resided in an impressive mansion called Chateau Edouard. Her father's favourite child, Meg was home-schooled, learning how to arrange flowers, play musical instruments, draw, and embroider – all intended to prepare her for her future destination as wife, mother, and society hostess. Although her childhood was privileged there were darker sides to life in the beautiful chateau: Édouard Japy was an alcoholic who was unfaithful and abusive to his wife, and mental instability ran in the family.

In 1890, Meg married a painter called Adolphe Steinheil. He was 19 years her senior, not very handsome, and only moderately successful. It was an unlikely alliance; however, Meg's father had died two years earlier, leaving the family in strained financial circumstances. There was pressure for her to marry as soon as possible, and for a girl without money the supply of suitors was not that great. When Steinheil proposed she accepted, mainly because they would live in Paris, the city of her dreams. Already during their honeymoon Meg seems to have regretted her choice, for she ran away from her new husband and returned to Beaucourt. Persuaded by her mother to give the marriage a chance, she reluctantly returned to Adolphe.

In Paris the couple lived in a villa with a garden, located at Impasse Ronsin in the fifteenth arrondissement. A daughter, Marthe, was born in 1891, but relations between Meg and Adolphe were far from optimal. They had very different attitudes to the outside world: she was energetic and socially ambitious; he was passive and introvert. Steinheil's paintings were in the old-fashioned, academic style and had nothing in common with the innovative art of the impressionists. Nevertheless, his wife set out to promote his work, employing her beauty and charm to establish a Parisian salon. Before long the Steinheils entertained composers, authors, painters, and politicians. Émile Zola was one of their frequent visitors.

In 1897, Marguerite Steinheil was introduced to Félix Faure, the President of France. He is mostly remembered for his role in the notorious Dreyfus affair, where the Jewish artillery captain Alfred Dreyfus – a victim of antisemitism within the army – was wrongfully accused of treason and imprisoned on Devil's Island. The affair quickly grew into a massive political scandal that divided the country. Faure obstructed all attempts to reopen the case, even after the publication of Zola's famous challenge *J'accuse*. That was in 1898, the year after the President met the charming wife of Adolphe Steinheil. He was immediately attracted to her, and they soon began a clandestine affair, meeting in the private quarters of the presidential Palais de l'Élysée. According to Meg (in her memoirs), the relationship was strictly platonic. She served as a 'consultant' to Faure, assisting him with his secret political memoirs, and helping him hide sensitive governmental documents from his enemies. Needless to say, few, if any, believed a word of this.

On 16 February 1899, Meg Steinheil and Félix Faure were alone in the private drawing room of the Palais de l'Élysée when screams suddenly were heard through the door. Rushing in, the President's aides found him unconscious on a sofa, having suffered a fatal cerebral haemorrhage. He died later that evening. Faure's unexpected death at the age of 58 naturally caused big headlines in the newspapers, and the publicity exploded when it became known that he had been in the company of his mistress when it happened. According to gossip, they had been in the middle of a passionate embrace when death intervened. The French press could not resist alluding to the embarrassing circumstances: 'Felix Faure passed away in good health, indeed from the excess of good health', was one of the comments.

After her brief fame as the President's mistress, Marguerite Steinheil disappeared from the headlines. Over the following years she had several love affairs to which her husband chose to turn a blind eye. Adolphe Steinheil had become addicted to opium as a remedy for sleeplessness, he was aging fast and did not produce as many paintings as before. In February 1908, Meg met the widowed Maurice Borderel, a wealthy industrialist from the Ardennes. They quickly became lovers and the relationship appeared to be more serious than her previous liaisons. Although Borderel had declared that marriage was out of the question, Meg may have thought she could make him change his mind – if her husband somehow was out of the picture…

In the morning of 31 May 1908, the dead bodies of Adolphe Steinheil and his mother-in-law, Émilie Japy, were found inside the villa at Impasse Ronsin. Both had been murdered: Adolphe by strangulation, Émilie by suffocation due to her false teeth being forced down her throat when a wad of cotton wool was squeezed into her mouth. The 17-year-old Marthe Steinheil was away from the house, but her mother Marguerite was found alive, gagged, and bound on the bed in her daughter's room. She told the police that she had been wakened by a gang of intruders, three men and a woman, who demanded money and jewellery. Dressed in long black garments, the men all had beards of different colour, one black, the others red and brown, respectively. The woman had wanted to kill Meg, but one of the men took pity on her because – she said – they mistook her for her young daughter in the darkness. She was not aware of what had happened to her mother or husband.

The police were suspicious of Marguerite Steinheil's story right from the start. There was no sign of forced entry, the intruders apparently having walked in through the slightly open front door. Apart from a few jewels and a little money, nothing of value had been stolen. Later, Meg would claim that important documents had been taken, but this could not be verified. The cord used to tie her up, and to strangle Adolphe, had come from the Steinheils' kitchen. Would professional criminals not have brought their own equipment with them? And the story about the robbers mistaking the 39-year- old Meg for her 17-year-old daughter was hardly credible. How did the gang know that Marthe slept in this bedroom, by the way? Why was the entrance door unlocked and the watchdog removed from the house the day before the murders? How come Adolphe's watch and money had not been taken from him? Despite their suspicions, the police could not act against Meg due to lack of hard evidence. The press had a field day, of course, bringing up the old scandal of Faure's death. There was even speculation that the intruders had been looking for secret documents belonging to Faure, possibly related to the Dreyfus affair.

The months went by without any arrest. In late October there was an unexpected development when Madame Steinheil accused her valet, Rémy Couillard, for having stolen a pearl she claimed had been missing since the night of the murder. The pearl was found in his wallet. Couillard, a young man of about twenty, vehemently denied that he had stolen it. The police made an investigation, concluding that the pearl probably had been planted in his wallet by Meg herself. Confronted with having lied, she quickly changed her story. Tearfully she admitted that the accusation against Couillard was false and only intended to shield the real culprit, Alexandre Wolff, son of her elderly housekeeper. Wolff had threatened to name her as an accomplice if she revealed his name to the police. When he flatly denied her allegations and could produce an alibi, time finally ran out for Madame Steinheil. She was arrested in November 1908, spending 11 months in the Saint Lazare prison before being brought to trial in early November 1909.

The prosecution could present several suspicious circumstances but no hard evidence linking Meg Steinheil to the crime. There was also the question of motive. From a financial point of view, she had very little to gain from the deaths of her husband and mother. Was her desire to marry Borderel so strong that she would murder her own mother to obtain her goal? In the end, giving a performance worthy of Sarah Bernhardt in a courtroom packed with spellbound onlookers, Meg Steinheil managed to convince the all-male jury to acquit her, despite the judge dismissing her story as 'a tissue of lies'. She immediately went to England, where she published her memoirs in 1912 and wed the 6th Baron Abinger. After being widowed in 1927, she remained in England where she died in a nursing home in 1954, aged 85.

What was the truth about *l'affaire Steinheil*? Everything points to what is now known as a staged domestic homicide: a crime scene arranged to give the impression of outside perpetrators, to direct suspicions away from the real culprit. The story of the four intruders was never seriously believed. Apart from what has already been discussed there is the curious fact that Madame Japy was found lying on a bed, as if she had been asleep, but was still wearing her dentures. If she had retired for the night, surely she would have removed her dentures? That she had not done so suggests that the murders took place earlier in the evening, and not in the middle of the night. Did Meg Steinheil have an accomplice, a man who was persuaded – perhaps paid – to kill her husband? Did Madame Japy happen to come across the killer strangling Adolphe, suffering a fatal heart attack from the shock? Was the cotton wool put in her mouth to give the appearance of intruders wanting to silence her? It is unlikely we will ever know. One thing seems certain: Meg Steinheil was somehow involved in the crime, and she was lucky to escape the guillotine.

For a reader familiar with *l'affaire Steinheil* it is easy to discern its influence on the plot of *Murder on the Links*. To begin with, the story is set in France – not in Paris though, but in the fictitious town Merlinville-sur-Mer on the Channel coast, halfway between Boulogne and Calais. Poirot and Hastings travel there at the request of Paul Renauld, a very wealthy man who has sent an urgent appeal for help to Poirot. Upon arrival at Renauld's house, Villa Geneviève, they find that the millionaire is already dead, killed during the night by intruders who forced him out of the house and took him to a nearby golf course under construction. His body – stabbed in the back – has been found in a newly dug, open grave. In the villa, the intruders have left Renauld's wife bound and gagged but unhurt. Madame Renauld describes the intruders as two men wearing false beards, of black and red colour, respectively. They gained entrance to the house via the front door, which was unlocked.

It turns out that the murdered man has been receiving visits from a mysterious woman called Jeanne Daubreuil, who lives in the neighbouring house, the Villa Marguerite. She has a young daughter called Marthe. The names of the villa and the daughter obviously allude to two of the central characters in *l'affaire Steinheil*; in addition, the description of Madame

Daubreuil is reminiscent of Meg Steinheil: 'Her hair…was dark and parted in the middle in the madonna style. Her eyes, half hidden by the drooping lids, were blue. There was a dimple in the round chin, and the half-parted lips seemed always to hover on the verge of a mysterious smile. There was something almost exaggeratedly feminine about her, at once yielding and seductive'.

Slowly Poirot unravels an amazing background story: about twenty years earlier, the attractive Madame Daubreuil – whose real name is Beroldy – stood trial for the murder of her husband, the wine merchant Arnold Beroldy. While he was an insignificant and unoffensive man, much older than his wife, she was 'young and good looking, and gifted with a singular charm of manner'. To friends she hinted of a secret in the past, of political intrigues and 'papers'. One morning Madame Beroldy was found lying gagged and bound on the floor; her husband was in a pool of blood on the bed, dead from a stab wound to the heart. Again, we hear about two masked, heavily bearded intruders turning up in the middle of the night, demanding secret documents. When Monsieur Beroldy refused to hand over the documents he was fatally stabbed, the killers escaping with a bunch of papers in the night.

Georges Conneau, the young lover of Madame Beroldy, confessed to the murder in a letter to the police, stating that he had done it at her instigation. He managed to escape justice by fleeing abroad. Jeanne Beroldy was put on trial, gave a star performance in court, and was acquitted. She has now resurfaced, together with her daughter, many years later. But why was Paul Renauld murdered in the same way as Monsieur Beroldy? Poirot finally solves the puzzle: Renauld was in fact identical with Georges Conneau. He made a fortune abroad, got married, and had a son. Upon returning to France, he was unlucky to buy a house whose immediate neighbour was Madame Beroldy/Daubreuil. She started to blackmail Renauld, who desperately tried to get away by restaging the drama of twenty years ago. A tramp who conveniently died of epilepsy on Renauld's grounds offered a chance for him to fake his own death. The plan, of which his wife was fully informed, was to stage a kidnapping, go to the golf course and dig a grave, then to put the tramp into it after destroying his features. The plan backfired, however, when someone suddenly turned up and stabbed Renauld in the back while he was digging the grave.

There are further twists and complications to the plot that cannot be linked to *l'affaire Steinheil*, but the main story – as we have seen – is clearly based on the famous French case. Possibly Christie also was inspired by the sad fate of Marthe Steinheil, who had been engaged to a respectable young man at the time of the murders. In the wake of the scandal, his family swiftly broke off the engagement. In *Murder on the Links*, the fictitious Marthe is in love with Jack, the son of Paul Renauld. They want to marry but Jack's parents are totally against it, due to the dubious past of Marthe's mother. The real-life Marthe briefly entered a Carmelite convent before marrying a young Italian painter called Raphael del Perugia in 1911. A year later she filed for a judicial separation from her husband.

Sources

Sarah Horowitz, *The red widow – the scandal that shook Paris and the woman behind it all* (2022)

Benjamin F Martin, *The hypocrisy of justice in the Belle Epoque* (1984)

Dr Hawley Harvey Crippen (1910)

The Man in the Brown Suit (1924), The Murder of Roger Ackroyd (1926), The Mystery of the Blue Train (1928), The Murder at the Vicarage (1930), Three Act Tragedy (1935), Five Little Pigs (1942), The Lernaean Hydra (in: The Labours of Hercules 1947), Mrs McGinty's Dead (1952), The Mirror Crack'd from side to side (1962), Third Girl (1966), Sleeping Murder (1976), Tape Measure Murder (in: Miss Marple's Final Cases 1979)

Dr Crippen is explicitly referred to several times, at least twelve, more than any other murderer (George Orwell referred to this case in several of his books, too) in Agatha Christie's stories. Although he 'only' killed one person, his wife, his story is probably one of the best known from the early twentieth century, despite the fact that there has only been one film (starring Donald Pleasance in 1962; in 1989 he was Jason Rafiel in *A Caribbean Mystery*) and one television drama, focussing on the court case. Domestic murders where the husband kills his wife or girlfriend, and sometimes vice versa, are a very common form of crime in real life; as Miss Marple states in *4.50 from Paddington* 'So many men seem to murder their wives' and she also observes that a doctor has greater opportunities than most. Possibly the domesticity of the crime appealed to the average middle class reader; they could imagine themselves or someone they knew being in such a scenario. Crippen certainly seemed to be the epitome of middle aged and lower middle class respectability and yet was carrying on an affair in secret with a young woman. Arguably his name sounds sinister and so is memorable.

Hawley Harvey Crippen, often known as Dr Crippen, or Peter to his friends, was an American, born in Coldwater, Michigan, in 1862. This quack chemist and dentist arrived in London in 1897. He was later employed as a commission only salesman for Munyon's Remedies. He shot to infamy in 1910 when he was charged with the murder by poison of his second wife, born as Kunigunde Mackamotzki (daughter of a Russian-German father and a Polish mother), who was also named as Corrine Cora Turner, chopping her up and hiding some of the body in the cellar of their house at 39 Hilldrop Crescent in north London. His wife was active in the theatre and music halls as a performer and from 1908-1910 was the treasurer of the Music Hall Ladies' Guild. Her stage name was Belle Elmore; Crippen even managed her for a time. On 31 January 1910, she was last seen alive at a dinner party at her home and then she disappeared and he pretended she had returned to California and had died there. Yet friends of his wife were suspicious, even more so when Ethel le Neve, Crippen's typist since 1900 and lover since at least 1905, was seen wearing some of Mrs Crippen's clothes and jewellery, after having moved to Crippen's house on 2 February to live with him as man and wife. On 10 July Chief Inspector Walter Dew visited Crippen on what was a fairly routine missing persons enquiry in which no foul play was suspected, to question him but found nothing untoward there at all. Crippen admitted that he had lied about his wife's death, now claiming that she had fled to the USA with a lover, Bruce Miller, but had done so to save embarrassment.

Crippen was safe, but then panicked. He and Ethel fled to Canada, via Belgium, on a liner, the SS *Montrose*, she disguised as a boy (they travelled as father and son), but were recognised by the ship's captain who contacted the police in London by wireless, the first time that this invention had been used to catch a criminal. Meanwhile, on 11-13 July the house at Hilldrop Crescent was more thoroughly searched and it was then that human remains were found and identified as those of Mrs Crippen, in part because a scar was found on the torso and she was known to have one of these. Inspector Dew took a faster ship across the Atlantic and was able to arrest Crippen and Ethel before they arrived in Canada on 31 July. On his return to England, he was tried for murder. Crippen took all the blame on his shoulders and was found guilty on 21 October at a trial at the Old Bailey. There it was stated that he had bought the poison hyoscine hydrobromide a fortnight before Cora was last seen. Medical evidence from three doctors, including

Dr Bernard Spilsbury, a rising young pathologist, was also decisive, as were the pyjamas found with the body parts. Crippen was hanged on 23 November at Pentonville Prison whilst Ethel was only stated to be an accessory after the fact, for which she was tried on the same day as Crippen. Crippen said that 'It is only fair to say that she knows nothing about it; I never told her anything'. Ethel was acquitted and left the country, to start a new life in Toronto, Canada, working there as a typist. Three years later she returned to London with a new name, Ethel Harvey and in 1915 she married Stanley Smith, with whom she had two children. They lived in Croydon, where she died in 1967.

In recent times the theory that Crippen was innocent has been postulated. This is on the basis that the corpse in the cellar was not that of his wife. However, this raises other questions; where was the real Mrs Crippen, who was not an insignificant personality, and why did she not take her jewels and other possessions with her? Whose body was in the cellar? Why did Crippen flee? The conviction of Crippen seems safe enough unless the pro-Crippen faction can resolve these difficult questions. In Agatha Christie's time, no matter how much people sympathised with Crippen, no one seriously doubted his guilt, whether in collusion with Ethel or not.

In the stories there have been various discussions on aspects of the case. There is some talk as to Crippen's character. The first reference is by Sir Eustace Pedler on a liner to South Africa in *The Man in the Brown Suit*, a little over a decade since the case. He says, 'Crippen, now, I believe, was one of the pleasantest fellows imaginable'. A similar comment is made In *The Mystery of the Blue Train*, a Poirot novel. George, Poirot's snobbish manservant, says 'I have always heard, sir, that Dr Crippen was a pleasant-spoken gentleman. And yet he cut up his wife like so much mincemeat'. In *The Mirror Crack'd*, Cherry tells Miss Marple, in relation to a very meek husband as a murder suspect, 'I've always heard that Crippen was ever so nice a man'. In *Five Little Pigs,* another Poirot novel, the Belgian detective remarks, 'People read with interest that Dr Crippen murdered his wife because she was a big bouncing woman and he was little and insignificant therefore she made him feel inferior'. In *Three Act Tragedy* there is a discussion about Crippen: 'An inferiority complex is a very peculiar thing. Crippen for instance, undoubtedly, suffered from it. It's at the back of a lot of crimes. The desire to assert one's personality'.

It is commonly thought that Crippen was a very mild mannered and polite little man and perhaps this heightens the horror of his crime. At the trial one witness stated that he was 'a kind hearted and good tempered man' and another said he was 'kind hearted and amiable'. He said 'I am very sensitive to any censure or scandal of that kind'. It has also led to a degree of sympathy for this murderer. Those in the legal profession and prison staff thought him polite and gentle. In contrast, many accounts of the case have nothing good to say about his wife. In fact, one non-fiction book published in 1977 and written by Tom Cullen about the case is titled '*The Mild Murderer*'. However, much that is known about Mrs Crippen comes from Crippen himself and he was not a disinterested witness. It is possible, too, that a degree of misogyny lies behind these comments in that some feel it is understandable at the very least for a man who is allegedly bullied by his wife to kill her. George Orwell once wrote that everyone feels sympathy for a man who murders his wife, though presumably not for women who kill their spouses.

Her friends described Cora as 'a stoutish woman, about 30 years of age, vivacious, bright and cheerful, a very pleasant woman generally, and enjoying the best of health'. Crippen gave a different version, alleging that she 'had developed a most ungovernable temper and seemed to think he was not good enough for her'. Apparently 'on frequent occasions … she got into violent tempers and threatened to leave him'. She was, he said, 'always finding fault with me' and he said she was having an affair with one Bruce Miller. He told how 'To the outward world' she appeared to be pleasant but this was not the case in their private life that only he knew about. As to Crippen's personality, some of Cora's relatives, far from disinterested parties to be fair, claimed he made unwelcome advances on women.

Whilst on board a liner to South Africa, Mrs Suzanne Blair, in *The Man in the Brown Suit*, declares, 'He was caught on a liner, wasn't he?' In *The Murder of Roger Ackroyd*, there is conversation about a suspect fleeing to America and Caroline Shepherd says 'That's what Crippen did' to which Dr James Shepherd, her brother, the narrator, replies, 'Without much success, I reminded her'. Mrs Ariadne Oliver mentions the case to Poirot in *Third Girl* four decades later, about a particular suspect 'he wanted like Crippen to go off with her [his mistress], and so he murdered the first one and nobody ever suspected'.

Certainly the dramatic flight and Dew's pursuit and arrest of the pair was an unusual feature of the case and probably helped the press to make even more of the case and so arouse public attention and indignation.

In the first Miss Marple novel, *Murder at the Vicarage*, Miss Cram, a secretary to an archaeologist, says of her boring boss, 'He'd a hundred times rather look at a nasty old bronze knife out of those humps of ground than he would see the knife Crippen cut up his wife with, supposing he had a chance to'. In the Miss Marple short story, *Tape Measure Murder,* the victim's widower and prime suspect is shouted at in the village street by a lad thus, 'Who's a Crippen' and he presumes he is a suspect therefore. The name Crippen is being used as he is so infamous that it is assumed that everyone at the time, children included, will have heard of him and know what that means. This is doubly hurting to the man in question because he would have known that not only was Crippen a murderer but a wife murderer as well.

In *Sleeping Murder*, the last Miss Marple novel, there is a reference to a murderer who has killed in the past and then sent letters purportedly from the missing victim overseas, 'It's the old Crippen touch again' says Miss Marple. Crippen claimed to receive letters about the wife he had murdered in order to make it appear she was still living. After all he initially told her friends that she received a telegram to request that she travel to California on urgent family business. When there, he alleged, she and family members sent cables and letters to say that she was ill. Finally, there was, he said, at the end of March, news that she had died and was cremated. No one saw these messages that Crippen claimed he had received. However, he also wrote two letters to her friends, purportedly from her, to state that she had left to go to help a sick relative in America.

Ethel was described by her landlady as 'most lovable and affectionate' and 'gentle, retiring and sympathetic'. A former employer claimed that she was 'a gentle and affectionate girl'. Yet in the Christie stories there is doubt about her involvement in the murder. A character in the short story '*The Lernaean Hydra'* in *The Labours of Hercules*, says 'I've always wondered if Ethel Le Neve was in it with him or not'. There are certainly grounds for suspicion for her involvement, though Crippen did his best to absolve Ethel of all guilt. Christie probably thought so, too. The subject is made even more explicit in *Mrs McGinty's Dead*, written just a few years after this story. It is impossible to know the extent, if any, of Ethel's involvement or even knowledge of her lover's crimes. He said she was wholly innocent and she never revealed anything. This proves nothing; but perhaps a straw in the wind against her utter innocence is that she emptied Mrs Crippen's post office savings account of almost £200 between February and June 1910 and she openly wore Cora's jewellery.

So far, all these books have referenced Crippen in a way that does not hugely impinge on the story's plot. This is decidedly not the case in the following book. In the Poirot novel, *Mrs McGinty's Dead*, the Crippen case casts a long shadow, but he is not mentioned by name. In the story Poirot discovers that the victim, Mrs McGinty, who has been knocked on the head in her little cottage in Broadhinny, had read in an illustrated newspaper article about four women involved in murder in the past and that she recognised one of them as a woman that she did the cleaning for. One of the four cases resembles that of Crippen. Another resembles another real life murder as shall be noted in a later chapter.

Poirot began to read this story as reported in the article, 'The name of Eva Kane he remembered, for the Craig Case had been a very celebrated one', as indeed the Crippen case had been. The names Eva and Craig even resemble those of Ethel and Crippen and the similarities grow. Alfred Craig had married 'a tiresome and temperamental wife…bullied him, nagged him'. The popular feeling about the Crippen case is that Cora Crippen was an absolute nightmare to her husband; though this version of events is reliant on Crippen's testimony which is hardly disinterested and a recent study questions whether this was the case, but it was a popular view at the time and since and one clearly adhered to here.

Eva Kane is a 19 year old young nursery governess who fell in love with Craig (the real Ethel was 26 and a typist to the childless Crippens at the time of the murder). Craig is 'a conscientious, rather nondescript little man, correct and pleasant in his behaviour' and though a Town Clerk (the chief executive of a borough council) rather than a chemist the personality of the two is apparently very similar. Then Mrs Craig disappears and Craig lets it be known that she has gone to a particular resort in France and then died. Suspicion falls on him when it is found that no one resembling her has been buried. In fact she has 'been cut up in neat pieces and buried in the Craig cellar'. She had been poisoned hitherto. This is very similar to the Crippen case.

Craig is arrested and sent for trial; Eva is charged as an accessory, but this charge is dropped. Craig is hanged and the pregnant Eva goes abroad and is forgotten about. The real Ethel was not pregnant, but for the plot purposes the fictional counterpart has to be.

Subsequently doubts are cast in the book about the innocence of Eva, just as characters in the other Agatha Christie stories have wondered if Ethel Le Neve was guilty. A female journalist says, 'I've no doubt that Eva Kane was a thorough little bitch and not an injured innocent at all'. In a later chapter, Superintendent Spence tells Poirot about what the police thought about it: 'That she was by no means the innocent victim that the public thought her'. Spence's old boss believed that Eva had the idea of murdering Mrs Craig – 'no evidence mind you' – and committed the deed herself. At the same time her lover was out and on his return he tried to dispose of the body and explain his wife's disappearance. On this coming unstuck he 'was frantic in his assertions that he'd done it alone'. Yet it was impossible to prove; either could have done it and the poison was in the house.

We are also told that the popular belief about Eva was that she was 'fragile and helpless'. Craig is said to be 'one of the most notorious criminals of the century – prominently placed in your Chamber of Horrors'. 'You remember the Craig case? Poirot asks a young woman?' She replies, 'Who doesn't? Why he's in Madame Tussauds! I was only a kid at the time, but the newspapers are always bringing him up and comparing the case with other cases. I don't suppose he'll ever be forgotten'. Much later the daughter of Craig talks about her father. 'My father was just – weak. And besotted by her. But he took the rap'. As to Eva, 'She was a nasty bit of goods alright…I've always believed that she did' [murder] whilst admitting that her father had been an accessory.

Crippen's waxwork did exist in the Chamber of Horrors for a very long time indeed, in a variety of incarnations. The Chamber focuses on criminals (for example, Jack the Ripper, the Krays, Haigh and John Reginald Christie who now all feature there). However, he appears digitally on a screen being portrayed by an actor being hanged at Pentonville Prison.

It transpires that Eva went to Australia (it was commonly and wrongly thought that Ethel le Neve moved there) after the case was over and that she died there. She had a son. The book was published in 1952 and there is a reference to the Craig case as being about 40 years previously which also ties it in with the Crippen murder of 1910.

However, Agatha Christie makes two slips with the children of Eva and that of Craig. Bearing in mind the case is said to have taken place 40 years ago, Eva's child would have to be about 40; his age is not hinted at but his supposed mother is said to be sixty odd. It is also revealed that Craig had a daughter by his wife; again she would have to be over 40; she is described as being 'a young woman'. Poirot would have doubtless smelt a rat here and in some mystery books such slips are used as vital evidence.

Crippen is mentioned in at least one of the televisations of these dramas. In the 1987 *Sleeping Murder*, Miss Marple tells the young couple,

'Of course, you're too young to remember the case of Dr Crippen, when something similar occurred'. This is in reference to Gwenda's stepmother who allegedly left home but it is feared that she was murdered instead, as per Cora Crippen.

Sources

Old Bailey online

Nicholas Connell, *Doctor Crippen: The Infamous London Cellar Murder of 1910* (2008)

Filson Young, *The Trial of Hawley Harvey Crippen* (1950)

Frederick Henry Seddon (1911)

The Mysterious Affair at Styles (1920),
After the Funeral (1953)

Poisoners rarely, if ever, evoke sympathy. To stand cold-bloodedly by, watching the victim suffer a slow and painful death over days, weeks, or months, seems crueller than the killer who, in a fatal moment of fury, attacks with a knife or a blunt instrument. But even among poisoners there are different degrees of evil. In bygone days, when a divorce was socially stigmatizing and difficult to obtain, an oppressed and abused wife's decision to put arsenic in her husband's soup might perhaps evoke some slight understanding. Some poisonings have doubtless also been the work of mentally disturbed people. Then there are those cases where the poisoner by all accounts is sane, being motivated solely by financial gain. For this category of killers, it is difficult to feel anything but contempt and disgust. One of the most famous cases belonging to the 'financial' category is that of Frederick Seddon, hanged in April 1912 for the murder of his tenant Eliza Barrow.

Frederick Henry Seddon was born in 1872 in Liverpool. He was employed by an insurance company and worked his way up to the position of superintendent. At a young age he married the even younger Margaret Ann and had five children. The family eventually moved to London, where in 1909 Seddon bought a fourteen-room house at 63, Tollington Park, near Finsbury Park. The family lived on one floor; the bottom floor was used as Seddon's office and the second floor was let out. In July 1910, four new tenants moved in: the 48-year-old Eliza Mary Barrow, her protégé or adopted son, 8-year-old Ernie Grant, and the married couple Hook. Eliza Barrow was unmarried and in possession of a small fortune consisting of £1,600 India Stock, the leasehold of a public house and an adjoining barber's shop, and some gold and banknotes kept in a cashbox. She is described as eccentric, very deaf, and irritable: 'Sometimes she would get offended over nothing and not speak to people for a week'.

Previously, Miss Barrow had shared lodgings with various relatives, but it had often ended in arguments and break-ups. For several years she lived in relative harmony with the Grant family, who were not related to her. It seems that Miss Barrow and Mrs Grant were happy to have a drink – or two – together. When Mr and Mrs Grant died a few years apart, Eliza Barrow took care of their children Hilda and Ernest (Ernie). The girl was placed in an orphanage while Ernie followed his benefactor to lodge with her cousin Frank Vonderahe and his wife in North London. After 11 months, this arrangement came to an end when Miss Barrow spat in Mrs Vonderahe's face. Shortly afterwards, she moved to Tollington Park.

Robert Hook was the brother of the late Mrs. Grant and Eliza Barrow was – according to him – an 'old sweetheart' of his. He and his wife had an agreement with her to live rent-free in the house at Tollington Park, in return for Mrs Hook helping with cooking and other household chores. There were soon arguments, culminating after two weeks, when the Hooks took Ernie on an outing without inviting Eliza Barrow. She became very upset and asked her landlord to evict the Hooks, explaining that she had a cash box in her room and was afraid that Mr Hook would steal her money. Seddon – annoyed at the disturbances – forced the Hooks to move, earning him Eliza Barrow's gratitude and trust.

Before long Miss Barrow had confided in Seddon that she was worried about her finances. New tax regulations might affect her income from the lease of the public house and, consequently, also the barber's shop. The India Stock had fallen. She was afraid of becoming poor and thought about how best to manage her assets. The subject of an annuity was brought up; apparently a friend of Eliza had acquired one. They finally agreed that she would transfer to Seddon her stock and titles to the property in exchange for her being allowed to live rent free and him paying her £3 per week for life. Upon her death the annuity would cease, meaning her relatives would not inherit anything. This came into effect in January 1911, everything being arranged through solicitors. There is no indication that Eliza Barrow was not fully aware of what had been agreed upon.

Seddon soon sold the India Stock and used the profits for new property deals. He is described as a man obsessed with making money, to the point that he took every little opportunity to earn an extra penny. For example, he was happy to jump in as an extra in theatres in the evenings, for half a crown a performance. He also ran a second hand clothes business in his wife's name. Miss Barrow is also said to have been obsessed with money and very careful with spending; she 'dressed rather poorly for her position' according to her cousin. Perhaps it was because landlord and tenant shared a passion for hoarding money that they both got along so well? When Seddon at the trial was asked if he liked Eliza Barrow, he replied: 'She was not a woman you could be in love with, but I deeply sympathized with her'.

From January to August 1911, nothing out of the ordinary occurred in the house at Tollington Park. Seddon punctually paid the weekly £3 to his tenant. His 15-year-old daughter Maggie looked after Miss Barrow for a small fee, Mrs Seddon sometimes cooked for her. Every morning Eliza Barrow walked Ernie to school and then picked him up in the afternoon. Ernie called her Chicky. At the trial the boy testified that the Seddons had always been kind to him and Chicky, and that he was much happier with them than he had been with the Vonderahes. At the beginning of August, Miss Barrow saw a doctor, who diagnosed 'congestion of the liver' and prescribed a harmless mixture. Shortly afterwards the Seddons, Eliza Barrow and Ernie Grant went on a few days holiday to Southend. On her return, Miss Barrow again consulted a doctor, now on account of asthma.

On 1 September 1911, Eliza Barrow fell ill with stomach pains, diarrhoea, and vomiting. The Seddons' family physician, Dr. Sworn, prescribed bismuth and morphine. It was unusually hot for the season and an epidemic of diarrhoea raged in the neighbourhood. The doctor assumed that Miss Barrow had contracted this infection. Her symptoms continued and Dr Sworn prescribed additional medication. He wanted to send his patient to hospital, but she refused. A slight improvement occurred although Miss Barrow was still weak and bedridden. On 11 September she dictated her will to Seddon, in which she gave all her personal assets to Hilda and Ernie Grant. As she had previously willed her estate to Seddon in exchange for the life annuity, it was only a matter of furniture, jewellery, and a watch. Two days later, Dr Sworn came to visit. He perceived Eliza Barrow's condition as serious but not life threatening; however, the next morning – 14 September – she died.

About an hour after Miss Barrow's death, Seddon went to see Dr Sworn. He said that he and his wife had been up all night to attend to Miss Barrow, that she had been in great pain but at last had fallen asleep, never to wake up. The doctor issued – on his own initiative – a death certificate, stating the cause of death to be epidemic diarrhoea. That same morning, Seddon visited an undertaker in the neighbourhood. He explained that a tenant had died and left only about £4, so he wanted to have the cheapest possible funeral. The undertaker offered to arrange everything for £4, but Seddon wanted to reduce the price because the doctor also had to be paid. In the end the two men agreed on £3 7s. 6d. Two days later, Eliza Barrow was buried in a public grave in Islington Cemetery, East Finchley.

Miss Barrow's relatives, the Vonderahes, knew nothing of the death or the funeral. By chance they learned of the matter and immediately sought out Seddon, who assured them that he had sent them letters which apparently had not arrived. He showed the will dictated by Eliza Barrow and informed the cousins about the arrangement regarding her annuity and the transfer of her assets to himself. One of the Vonderahe ladies remarked that 'whoever persuaded Miss Barrow to part with her property must be an extremely clever person'. She also pointed out that the dead woman should have been buried in the family's private vault in Highgate. Seddon dismissed the cousins' objections with a shrug and went on another holiday with his family. But time was about to run out for him.

The Vonderahe family went to the police, relating their suspicions against Seddon and insisting on an investigation. Eliza Barrow's corpse was exhumed on 15 November and examined by Dr William Willcox, who discovered 2 grains of arsenic (a lethal amount) in various internal organs. The pathologist believed that a fatal dose of arsenic had been administered within two days of death, his calculations indicating that at least five grains had been present at the time of death. On 4 December Frederick Seddon was arrested and in January so was his wife Margaret Ann. They were charged with wilful murder and put on trial at the Central Criminal Court (Old Bailey) on 4 March 1912. The Attorney-General, Sir Rufus Isaacs, led for the prosecution. Edward Marshall Hall defended Frederick Seddon, Gervais Rentoul defended Margaret Seddon and the judge was Mr Justice Bucknill.

The evidence against the Seddons was entirely circumstantial. The prosecution presented the financial transactions between Frederick Seddon and Eliza Barrow, emphasizing Seddon's obsession with money. His claim that she left only £4 seemed dubious: there was evidence that she had withdrawn her entire deposit (£216) from the Savings Bank in gold in June 1911. What had happened with all this money? Carl Taylor, employed at the same insurance company as Seddon, testified that on the evening of 14 September, Seddon – who was his immediate superior – had been sitting at his office desk counting gold coins, about £200, and joked with another employee that it was that man's salary. However, it could not be proven that the gold coins had belonged to Miss Barrow. Seddon naturally denied this: 'That would make it out that I was a greedy, inhuman monster, and that having stolen this woman's money I should bring it down and count it in the presence of my two assistants and flaunt it like that; the suggestion is scandalous'.

How the Seddons got hold of arsenic was not fully established. The prosecution's theory was that the poison had been extracted from arsenical flypapers, soaked in water. A pharmacist identified young Maggie Seddon as the girl who bought a packet of flypapers containing arsenic from him a few days before Eliza Barrow fell ill. Maggie denied that she was the one who made the purchase. Mrs Seddon stated that Eliza Barrow's room had been full of flies (this was confirmed by Dr Sworn) and that she herself bought arsenical flypapers a few days after the tenant fell ill. The pharmacist's identification of Maggie Seddon was challenged by Marshall Hall. He also managed to create uncertainty regarding Dr Willcox's quantification of arsenic in Miss Barrow's body, which was based on calculations with a considerable margin of error (he was to do this again in the Harold Greenwood case, as we will see later). Marshall Hall pointed out that arsenic was detected in the distal ends of the hair, which indicated ingestion over a long period of time, probably via various medicinal preparations.

It is possible that Frederick Seddon would have been acquitted if he had not – against the advice of his barrister – insisted on giving evidence himself. In the witness box he came across as conceited, arrogant, and condescending. It did not matter that he could provide plausible answers to most questions; the jury got an unfavourable impression overall. Things did not get any better for him when the judge gave his summing-up, which seemed to be prejudiced against Seddon while his wife was treated with great indulgence, the judge almost instructing the jury to acquit her. After an hour's deliberation the jury found Margaret Seddon Not Guilty and Frederick Seddon Guilty. Asked if he had anything to say, Seddon replied calmly and at length, explaining some of the economic transactions. Finally, he made a Masonic sign with his hand in the air and solemnly stated: 'I declare before the Great Architect of the Universe, I am not guilty'. Mr Justice Bucknill was also a Freemason, and it is said that he was greatly moved by Seddon's words. However, that did not stop him from delivering the death sentence, a moment that was photographed and preserved for posterity.

Frederick Seddon was hanged in Pentonville Prison on 18 April 1912, just three days after the Titanic disaster. Later that year his widow – who quickly remarried and was now Mrs Cameron – gave a sensational statement to *The Weekly Dispatch*, in which she claimed to have seen her husband poison Miss Barrow. He had threatened to shoot Margaret with a revolver if she revealed anything. She also claimed that Frederick had been abusive to her from the beginning of the marriage, at one point knocking out some of her teeth. Curiously, Margaret retracted the entire statement under oath a few days later. Shortly thereafter, she emigrated with her new husband and the five children to the United States.

No doubt Frederick Seddon was an unsympathetic, greedy man who took advantage of Eliza Barrow's vulnerable situation (single, at odds with relatives, worried about her money) to enrich himself. That he ultimately poisoned her with arsenic is likely, although the evidence was purely circumstantial. One question remains regarding the motive: when Miss Barrow died Seddon was freed from paying the annuity, but he undertook to provide for Ernie Grant, who had become good friends with his own children and was accepted as one of the family. The cost for the boy's education, clothing, food and so on for several years to come would be considerable. Did Seddon really make so much money from Eliza Barrow's death that it was worth taking the risk of murdering her?

In *After the Funeral*, the solicitor Mr Entwhistle reflects:

> 'Murderers, as far as he could judge, seemed to be of all sorts and kinds. Some had over-sweeping vanity, some had a lust for power, some like Seddon had been mean and avaricious'.

Entwhistle then goes on to briefly characterize some other real-life murderers, the common denominator being their comparative ordinariness. The assessment of Seddon is in line with that of most other observers, both contemporary and modern. Indeed, it is difficult to find a single positive statement about him, although the weakness of the evidence is commented upon by several writers.

There is probably an indirect reference to the Seddon case in Christie's famous first novel, *The Mysterious Affair at Styles* (1920). After the murder by strychnine poisoning of wealthy Mrs Emily Inglethorp, there is strong suspicion against her second husband Alfred, a much younger man who appears to be a fortune-hunter. Evelyn Howard, Mrs Inglethorp's companion, urges John Cavendish (Mrs Inglethorp's elder son by her first marriage) to do something about the unpopular Alfred:

> 'What do you want me to do?' asked John, unable to help a faint smile. 'Dash it all, Evie, I can't haul him down to the local police station by the scruff of his neck.'
>
> 'Well, you might do something. Find out how he did it. He's a crafty beggar. Dare say he soaked fly papers. Ask Cook if she's missed any'.

Later, Poirot asks Evelyn if she still believes that Mrs Inglethorp was poisoned by her husband. The companion lady retorts:

> '…I'll admit that it wasn't he who bought strychnine at the chemist's shop. What of that? I dare say he soaked fly paper, as I told you at the beginning.'
>
> 'That is arsenic – not strychnine,' said Poirot mildly.
>
> 'What does that matter? Arsenic would put poor Emily out of the way just as well as strychnine. If I'm convinced he did it, it doesn't matter a jot to me how he did it.'

The Mysterious Affair at Styles was written in 1916, only four years after the Seddon trial. It seems reasonable to believe that the references to soaked fly paper were inspired by young Maggie Seddon's purchase of arsenical flypapers and the prosecution's theory that they were soaked with water to extract the poison.

Murder for financial gain figures frequently in Agatha Christie's novels and it is possible that the Seddon case – at least partly – may have inspired not only *The Mysterious Affair at Styles* but also *Dumb Witness* (1937), where the wealthy and unmarried Emily Arundell falls victim to poisoning (with phosphorus, not arsenic) shortly after having revised her will. In the short story 'How Does Your Garden Grow?' (1935) we encounter another wealthy and unmarried lady, Miss Amelia Barrowby, who gets poisoned for financial reasons, this time with strychnine. Perhaps the choice of surname for the victim is not a mere coincidence? Barrowby – very similar to Barrow – may well be an allusion to the Seddon case.

Curiously, there is a solicitor named Seddon in the novel *Sad Cypress* (1940). His first name is not Frederick but Edmond, and – although he gives his clients financial advice – he does not appear to have anything more in common with his infamous namesake.

Sources

Mark John Maguire, *They got away with murder II* (2023)

F.E. Smith, first earl of Birkenhead, *Famous trials* (no date; 1920s)

Proceedings of the Old Bailey, Trial account of Frederick Henry Seddon and Margaret Ann Seddon for wilful murder of Eliza Mary Barrow (accessed at https://www.oldbaileyonline)

Brides in the Bath

George Joseph Smith (1912-1914), *Murder on the Links (1923), The Listerdale Mystery (1934), After the Funeral (1953), A Caribbean Mystery (1964)*

One of the most infamous murder cases of the early twentieth century was that of The Brides in the Bath. As with Jack the Ripper, a nick name was given to the case, albeit not to the killer, whose identity is known, but rather it refers to the victims. It was and still is a very well known case, being referred to by George Orwell as well as being the subject of several books and dramas.

The central protagonist was George Joseph Smith, born in London's East End in 1872. He was a career criminal, motivated by money. Initially he was a thief and was in trouble with the law from his youth onwards. He then began to use female accomplices to make life easier for him, taking the gains but exposing them to the danger of arrest and imprisonment. He certainly had an attraction for women and he exploited this to the full. As Sir Edward Marshall-Hall, the barrister who defended Smith, noted 'I am convinced he was a hypnotist' and one woman of the several whom he married agreed with the assessment. She added, 'The power lay in his eyes. When he looked at you for a minute or two you had the feeling you were being magnetised. They were little eyes which seemed to rob you of your will'.

He was also a serial bigamist as well as, eventually, a killer. His first and only lawful wife (he never divorced her) was Caroline Thornhill, who he married in Leicester in 1898. He also had a penchant for using various aliases, and he married her under the name of George Oliver Love, and this was to assist him in his criminal exploits. In the next few years they lived in London and Hastings; she would gain employment in domestic service and then would leave with stolen goods, which her husband then sold. He also committed bigamy for the first time in 1899. His crime spree came to a temporary end in 1901 when he was arrested and imprisoned for two years. Caroline left him at this time and emigrated to Canada.

Smith's whereabouts for the next few years (1902-1908) are unknown; he may have been in the army or he may have emigrated. In 1908 he established what was to be his subsequent modus operandi. Meeting a widow in Brighton with some money to her name, he promised marriage but told her that his business needed her savings for it to prosper. The unsuspecting woman handed her savings over and he promptly deserted her with it. He then married one Edith Pegler later that year and she was to be his only constant companion. Next year he married again, to one Annie Falkner, after meeting her at another seaside resort, and took £400 in cash and property.

There was an even more exciting prospect for this unscrupulous man. In 1910 he met Bessie Mundy, a wealthy spinster. They married, Smith giving his name as Henry Williams, bachelor, and soon asked her what money she had. The trustees passed the accumulated interest of her funds to him (they could not touch the capital of £2,500), and he promptly abandoned her. Two years later they were reunited and, amazingly, he was forgiven. They then made wills in favour of each other.

The couple rented a house in Herne Bay, Kent, and Smith also rented a bath tub. Smith told a doctor he was concerned for his wife's health as she had fits, thus preparing the ground for what was to follow. Shortly afterwards, on 12 July 1912, Smith told how, returning from an evening stroll, he came home to find his wife drowned in her bath. There was an inquest and the verdict of accidental death was announced. This was reported only in the local press. Smith then inherited his wife's money and though her family were unhappy they could not stop him. He invested his windfall in property.

Next year, in 1913, Smith met Alice Burnham, a farmer's daughter. He persuaded her to part with her money, and when they married (in his real name), had her take out a life insurance policy. The two honeymooned in Blackpool. They took lodgings in a house with a bath tub, rejecting the first house because it did not have such an amenity. Again, Smith went to see a local doctor about his wife's health. As before, Smith went out for a walk on the evening of 12 December. Returning to his lodgings, he found his wife with her head and shoulders underneath the water. She was dead.

Smith showed a callous attitude and scrimped on the funeral costs, which upset the landlady's family. The inquest once again recorded a death by accident and achieved only local prominence. Smith cashed in the insurance policy and was richer by just over £600.

In the next year, Smith, calling himself John Lloyd, met Margaret Lofty, an unmarried vicar's daughter of Bristol. He promised marriage on his return from his non-existent trip to Canada. In the interim he married again, in Woolwich, as Charles James, and took £76 from Alice Reavil. Deserting her, he met up with Margaret. As with Alice Burnham, he persuaded her to take out an insurance policy on her life, for £700. They married in Bath and then travelled to London.

The couple found rooms in a house on Bismarck Road, north London. Margaret withdrew her meagre savings for her husband's benefit and the two visited a doctor where Smith talked about his wife's ailments. They also went to a solicitor to draw up wills benefitting each other. That evening, 18 December 1914, Margaret went to have a bath and her husband said he was going for a walk. When he returned, he could not get his wife's attention. So he and the landlady entered the bathroom and made a grim discovery. She was in the bath tub, dead.

Next day the calm widower arranged an economical funeral. He attended the inquest – as ever a verdict of accidental death was concluded, despite some bruising on the corpse. Smith arranged early next year to collect the insurance money and have probate granted. Again the inquest was reported in the press, but this time there was a crucial difference. One of the newspapers which reported it was a national newspaper, *The News of the World*, and nationals reported London news, but provincial news usually did not feature therein and in this was the seed of Smith's downfall.

The newspaper was read by both Charles Burnham, Alice's father, and Joseph Crossley, a Blackpool man who recalled her death. The name of each husband was different, as was the location, but the unusual method of death was the same. They contacted the police, enclosing newspaper cuttings to probe the similarity. Smith was arrested and stood trial for murder. It was a high profile case and an unusual one, as the jury were to take on board the fact that there were three similar murders committed by the same man. This was known as evidence of a system. Smith was found guilty and was executed on 13 August. As with Cream and Crippen, the notoriety of the case persisted for a waxwork model of the killer was subsequently included in Madam Tussaud's Waxwork Exhibition, with Smith appearing alongside the actual bath he had used to murder Margaret Lofty in the house in London.

Smith had hit upon a formula. He would marry a woman who had some money and have her write a will in his favour and/or have her insure her life. He would then have her visit a doctor in his company and suggest that she might be unwell. He would have a different name when meeting each woman and would do so in a different place. He would drown her in a bath shortly after marriage. The death would appear to have been a tragic accident in all cases. And he would be so much richer afterwards. Providing no one ever made a connection between these deaths it was a winning formula for him, but lethal for those he married.

There are references to this case in several of Agatha Christie's stories. The first to include it, is *Murder on the Links*, which was written just a few years after Smith's execution. Poirot tells us of 'The English murderer who disposed of his wives in succession by drowning them in their baths was a case in point. Had he varied his methods he might have escaped detection to this day. But he obeyed the common dictates of human nature, arguing that what had once succeeded would succeed again, and he paid the penalty of his lack of originality'. This is also in reference to the fictional mysterious murder in this book, that of Paul Renauld, a rich man, whose body is found on a golf course in northern France to a similar crime occurring in the past. Here, 22 years ago, a husband is killed by his wife and her lover, one George Conneau. Could the cases be linked? See further the earlier chapter on Marguerite Steinheil.

There is another reference to the case by elderly lawyer, Mr Entwhistle, in *After the Funeral*, published in 1953, in which he refers to Smith having 'an incredible fascination for women'. This has already been discussed. Women certainly were taken in by him. Margaret, the last woman he bigamously married wrote to her family on the day after marriage, 'He is a thorough Christian man…I would do anything to secure the one I love, and I have every proof of his love for me. He has been honourable and has kept his word to me in everything. He is such a nice man, and I am certain you would have liked him. I am perfectly happy'. Bessie Mundey once wrote, 'I am very happy indeed'.

Smith was able to marry at least eight women and to beguile others into thinking that he was in love with them. Even after he deserted Bessie in 1910 and stole her money he was able to rekindle her love for him on meeting up again two years later. His hypnotic powers have already been referred to. Yet a detective was unconvinced, writing 'To this day it has always been a poser to me what a woman could see in a man of this type… just like any butcher'. However, he was a mere man and was being wise after the event.

A Caribbean Mystery, published in 1964, features the story far more strongly. A retired soldier, Major Palgrave, is telling old stories to Miss Marple on the fictional Caribbean island of St. Honore. He tells the story he has been told by a doctor of a man whose wife tries to commit suicide. The man is able to find the doctor in time and she is saved. However, a few weeks later she succeeds in her aim and the widower is distraught. The same doctor later discusses the case with a fellow physician and he too, knows of a very similar story, though the locations are different as is the name of the man. To clinch matters, the first doctor has a photograph of the man in question and when he shows it to the other doctor, he recognises it as the same man. No further action is taken, however. The major has a copy of the photograph of the murderer.

Miss Marple replies, 'If a man gets a formula that works – he won't stop. He'll go on' and so the major retorts, 'Brides in the bath'. He could, of course, have chosen to refer to the far more recent case of the acid bath murders (see chapter on John George Haigh). The major is about to show Miss Marple the photograph but then looks over her shoulder, is startled by who he sees and then changes the subject. It is later surmised that he has seen the man whose picture he was about to reveal. He is subsequently found dead.

The case is referred to again in the story. Miss Marple is talking to Jason Rafiel, a disabled, rich and rude elderly man. Miss Marple says, 'Supposing there was a murder planned. If you remember, the story Major Palgrave told me concerned a man whose wife died under suspicious circumstances. Then, after a certain lapse of time, there was another murder under exactly the same circumstances. A man of a different name had a wife who died in much the same way and the doctor who was telling it recognised him as the same man. Well, it does look, doesn't it, as though this murderer might be the kind of murderer who made a habit of the thing?'

Mr Rafiel replies, 'You mean like Smith, Brides in the Bath?' and Miss Marple agrees, and adds:

> 'As far as I can make out…and from what I have heard and read, a man who does a wicked thing like this and gets away with it the first time, is, alas, encouraged. He thinks it's easy, he thinks he's clever. And so he repeats it. And in the end, as you say, like Smith and the Brides in the Bath, it becomes a habit. Each time in a different place and each time the man changes his name. But the crimes themselves are all very much alike'.

She adds:

> 'If you remember, that was exactly the way Smith got caught. The circumstances of a crime attracted the attention of somebody who compared it with a newspaper clipping of some other case'.

Miss Marple is correct about the newspapers being the vital clue, as already noted. In the story a married man who has already killed two wives for their money and got away with it by passing off the deaths as suicides, is planning to do so again. Of the three couples at the holiday resort, Mr Dyson's first wife died some time ago, though nothing is known of the antecedents of that of fellow guest, Colonel Edward Hillingdon or Tim Kendall, hotel proprietor. If the major did recognise an undetected murderer who was perhaps about to kill again, then he would be a target, as he is. The killer strikes again, but his ultimate plans are thwarted by Miss Marple and a woman's life is saved.

The parallels are striking. In both cases there is a man who marries women, kills them for their money but passes off their deaths as being suicides (rather than accidents) and so are uninvestigated. He changes his name and moves about in order to do so and to escape any chance of detection. His modus operandi is the same throughout.

A Caribbean Mystery has been televised three times but only in the most recent one (2013, starring Julia McKenzie as Miss Marple) is there a reference to the 'Brides in the Bath' case, made by Major Palgrave. As an aside, in Molly's room (in the Joan Hickson Miss Marple drama of 1988) a book is found by Professor Henry Yellowlees, *To Define True*

Madness: Commonsense Psychiatry for Lay People, published in 1955. The author was the medical expert for the defence in the trial of acid bath serial murderer Haigh in 1949 when the doctor attempted to show that the defendant was suffering from mental disorder and so should be assigned to Broadmoor rather than the gallows. He failed in this. Haigh admired Smith. Oddly enough the David Suchet drama of *The Clocks* (2011) has a suspect make reference to the Brides in the Bath case, which is not in the book it is loosely based on.

It is arguable that the short story 'Philomel Cottage' from *The Listerdale Mystery* has some inspiration from the case when the bride, Alix, finds that her new husband, Gerald Martin, was once charged with bigamy and murder, but was found not guilty of the latter. He has clearly married her for her money and is planning to kill her. Fortunately she is able to outwit him and survive.

Sources

Jonathan Oates, *London Serial Killers, 1888-1965* (2022)
Jane Robins, *The Magnificent Spilsbury and the Brides in the Bath* (2014)
Eric Watson, *The Trial of George Joseph Smith* (1930)

Harold Greenwood (1919)

The Tuesday Night Club (in: The Thirteen Problems, 1932),
The Lernaean Hydra (in: The Labours of Hercules 1947),
A Murder is Announced (1950),
The Cornish Mystery (in: Poirot's Early Cases 1974)

This case is not mentioned explicitly by name in the Agatha Christie canon but a knowledge of true crime will enable the reader to discern it. After all, it occurred when Christie was a young woman and it hit the headlines in the same year that her first novel, The *Mysterious Affair at Styles*, was published. This was another middle-class poisoning case, of a wealthy woman, just as the fictional Styles case had been, and as in that case, suspicion instantly fell on the husband, a younger man with a financial dependence on his rich wife. As with the fictional Alfred Inglethorp, Greenwood had an extra marital love interest.

Greenwood was a solicitor, born in Ingleton, Yorkshire, in 1874 and married to Mabel Bowater in 1896, three years his senior. They had lived in a detached house, Rumsey House, in Kidwelly, Carmarthenshire, since 1916 after having lived elsewhere in the little town since 1898. They had four children, the eldest being Edith Irene, born in 1898. The others were, in 1919, seventeen-year-old Mabel and two boys, Norman aged 15 and John Kenneth aged 9. The first and last lived at home in 1919.

Greenwood was not an outstanding specimen of humanity, if the police assessment of him is to be believed:

> 'Harold Greenwood may be described as a man of little ability, a certain amount of simple cunning, and a large measure of conceit, is a solicitor and has an office in Llanelli. His small practice has mostly to do with Jews, moneylenders and dealings in house property.

> 'He has a poor reputation, both as a lawyer and generally, no one seems to have good word for him.
>
> 'He was too friendly with other women, during his deceased's wife's life, which caused a certain amount of domestic infelicity, so that their married life could not be described as a particularly happy one'.

Two women in particular had caught his eye. They were Miss Mary Adeline Griffiths, the younger sister of the doctor who lived opposite the Greenwoods, and Gwladys Jones, who worked in the family business, which was *The Llanelli Mercury* newspaper. On one occasion in 1918, when Mrs Greenwood had been absent for a weekend, Miss Jones stayed at Greenwood's house for the weekend. However also present were Irene Greenwood, Alice, Gwladys' sister and the children's governess, Miss Davies. The two were also seen lunching together locally.

Mabel was involved in the business side of running a local tennis club and was involved in church work. However, she 'did not enjoy particularly robust health'. She was also privately wealthy with her own income.

On Saturday 14 June 1919 Mrs Greenwood went to Ferryside, four miles away, to attend a business meeting of the tennis club, though she did not play the game herself. That evening her friend Florence Phillips visited and Mrs Greenwood seemed 'unusually well and cheerful' and her complexion seemed improved, 'a lovely sort of pink'.

Next day the family had breakfast together, on poached egg, bread and butter and coffee. Mrs Greenwood then went outside and wrote letters whilst sitting on the lawn. Then there was lunch. Both Greenwood parents were there, along with Irene and Kenneth. The 18-year-old parlourmaid, Hannah Williams, 'quite an intelligent girl', waited at the table. They all ate the meat and vegetables followed by gooseberry tart and custard. Greenwood drank whisky and, according to Hannah, his wife drank port wine; the children had water. Hannah later recalled that she had twice seen Greenwood visit the room where the wine had been stored prior to the meal. The bottle and its remaining contents disappeared on the following day. Hannah stated 'She [Mrs Greenwood] always took port wine and was never known to take whisky'.

That afternoon, Mrs Greenwood was in the garden as before lunch. The family had tea at 4pm. Mrs Greenwood began to show symptoms of being unwell, being 'taken with pains in the stomach'. Her husband gave her a glass of neat brandy. This did nothing to alleviate the pain.

At about seven o'clock, Greenwood went across the road to fetch Dr Thomas Griffiths. He came over quickly and prescribed a mixture of bismuth to soothe Mrs Greenwood's stomach. He also recommended small and frequent doses of brandy and soda, and milk and soda with ice if it was available. He also ordered her to take to her bed. The district nurse was also summoned, and she came along. However, the patient was very sick with vomiting and diarrhoea. Greenwood went over to the doctor's again.

He was allegedly an hour there, spending most of his time in the drawing room, with the doctor's sister with whom he had had 'a longstanding flirtation'. They later claimed it was only 10 minutes. Miss Griffiths said that Greenwood was 'in very good spirits and jocular in his manner'. Greenwood told her about his wife: 'She is worse than usual and I don't think she will get over it this time'.

Irene came over to the house to find her father and to hurry the doctor along. The two men found Mrs Greenwood in her room with her eldest daughter. The doctor then gave the nurse two tablets; variously described as being morphia tablets and later opium tablets and these later became a subject of much controversy. At 11pm the nurse and Greenwood remained with Mrs Greenwood. She got no better, being repeatedly sick and suffering from diarrhoea of a kind not known to the nurse and at 3am she thought that the pulse had stopped. Dr Griffiths was recalled.

Death took place at 3.30am on Monday 16 June. Incredibly, Dr Griffiths put her death down to 'valvular disease of the heart', duly recording it on the death certificate, and she was buried in the churchyard on 19 June. The doctor was surprised at her death, but recalled that she had had a history of being unwell. A month ago he had prescribed her with a tonic because she was going through the menopause. Apparently he was 'not regarded by many who are quite friendly with him as particularly competent'. No memorial was erected to her. Fifteen weeks later, on 1 October 1919, at Bryn chapel near Llanelli, Greenwood married Miss Jones (of the newspaper business). They went on a motoring honeymoon and then returned to live at the family home.

However, as a policeman later stated, 'The case has excited an uneasy feeling in this district of Wales and this is being kept alive by the presence of a number of newspaper reporters who appear to be spending money quite freely for sensational copy'. Nurse Jones talked to the vicar, the Rev.

David Ambrose Jones. It was not that she thought the death was a suspicious one, but she felt that a post mortem would have been in order. It was also 'agreed by all who knew her that she was decidedly not a person who would seek to take her own life'.

Such local suspicions led to a police investigation led by the local policeman, Sergeant Lewis, and enough material was found to request that the Home Office gave an exhumation order. When being told of this, Greenwood said 'Just the very thing. I am quite agreeable'. On being questioned he gave a very unfavourable impression to the police, as he 'did not act in the manner one would regard as that of an innocent man… He showed no indignation and did not resent in any way the implication that he was suspected of being involved, and acted as if he knew there was something to explain'.

On 16 April 1920, there were diggings in the churchyard and certain organs were removed from Mabel's body by one Dr Alexander Dick, the police surgeon, and sent for analysis at St. Mary's Hospital in London. The conclusion of Dr William Willcox was that there was arsenic in the body. This agreed with the symptoms noted in the last hours of Mrs Greenwood's life. An inquest was held at Kidwelly Town Hall. Although he was summoned to attend, Greenwood did not do so. On 16 June, the second day of the inquest, and exactly a year after her death, the jury concluded that Mrs Greenwood had been wilfully murdered by her husband.

Matters were looking black for Greenwood. On 2 and 8 June 1917 he had bought two quarts of Cooper's Weedicide from Jones the chemist in Kidwelly. He had signed the poisons book as was necessary and told Jones that he needed the poison to destroy weeds. This preparation was almost entirely made up of arsenic. He had also bought Eureka weedkiller earlier in 1919. Greenwood had previously denied ever buying arsenic which was 'so palpably untrue'.

Greenwood was arrested on the last day of the inquest and following a series of court appearances, was to be tried at the Carmarthen assizes. This began on 2 November. Fortunately for him, he had Sir Edward Marshall Hall as his defending barrister. Hall had a reputation for securing not guilty verdicts, as in the case of Ronald Light earlier that year. Crucially in the trial, Irene told a stunned court that she too had drunk from the wine at the fatal lunch and had suffered no ill effects from it. She had never said this before and this dealt a mortal blow to the prosecution case. If what she said was true then her mother did not die from poisoned wine. It was also suggested that if the doctor had given Miss Greenwood morphia tablets these would have killed her. On 8 November the judge gave his summing up speech, lasting three hours. The jury took a long time over their verdict and gave Greenwood the benefit of the doubt, 'not guilty'. However, it should be noted that all this meant was that if Irene was truthful, her mother had been poisoned by another method as there was no doubt about the arsenic in her remains and it is hard to think that anyone but her husband could have been responsible, having both motivation, opportunity and means. Yet he was now a free man. Greenwood then had his own story published in a newspaper.

By 1923 Greenwood left Kidwelly with his second wife and eventually settled in Herefordshire, where he died in the village of Walford on 17 January 1929, under the name of Pilkington. He was aged 55. His widow returned to live in Llanelli and died there in 1962. Shortly after Greenwood's death, the case was covered in a volume of the Notable British Trials series and the editor is sympathetic towards Greenwood.

The consensus of later opinion is ambiguous as to whether Greenwood got away with the murder of his wife in order that he could remarry a younger woman. However, a recent assessment is that he inserted arsenic into the wine which he knew that only his wife would drink, then disposed of the bottle and the remaining wine, which presumes his daughter was a liar. Initially it seemed that all was going well, as no one was suspicious and there was no investigation. Then he did everything he could to invite suspicion; remarrying indecently soon after the death of his wife and then remaining in the same family house as if nothing untoward had occurred. He had upset all the social norms and so brought down local hostility on his head which eventually led the police to act. He was very lucky that he had secured a top barrister who was able to cast enough doubt on the testimony of the witnesses to have him to be found not guilty. A recent commentator, Mark John Maguire, has suggested that Greenwood was assisted in the murder by Dr Griffiths who he was friendly with.

This well-known middle class poisoning case is referred to in *A Murder is Announced*. Miss Marple tells Bunch Harman:

> 'Family solidarity is a very strong thing. Very strong. Do you remember some famous case – I really can't remember who it was. They say the husband poisoned his wife. In a glass of

> wine. Then, at the trial, the daughter said she'd drunk half her mother's glass – so that knocked the case against her father to pieces. They do say – but that may be rumour – that she never spoke to her father or lived with him again'.

Irene, his daughter, claimed to have drunk from the same bottle but without ill effect. However, following her mother's death she left the family home and lived with her mother's family, the wealthy Bowaters, in London and in 1921 was employed as a governess in Cheshire. Her father had given Irene her mother's wedding ring but then demanded it back to give to Miss Jones – and he only told Irene about his forthcoming remarriage two days before the date. She was clearly able to support her father to the extent that she did not want him to suffer the ignoble fate of hanging and to have the notoriety of having a convicted murderer as her father, which would certainly not help her future prospects. On the other hand, after taking that crucial step, she did not want to have anything more to do with him and she and her sister did not attend their father's funeral, which suggests hostility.

However, the argument for Greenwood's innocence could rest on the fact that he gained very little from his wife's death. Her estate was only £378 and her income went to the children. As to his remarriage, there is conflicting evidence for a romance between him and Miss Jones prior to his wife's death. Short engagements were more common during and after the First World War. Perhaps the whole case rested on small town gossip? Certainly Greenwood claimed so. His life after 1920 was one of relative obscurity and genteel poverty, though that is not definite proof of innocence.

In the novel, the central household is that of Miss Letitia Blacklock, who lives with two young people who are her distant relatives. Although comfortably off, Miss Blacklock is not fabulously wealthy. However, her sister is, and she is ailing. When she dies Miss Blacklock will become very rich indeed. Yet her life seems to be in peril. Someone seems to have paid a disreputable hotel employee to shoot her, but he is instead killed. The killer would appear to be a relative of the unmarried and childless Miss Blacklock, for after her sister's natural death and that of Miss Blacklock, that unknown relative will inherit a good deal. However, the plot of the book has little or no connection with that of the Greenwood case. The killer goes on to kill twice again and is motivated by money. Their methods are dissimilar; shooting, poison and strangulation. Miss Marple is using it as an example about family solidarity in a murder case.

'The Cornish Mystery', published in *Poirot's Early Cases,* feels similar to the story. A married woman in a small Cornish town is being poisoned and her husband, a dentist is the suspect. He is apparently having an affair with his young assistant. The woman dies and the doctor passes it off as a gastric death. Yet when the widower announces his engagement to his assistant, gossips feel he must have murdered his wife. An exhumation is ordered and sure enough, arsenic is found. The dentist is put on trial for the murder of his wife.

The story 'The Tuesday Night Club', the first Miss Marple story from *The Thirteen Problems*, has elements of the Greenwood case in it. Here there is a gathering of three people for a meal and the wife, a Mrs Jones, dies. The doctor, who had visited her that evening and given her pills, puts the death down to natural causes. Her husband, a philanderer married to a richer spouse, is suspected and an exhumation reveals arsenic as the true cause of her death. Yet it is unclear how he could have administered it.

We could also link this case to that in 'The Lernaean Hydra' in *The Labours of Hercules*, though that also links with that of Major Armstrong as shall be noted (in real life the cases of Greenwood and Armstrong were linked by commentators then and now; both were small town solicitors accused of wife poisoning in 1919 and 1921 in Wales). In fiction the invalid Mrs Oldfield dies, apparently of gastric trouble; as Poirot remarks, 'the symptoms of gastric inflammation and of arsenical poisoning are closely alike – a fact which everybody knows nowadays. Within the last ten years there have been at least four sensational murder cases in which the victim has been buried without suspicion with a certificate of gastric disorder' (a reference to the Armstrong, Croydon poisonings, Annie Hearn and Greenwood cases).

In a discussion of these murderers, a character in the story says 'Armstrong, for instance, and that other man – I can't remember his name'. This is an implicit reference to Greenwood, and as with the Miss Marple quote above, Christie does not name him explicitly. Since he had died in 1929 and this had been widely reported, it is not certain why she could not have done so without fear of any legal consequences. In this case, it is the gossip of neighbours that led the authorities to act; Greenwood said, 'I am a victim of village gossip, of village scandal' and in the story it is the gossips that lead the widowed Dr Charles Oldfield to summon Poirot following the death of his older wife. As the doctor tells him, 'I don't know how to fight this – this vile network of lies and suspicion'. In both cases there is the rumour that the widower poisoned his wife because he wanted to marry a younger woman whom he is friendly with.

There are several solicitors in Christie's books. Many only have fleeting roles in reading wills and other strictly legal duties; eg Seddon in *Sad Cypress*. Some are suspects; as with Walter Fane in *Sleeping Murder*; Mr Abbott in *Murder is Easy*, and Charles Vyse in *Peril at End House*. However, none of these men are accused of murdering their wife; all are bachelors. And then there is Richard Symmington in *The Moving Finger*. He is a solicitor in the small Devon town of Lymstock, a married man with two boys. His wife, Mona, dies of potassium cyanide but there is no doubt that that is what it is and an inquest is held. Apparently she received an anonymous letter to say that her second son is illegitimate. A note from her reading 'I can't go on' is found. This evidence is thought conclusive and the verdict is suicide. Unlike the allegedly womanising Greenwood, Symmington is very proper and respectable.

Finally, we might cite a comment made by Miss Marple at the end of one novel in which the spinster sleuth states, 'He wanted to marry the girl, you see. He is very respectable and so is she. And besides, he is devoted to his children and did not want to give them up. He wanted everything, his house, his children, his respectability and Elsie. And the price he would have to pay for that was murder'. Perhaps this provides a motive for Greenwood as well as the one in this story.

There is an even better known case of a real life solicitor being accused of murder and this will be the focus of a later chapter.

Sources

Stephen Bates, *The Poisonous Solicitor* (2021)
Winifred Duke, *The Trial of Harold Greenwood* (1930).
Jonathan Oates, *Harold Greenwood and the Kidwelly Poisoning* (2025).
Mark John Maguire, *They got away with murder I* (2023)

Katie Whistance (1920)

Mrs McGinty's Dead (1952)

When Poirot investigates the mysterious death of charwoman Mrs McGinty in the village of Broadhinny, he finds that not long before she died, she had read a Sunday newspaper story about four people who had been involved in crimes in the past. One of these four was Eva Kane, whose story has already been told. Another is that of Lily Gamboll, perhaps the most disturbing of these because she was a child who killed. Three decades before the publication of *Mrs McGinty's Dead*, a real-life murder occurred which may have been the basis for the fictional crime of Lily Gamboll.

This shocking story took place at Rose Cottage, Llanvetherine, a small hamlet on the old road between Abergavenny and Ross. This was the lonely home of Mrs Sarah Ann White, aged 53, who had lived there for some years. She had been a widow for 16 years and derived her income from rents from six cottages in Ross bequeathed to her by her late husband, George White, a gardener. This yielded £50 per annum. Police found that she was 'spoken of as a respectable woman reputed to be in comfortable circumstances'. The cottage itself was a substantial one, with seven or eight rooms. There were stables and outhouses. An elderly labourer, Edwin Pritchard, who was very deaf, lived in one of these. There was another labourer of no fixed abode who lived nearby, one George Wilkins, who lived in the coach house, but occasionally visited the cottage.

Mrs White had few visitors, but nearby lived her brother, James Albert Whistance, a farmer of Terew Farm and her married sister, mother to fifteen-year-old, Primrose Catherine Alice Whistance (known as Katie). She had lived with her aunt, Mrs White, for the past four and a half years. She was described as 'a buxom, pretty girl of 16 [this was a year out], with large blue eyes and a profusion of dark hair'. She had been born on 15 January 1905 at Abergavenny to Rose Hannah Whistance, a single woman who had two other illegitimate children. The teenager slept at Rose Cottage, as company for her aunt and helped with housework in the morning, spending the afternoons with her uncle at Trerew Farm.

Her mother, aged 43, was 'generally spoken of as a disreputable character in the district. She lives in a very poor hovel and apparently has for a long time past not had sufficient nourishment for herself and children'. She lived at Coedoe cottage in Pont. She was not living with the man she eventually married.

On Friday 11 June 1920, at 7.30 in the morning, Katie went to the nearby police station and told Sergeant Hathersall that she was very worried about her aunt. She said 'Will you please come down at once, my auntie' and the sergeant asked, 'What is the matter with your auntie'. The girl replied ' I think she's gone out of her mind'. Elaborating, she said that on the previous night the woman had told her to prepare to leave because she would not be around much longer, as she could not keep her anymore and gave her a little money.

She asked them to come to the cottage to investigate. Hathersall did so and told her that there was shocking news. Her aunt had been murdered. They had found the body of the murdered woman on the floor of her bedroom. It was dressed in her night clothes. There were four wounds on her head, inflicted with a heavy wooden mallet, which was found in the bedroom. There was no sign of a struggle and the rest of the house was in order. She had been hit once in bed, then rolling out had been struck down another three times.

Katie told her story 'with remarkable composure and self possession'. She had been recently bought a new bicycle by her aunt, and was out riding it in the days before the murder. She was thus unaware if there had been any visitors to the cottage, though on the days she was at home did not think there had been any. On the Thursday she said that her aunt was behaving oddly and did not sleep well that night. She eventually told her niece to leave the house in the early hours of the morning. She told her to be back soon and if there was anything amiss, to go to the police. She went for her bicycle ride, visited her mother who lived nearby to tell her that her aunt was saying strange things and behaving oddly, and then returned home and found the front door shut but unlocked. She entered, thinking that she would find her aunt downstairs, but could not find her at all. She called out but without hearing a reply.

Mrs Whistance said that her sister did not have an enemy in the world. She said that she did not have many men friends. The Glamorganshire police were baffled and the chief constable contacted Scotland Yard on the same day to ask for help. Chief Inspector Albert Helden and Sergeant Alfred Boden arrived to begin the investigation.

They arrived in the afternoon on 12 June and saw the scene of the crime. They took witness statements, spoke to their colleagues and the doctor. A solution was not long off.

On the evening of Monday 14 June, the two detectives visited Katie's mother's house (Katie was now living there). They talked to her until Katie arrived. Helden said she should come to the police station with them. Helden added 'We are police officers from London and I arrest you for the murder of your Aunt at Rose Cottage on the 11th of June'. She replied, 'I did not do it, what makes you think I did'. On their way by car to the police station, she fainted.

At the police station they gave her tea and Sergeant Hatherall was present. It was then that she made the following statement to Helden and Boden:

> 'I make this statement of my own free will after being duly cautioned. On Thursday night 10th June, my Aunt grumbled at me for being out late about a month ago and told me I should have to go. She then packed my box and told me I could take it in the morning. We had supper together and went to bed about half past nine. Auntie went to sleep and I also went to sleep. I woke up some time in the night. I went downstairs to the back kitchen and got the Beetle [mallet]; Auntie had told me to bring it in on the Thursday evening from the stable. I went upstairs and hit Auntie with it and she fell out of bed. I hit her again on the floor. I then got my box and bicycle and went to my mother's. The story I told my mother was untrue. I worried about my Auntie turning me out and knew I would lose a good home. This statement has been read over to me and it is true'.

There was additional evidence that she was guilty. Bloodstains were found in her chemise and nightdress, and her stockings were saturated in blood from her feet. The weapon was a 'heavy formidable cudgel' and would not need much physical strength to wield it. Dr Edward Lloyd thought that the blows could have been struck by a 'short person of very moderate physical strength'.

She appeared before the magistrates' court on the next day and was remanded in custody. The inquest gave proof of identity of the corpse but was otherwise adjourned.

The motive seemed slight: 'it cannot be seen how she could be benefitted by the death of her Aunt'. Theft did not seem a motive as little if anything of monetary value was missing. Insanity was a possibility. 'Considering that one of her Aunts was in a Lunatic Asylum some years ago and the apparent weak mindedness of her mother it may be possible that the girl is suffering from some form of insanity'.

It was probably a case of adolescent rage and anger about her aunt's attitude towards her, and perhaps petty grudges had been built up over time, possibly due to misunderstandings due to the age gap and isolation from others of her own age whom it would be more ordinary for her to have associated with. There does not seem to have been any major attempt at analysing her psychology. Certainly she was not thought to have been insane by the standards of the day, as ajudged by the MacNaghten Rules, which decreed that a defendant was unfit to stand trial and thus be convicted if they were either unaware of the gravity of the offence or did not know that it was wrong.

The case was heard at the Monmouth Assizes on 6 November of that year (at the same time that the Harold Greenwood case was bring tried at Carmarthen), before Mr Justice Sir Charles Montague Lush. Katie was defended by Mr St. John Micklethwait and the prosecuting counsel was Mr B.R. Vachell. Defence argued that her confession should not be admitted as evidence as they suggested that it was obtained by 'promise or threats'. However, the judge allowed it. The trial lasted from 10.30 am to 7.15 pm. The jury discussed the evidence for 35 minutes and on their return to the court they concluded that Katie was guilty as charged of murder, but with a recommendation to mercy because of the unfortunate circumstances of her upbringing. Because she was under sixteen, she could not be executed.

Katie was sent to a borstal, a secure institution for young offenders, at Aylesbury in Buckinghamshire. She did get into some trouble with other inmates, though it was not serious and she often appeared withdrawn. On the whole she behaved well under close supervision (most prisoners do if only because it is in their best interests to do so). She remained there until she was released on parole at the end of 1924. She gravitated to London and secured menial employment whilst living in a variety of hostels for young women. In 1925 she worked as a servant, and allegedly as a prostitute in Hyde Park, but became pregnant. She married one Edward Thompson in London in 1926 and moved with her husband, a young soldier who later worked as a miner, to Shuttlewood, Derbyshire. She had another two children and by 1938 was noted as being well conducted and had regular habits. She still had to regularly report to the authorities, which ceased in 1939.

She died in Ardwick, Yorkshire, in 1954, having apparently no further entanglement with the law.

In late 1920 a waxworks museum in Cardiff put a wax model of Katie Whistance in the Chamber of Horrors. It was near to that of Harold Greenwood, who had recently been acquitted of poisoning his wife in Kidwelly as noted in the previous chapter.

In the 1952 story (whilst Katie was still alive), *Mrs McGinty's Dead*, Lily Gamboll was a 12-year-old who came from poor circumstances, having been saved from 'an overcrowded home' by an aunt. She killed the aunt, who apparently was strict, but 'small and frail', with a meat chopper when she refused her permission to go to the cinema. The weapon was snatched from a table and the murder was with a single blow. Because of her age, there was no trial, but she was sent to an approved school, where her conduct was said to have been exemplary. She learnt office skills there and then was put on probation. Lily was last heard of in Ireland. Her current whereabouts are unknown and cannot be easily ascertained. As a child she was said to be 'well developed and muscular', but 'hideously ugly' and 'a plain child with an adenoidal appearance of open mouth, hard breathing and thick spectacles'.

The problem in the book is not with the past but with its effect on the future. Poirot surmises that one of the four killers from the past has been recognised, years or decades later, by Mrs McGinty. This individual wants to preserve their good name and not be revealed as having been a murderer decades ago. There are several young women in the village, including the doctor's wife and the wife of a businessman and prospective MP, who would have been old enough now to have been Lily in the past. The fact that Mrs McGinty was killed with a type of cleaver points to Lily as the murderer in the present as well.

Lily's past crime is not viewed sympathetically by those who comment on her actions. 'I wouldn't care to have her gambolling about me with a meat chopper' says a female journalist. Poirot says that his sympathies are with the aunt not the girl, 'not a nice child'. Similar attitudes can be read in other books by the author, who is not averse to having a young girl as the killer in another novel; and again there is little sympathy for her.

The main similarities between the fact and fiction is that both murderesses were very young (12 and 15 years of age). Both lived with their aunts and both had objectively minor grievances. Both killed their aunts by blows to the head, though in reality there were several blows not one. Katie was not the plain or ugly girl that Lily is made out to be. As she was older she did face trial. Nor did she work in an office when released on probation or go to Ireland. It may be a coincidence, alternatively a clue to the real-life story, that Lily Gamboll's aunt lived in Buckinghamshire – which was also the location of Katle Whistance's borstal.

Murder by children was not entirely unknown at that time, even though, with even more heinous crimes occurring in the later twentieth century (see the chapter Something wicked this way comes) and beyond, such have disappeared from the collective memory which yearns for a golden age of innocence that never was. There has never been a book on this case and there is very little about it online, unlike the Abertillery murders of Harold Jones (tried at the same assize county in the following year), where the criminal was of the same age, the same part of the country and in the same time period as Katie Whistance. The newspaper reading public of the early twentieth century, including Agatha Christie, would have been aware that their present was far from perfect, and this terrible story, though not its aftermath, would have been common knowledge.

Sources

The National Archives files:
Murder of Sarah Ann White, MEPO3/270
Primrose Whistance, detained at His Majesty's pleasure, PCOM8/427

Major Herbert Rowse Armstrong (1921)

Peril at End House (1932), Three Act Tragedy (1934), Murder is Easy (1939), The Lernaean Hydra (in: The Labours of Hercules 1947), They Do It with Mirrors (1952), After the Funeral (1953), At Bertram's Hotel (1965), By the Pricking of My Thumbs (1968), The Chocolate Box (in: Poirot's Early Cases, 1974), Sleeping Murder (1976)

One of the most celebrated cases of the 1920s that has been the subject of four significant books and a TV drama is that eminently middle-class case surrounding Major Armstrong of Hay on Wye in Wales. It shares some similarities with that of the far less well-known Harold Greenwood.

Herbert Rowse Armstrong was a Cambridge educated solicitor, born in 1869 and practised from 1895, first in Liverpool and then in Newton Abbott. He was married to Katherine Mary Friend in 1907, born in 1873 and whom he had known for years. They were to have three children. Katherine was often in poor health, however, both mentally and physically; being rheumatic and described as 'never a robust woman', 'a martyr to indigestion' and an enthusiast for homeopathic remedies. However, witnesses claimed that the two were on 'very affectionate terms'. Armstrong was a little man, five feet six high, and his wife was taller than him. They moved to Cusop, on the Welsh border, in 1906 and Armstrong bought into a local solicitor's firm, later becoming the sole proprietor following the death of his elderly partner. From 1910 they lived in a detached house, Mayfield, in its own grounds; where they lived with servants. His office was on the Broad Street, Hay on Wye, in Herefordshire.

Armstrong was also an officer in the Engineers' section of the Territorial Army, from 1901 and used his rank in civilian life. He was well respected locally; a churchwarden and a Freemason, as well as being clerk to the justices of the peace and clerk to the commissioner of taxes. However, he had the reputation of being henpecked by his wife on issues such as his bath times, consumption of alcohol and tobacco, even in front of servants and friends. For him the First World War, when he was promoted to the rank of major, was a liberating experience, though he never saw any active service, working efficiently in administrative matters. He did, however, meet a single woman, Marion Gale, and they formed a friendship.

Armstrong was a longstanding local resident. Tributes to him include the following by Frank Talbot, a local tax inspector:

> 'I found him an agreeable person. He was short and slightly built, his voice was pleasant and his manners easy, but the physical characteristic I thought most remarkable was the luminosity of his penetrating blue eyes'.

Katherine was also mentally unstable, suffering from melancholy and delusions and was reputedly even suicidal and from 22 August 1920 to 22 January 1921 was in Barnwood private asylum. She seemed to be getting better physically and so returned home as her husband requested. There she began to be physically unwell, being unable to retain food and suffering from indigestion, abdominal pains, vomiting and diarrhoea. A private nurse was employed and Dr Henry Hincks visited daily. She took her meals in her bedroom and was bedridden by 18 February. Armstrong removed his razors and gun so his wife could not access them. On 22 February 1921, she died, apparently of gastritis and heart disease and the death certificate was made out to this effect. There was no inquest as she had been in the hands of medical professionals at the time of her death. Armstrong did not show many signs of grief and few mourners attended the funeral, which was three days later. She was laid to rest in the churchyard in an unmarked grave. Her will left just over £2,000 to her family.

For Armstrong life went on. He took a break and went on holiday in the Mediterranean. He discussed marriage with Marion Gale. His children remained at their boarding schools. He invited people over to tea and dinner.

Professionally he was acting for clients in a farm sale that was in opposition to Oswald Martin, a young newcomer to the town and a rival solicitor. Wanting to talk the matter over with Martin he invited him to Mayfield. Serving tea, buttered currant loaf and scones on 26 October,

Martin later alleged that Armstrong, behaving unusually with great social maladroitness, handed him a scone to eat (Armstrong denied this social faux pas) and said 'Excuse my fingers'. Later that day Martin was ill and apparently had been given a small dose of arsenic. This was not the first time that a similar event had happened. On 21 September 1921 a box of Fuller's chocolates had arrived at the Martins' house and with relatives dining with them, Martin's sister in law, Dorothy, ate two and was later sick. Arsenic poisoning was diagnosed, but the sender of the chocolates was unknown. On examination, small holes had been drilled into some of the chocolates and arsenic inserted with a nozzle.

Despite Armstrong's local popularity a number of his neighbours, including Dr Hincks, began to suspect him of being a secret poisoner, having not only poisoned the Martins but also his wife. There was communication with the Home Office and Scotland Yard. Discreet enquiries and discussion then ensued, with Armstrong being wholly unaware of such. Armstrong was arrested by Chief Inspector Crutchett of Scotland Yard at his office on 31 December 1921, accused of poisoning Martin. He then made a statement. His wife's corpse was exhumed from the churchyard on 2 January 1922. On examination by Spilsbury it was later found to contain arsenic. Certainly Armstrong had purchased liquid weedkiller and solid arsenic locally, at Mr Davies' chemist's shop, to purportedly use as weedkiller on several occasions and had signed the poisons register. He made up small packets of arsenic and had some on his person when arrested and also hidden in his desk drawer. There was no evidence that Armstrong had sent the poisoned chocolates however. He denied all the allegations made against him. He was charged with his wife's murder on 19 January, which he naturally denied.

There was great indignation in the little town over Armstrong's arrest. He had lived there for over a decade and was well respected by many of its inhabitants who had come into contact with him socially and professionally. As a newcomer, Martin was not wholly popular and this rebounded to Armstrong's credit. Some refused to believe that Armstrong could be guilty of murder.

Armstrong was put on trial at the Hereford assizes, charged with the murder of his wife. He pleaded not guilty. This was Justice Darling's last case. The prosecution was the work of the Attorney General, Sir Ernest Pollock. Sir Henry Curtis Bennett was the defending barrister. However, he also had to contend with the judge who took the side of the prosecution. Armstrong was accused of killing his wife so he could marry Marion

Gale, and indeed he had made this suggestion to her after his wife's death though there had not been anything official. His defence argued that Katherine could have committed suicide by taking arsenic, as she knew where it was held and would have been able to have taken it. She had talked of suicide and her mental health was none too good. Curtis Bennett was pretty certain that an acquittal would result. Yet the case went against Armstrong. He was found guilty on 13 April after a two week trial. There was an appeal, which failed.

There was no confession and Armstrong was determined that 'he should meet his fate in a manner becoming an officer and a gentleman'. In prison he was light hearted and talkative: 'The warders like him, except they wish his talkativeness were a little modified'. He knew the names of all those who guarded him. Armstrong was hanged on 30 May 1922 at Gloucester Prison and has the distinction of being the only British lawyer ever to have been executed (Harold Greenwood having had a near miss from such in 1920). A waxwork of him was soon put up on display at Madam Tussauds' Waxworks. Some of his friends, such as the vicar, and his children, were certain of Armstrong's innocence to the last.

Armstrong's house still stands and his workplace is still there; even his nameplate has been retained and is on view. Such a memorial to a convicted murderer is not commonplace.

Since then there have been four books on the case. The first was in the Notable British Trials series, not long after the trial and in which there is no doubt about Armstrong's guilt. Then there was the book in 1975 by veteran true crime author Robin Odell, taking the line that Armstrong was indeed guilty as charged, as well. The evidence was circumstantial but in conjunction with his character, conclusive. The TV drama *Dandelion Dead*, broadcast in 1994, though sympathetic to Armstrong as a man, did not doubt that he was a murderer. A year later a book came out by a Hay on Wye solicitor, Martin Beales, in conjunction with Armstrong's surviving daughter, with a radically different view. It took the angle that Armstrong was innocent and that his wife did indeed commit suicide. Then Martin's father in law, Fred Davies, a chemist, framed him for the alleged attempt on Martin's life. Armstrong is generally given a whitewash (his war service, his general character and popularity are held up as proofs of innocence). More recently there has been a fourth book on the topic. It is sympathetic towards Armstrong, focusses on his unfair trial, but then shows that Armstrong did poison others (not fatally) and so implicitly upholds the original verdict.

The evidence against the major is indeed circumstantial, as no one saw Armstrong poison his wife nor did he confess. But this is the case with most poisoning cases. It is undeniable that Mrs Armstrong died of arsenic poisoning. It is possible that it was self inflicted. But this is unlikely on two grounds. Firstly, taking arsenic as a means of committing suicide is highly unusual. It is a slow and painful way to die. Secondly a God fearing and socially conventional lady as she was would not seek to disobey the laws of God and Man and also embarrass her husband and children. This only leaves her husband who routinely carried arsenic packets on his person for no obvious lawful reason and benefitted financially and romantically by his wife's death; he may also have poisoned others. His guilt is at least highly probable.

Christie refers to the case in many of her stories, both by direct reference to the major and in the use of one of his alleged attempts at murder. Perhaps this is no surprise; the case broke into the headlines in 1922, just two years after her debut novel *The Mysterious Affair at Styles* was published. It was a domestic poisoning case among the middle classes. As with the Charles Bravo case it was one which chimed into her milieu.

Armstrong is referred to in a short story 'The Lernaean Hydra', in *The Labours of Hercules*, when it is announced that the body of Dr Charles Oldfield's wife will be exhumed to check for poison. As with Armstrong, this occurs in a small country town. She had apparently died of a gastric ulcer and in her will her money went to her husband. There is a great deal of gossip about him and a young woman he works with. His wife's body is exhumed and her corpse does indeed contain arsenic. However, though the doctor's affections are directed otherwise, neither he nor his love are involved in the murder. The parallels of a professional man accused of wife murder so he can perhaps marry another are clear.

There is a lengthier direct note about this in *By The Pricking of My Thumbs*. Dr Murray tells Tommy Beresford:

> 'You remember in the case of Armstrong, anyone who had in any way offended him or insulted him, or indeed, if he even thought anyone had insulted him, that person was quickly asked to tea and given arsenic sandwiches…His first crimes were obviously mere crimes for personal advantage. Inheriting of money. The removal of a wife so that he could marry another woman'.

This implies that Armstrong was a mass poisoner, but he only killed one person and perhaps attempted to kill another. Recent research has noted that he indeed did try and poison others.

In *And Then There Were None* (1939), one of the ten people summoned to the island is a Dr Armstrong, who once killed a patient, and this name may not be coincidental, though in *Murder on the Orient Express* the upright Colonel Armstrong in the backstory has absolutely no connection with this case. In *Murder is Easy*, there is a Major Horton, a respected inhabitant of the village of Wychwood. His wife, Lydia, is unwell and eventually dies, initially it is thought, of gastritis. It later transpires that she has been poisoned. However, in this instance, the major was a retired regular soldier, not a solicitor, and it transpires that he did not poison his wife. In the novel Miss Pinkerton refers to the 'Abercrombie case', which is probably meant to be the Armstrong case, 'you know the Welsh poisoner'. It is also said 'Of course he'd poisoned quite a lot of people before anyone's suspicion was aroused', which is an exaggeration, but had not the attempt on Martin's life being suspected the death of his wife would not have been investigated. Nor was Armstrong Welsh but he did live there.

Another explicit reference to Armstrong the poisoner comes in *Sleeping Murder* where Giles Reed is discussing murderers with his wife, Gwenda, and he says 'Armstrong who everybody said for years was such a kind unassuming fellow'. Likewise, Mr Entwhistle, in *After the Funeral* relates Armstrong was a pleasant fellow. These references, as well as the quotation from *By the Pricking of My Thumbs* shows that Christie was in no doubt about Armstrong's guilt. But she was also less well informed about Armstrong's crimes. She is also correct about Armstrong being a popular member of Hay on Wye's middle-class community and that he was a modest man, and one who bore his wife's comments without apparent comeback.

The idea that another wife killer, Crippen, was a pleasant fellow has already been noted. In this case, there seems little dissension in the idea that Armstrong was personally a very decent fellow. Yet as Poirot notes in *Dumb Witness*, with reference to previous killers he has encountered, there is no contradiction in a killer also being a very amiable man.

One of the defining moments in the Armstrong case was the box of Fuller's chocolates sent to the Martins, the sender of which was never discerned. Poisoned chocolates appear several times in Christie's books. In 'The Chocolate Box', a short story in *Poirot's Early Cases*, the French politician, Paul Deroulard, dies from heart failure. It transpires that death was due to chocolates stuffed with trinitrin. It is well known that he eats chocolates after dinner and these were given by a friend, John Wilson. Then there is *Peril at End House,* a Poirot novel, which involves a box of poisoned chocolates being sent as part of the alleged plot to murder heiress Magdala Buckley. They are laced with cocaine and allegedly sent by Poirot. She eats one and is very sick but does not die. This also happens in *Three Act Tragedy*. There is a similar device in *They Do It with Mirrors*, when Mrs Serrocold is sent a box of chocolates, and they are found to have been poisoned. In 'The House of Lurking Death', a short story in *Partners in Crime*, a box of poisoned chocolates is sent to Lois Hargreaves' family and they contain arsenic. Finally the motif is used in the Miss Marple novel, *At Bertram's Hotel.* Elvira Sedgwick, a wealthy young heiress, who has apparently just witnessed a fatal shooting, recounts how a murder attempt, using chocolates, happened to her when she was in a finishing school in Italy.

A big box of chocolates was found in her room, with a message on, apparently written by an Italian admirer. Elvira eats one or two violet creams, her favourites, 'And afterwards, in the night, I felt terribly ill'. She later found that there were holes in the bottom of the chocolates for poison to have been inserted there. Yet when her friend Bridget is asked about the incident all she can recall is the arrival of a chocolate box, of her friend eating some and later being sick, but not that there was any evidence of the chocolates being tampered with.

Some of the above poisonings are in fact red herrings, used by the murderer to distract suspicion from them, with the killer suffering mild effects of poisoning at worst. Proponents of Major Armstrong's innocence have suggested that this was the case with Martin in order to ruin his local legal rival. At the trial, because it could not be known who sent the chocolates in the post, this aspect of the case, though reported in the press pre trial, was not discussed. It would have put some doubt on the prosecution case had they attempted to use it and it was of no use to the defence. The chocolate was clearly sent by someone who knew the Martins for they had recently moved house. Armstrong would have fitted the bill and given his probable poisoning of Oswald Martin later it is implicit that he did it. Of course, it is also possible that the Martins may have had another enemy and he was not popular locally.

There was an earlier case of poisoned chocolates which is less well known but perhaps it was one known to Agatha Christie. This was the case of Christiana Edmunds, born in 1829 and once resident in Brighton. She was apparently of good character, well educated, of temperate habits and an Anglican. However, at the Old Bailey in January 1872 she was on trial for the murder of four-year-old Sidney Albert Barker, by poisoned chocolates. She was found to be guilty and was sentenced to death. She was reprieved and in 1875 was eventually sent to Broadmoor following a prolonged debate about her fate.

Sources

Stephen Bates, *The Poisonous Solicitor* (2021)
Martin Beales, *Dead not buried: Herbert Rowse Armstrong* (1995)
Robin Odell, *Exhumation of Murder* (1975)
Filson Young, *The Trial of Major Armstrong* (1927)

Frederick Bywaters and Edith Thompson (1922)

Crooked House (1949), Mrs McGinty's Dead (1952), A Pocketful of Rye (1953), After the Funeral (1953)

This case is a well-known one, not because it was unsolved but because the court's verdict and subsequent double execution is controversial; and increasingly so as discussed in more recent books.

It concerned the eternal triangle; in this case, two men and a woman. Percy Thompson, born in 1890, was employed since 1909 as a shipping clerk at O.J. Packer and Co, shipping agents at 20 Eastcheap, in the City of London. In 1922 he had a minimum annual income of £300. On 3 January 1915 he married Edith Jesse Graydon, two years his junior. In 1916 he was conscripted into the armed forces, in a battalion of the London Scottish regiment, at the height of the First World War. Yet he was medically unfit and so was discharged from service in the same year. The couple were childless. Edith was progressing well at work, as book keeper and manageress at Carlton and Prior's, a wholesale milliners, of 168 Aldersgate Street, London, earning £6 per week, a remarkable sum for a young woman at the time. A colleague described her as 'a very capable business woman'. They lived at 65 Mansfield Road in 1919 and from 1920 at 41 Kensington Gardens in Ilford, East London.

Edith had met Frederick Edward Francis Bywaters, born on 27 June 1902 and thus ten years her junior. He had been employed as a clerk after leaving school and then as a sailor from the age of 15 on SS *Morea*. They had known each other since early 1915 when some of his siblings attended the same school as she did. Often, in 1921 and 1922, they had lunch or coffee together, usually near her workplace, when he was not at sea. Bywaters lodged with the Thompsons from June to August 1921, paying 25s per week in rent. The three of them went on holiday to the Isle of Wight. Relations between the Thompsons were not good and in August 1921, there was a quarrel over a minor matter, Edith claiming it concerned a pin, resulting in Thompson hitting his wife (so she and Bywaters later claimed). Bywaters intervened on her behalf with the result that Thompson told him to find new lodgings on the next day.

Whilst all this may well seem to be a rather commonplace domestic strife, perhaps what lifted it out of the ordinary was that not only did Edith write to Bywaters when he was abroad, from August 1921 to August 1922, but he kept the letters she sent him. The content of the letters was a key feature in the ensuing drama.

Meanwhile the story unfolded. Bywaters' ship arrived back in London on 23 September 1922 and he went to the house he now usually stayed at when on shore leave. This was 23 Shakespeare Crescent, Manor Park, not far from where the Thompsons lived. He also bought a knife for 6s 6d from a shop next door to Edith's workplace. He met Edith on several occasions in the next ten days, often telephoning her in the morning to make arrangements with her. They usually met near her place of work and were often witnessed together. On 2 October he told those he lodged with that the Thompsons were going to the theatre in Piccadilly on the next evening; clearly Edith had informed him of such. On the evening of 3 October, John Laxton and his wife went with the Thompsons to see a play, 'The Dippers' at the Criterion Theatre in Piccadilly. They met at 5.45 pm, both the Thompsons being at work earlier that day. At 10.50pm they said their goodnights and by midnight the Thompsons had returned to Ilford by train, via Liverpool Street Station.

They then began to walk from Ilford Station to Kensington Gardens, via York Road and Blagrove Road. It was now at 12.30 am and they were 100 yards from home. A witness later recalled hearing Edith exclaim, 'Oh my God, will you help me, my husband is dying'. She was 'in a hysterical condition and incoherent'. She soon told PS Mew, 'They will blame me for this' and that 'We were walking along and my husband said "Oh"'. He then apparently collapsed. She also claimed that Thompson just fell over because of an illness and that she had seen no one else. This was not quite the case.

The police surgeon found a rather more precise form of death. Although there were a number of cuts to the torso, the main injuries were three stab wounds to the neck; the stab on the right side of the throat had pierced an artery. These were struck from behind and Thompson would have died two or three minutes after being attacked.

Bywaters was arrested on the next day. His landlord said that he had left the house at 10.50pm. When Edith was told of this she said 'Oh God, oh God, what can I do? Why did he do it? I didn't want him to do it'. She gave a less inaccurate version of the events of the fatal morning, 'When we got near Endsleigh Gardens, a man rushed from the garden and knocked me away, pushed me away from my husband. I was dazed for a moment. When I recovered, I saw my husband scuffling with a man. The man I know as Freddie Bywaters, was running away'.

Bywater's version of events was as follows. In contrast to Edith's versions, he claimed that he first conversed with Thompson, telling him,

'You have to separate from your wife'.
'No'.
'You will have to'.

A struggle then ensued and Bywaters knifed Thompson. He then fled back to his mother's house in Norwood, south London, throwing the knife down a drain in Endsleigh Gardens and reaching his mother's at 3am. He added that Thompson had failed to act like a man in relation to his wife, that he loved Edith and that he had not intended to kill him. He added 'He always seemed several degrees lower than a snake. I loved her and could not go on seeing her lead that life…I gave him an opportunity of standing up to me as a man but he wouldn't'. He clearly entertained a great hatred against Thompson despite not having seen him since August 1921 and this hatred can only have been instilled in him by the content of Mrs Thomspon's letters and probably topped up by the almost daily conversations the lovers had had in the days running up to the murder. He added that he thought Thompson would kill him and that he was armed with a knife or gun (none were found), so acted in self-defence and had no intention to kill. There is no evidence for such; it was a premeditated murderous attack.

Among his possessions were the letters sent from Edith and also a number of news cuttings. The latter had several articles about poisoned sweets and chocolates, overdoses and drug related deaths. The correspondence, and only Edith's letters are known to have existed (she routinely destroyed all the letters sent to her as a sensible routine precaution and lied to her husband about receiving any), were described by the police as being 'couched in extravagantly affectionate language'. There is much in them about her great love for her 'darlint', and about how she longed to see him again. Some passages from one read thus:

> 'You felt you wanted all me in exchange for all you. I know this – felt this – wouldn't say "no" for that very reason.
>
> 'Darlint, I feel that I never want to withhold anything from you – if you really want it and one of these days you're going to teach me to give all and everything quite voluntarily – aren't you? Please darlint.
>
> 'Darlint I do know how much you do love me – how much I love you – I'm pleased to because it's a lot for me and a lot for you. Its such a lot it hurts – terribly hard sometimes – just when I think and hope without much thought of that hope ever being realised'.

There is much, much more in a very similar vein, interspaced with various domestic and everyday items of news. So far, so normal for love letters.

The issue with them was that they described her hatred for her husband and her attempts to poison him, whether real or imagined. She wrote of a woman who had lost three husbands and others could not lose one. On 10 February 1922 she wrote 'You must do something this time. Prescription – witnesses. So easy if I had things'. Enclosed was a newspaper cutting about the poison hyoscine, poison in chocolates and ground glass in victims' food. A month later she wrote 'I am relying on you for all plans – only just the act I'm not'. Some letters suggest action on her part, as on 31 March, 'There will be no failure next time' and then on 15 April, 'Not going to try again till you come back. Tea bitter – 28 March. Going to try the glass again'. Next day she wrote 'Used light bulb three times' and 'Enough for elephants. Try to make pills'. As to the light bulb she wrote 'I used a lot – big pieces too not powdered and it has no effect quite expected to send that cable but no – nothing has happened from it….'

All this suggested that she either had tried to kill her husband by putting ground glass in his food or drink or that she fantasied about such. What is undoubted is what she wanted to see happen, whether or not she actually practically went about it. There does not seem to have been an enquiry about whether Thompson sought medical advice. He was certainly physically unwell generally, suffering from fits and with a bad heart and as seen his brief military service showed him to be unwell (unable to complete a three mile route march, falling out after only a mile despite being in his mid twenties).

Edith also sent Bywaters a number of romantic novels to read. One was titled *Bella Donna*. In it a female character systematically poisons her husband with digitalin. There were other references to poison and poisonings in the same book. In the accompanying letters of 18 and 23 May 1922, she wrote, 'Digitalin – Bella Donna – any use' and later 'Read Bella Donna – you may learn something in it to help us'. Her meaning was very clear in all these letters. It is probable that as with all lovers Bywaters would have read them more than once and the implications would have been obvious. His reactions cannot be wholly known because none of his letters survive. That he kept them showed how much he valued them and so it seems reasonable to assume that he took their messages to heart.

Without the letters it seems unlikely that Edith would have been charged with anything. Adultery, as was pointed out at the time, is not the crime it was in Biblical times (punishable by stoning). They were deemed incriminating. It is dangerous for lovers to keep written evidence of their feelings for one another, however understandable this may be and this is especially the case if one or other, as here, are married.

Frederick Bywaters and Edith Thompson were jointly charged with murder. The trial took place at the Old Bailey on 5 December. The judge was Sir Montague Shearman (who had tried the Greenwood case); and among the prosecution barristers were Travers Humphreys; Sir Henry Curtis-Bennett was leading for the defence, as he had in the Armstrong case. After five days, on 11 December, the hearing was over. The verdict was guilty for both parties and there was no recommendation for mercy in either case. There was an appeal on Edith's behalf on the grounds that the judge had misdirected the jury by not emphasising the main points made by the defence and on focussing on the moral aspects of the case. It failed. Despite a large public petition to save them, in part doubtless because of the rarity of women being hanged, both were hanged on 9 January 1923, she at Holloway and he at Pentonville. John Ellis, who hanged her, later wrote, 'we were all to witness a scene that will never fade from my memory... Mrs Thompson was in a state of complete collapse, and had lost all control of herself. --- My own feelings defy description. The woman's cries and semi-demented body movements all but unnerved me.'

The controversy here concerns, not the execution of Bywaters, as there is no doubt that he struck the fatal blows to Thompson. Rather it is the hanging of Edith, who did not strike the blows in question. Whether she was aware of Bywaters' plan is another question and can never be known for certain. The letters reveal that she thought about her husband's death, that she sought it and she had sent Bywaters information about poisonings, but he was not killed thus. She was not an accessory or an abettor, though was at the scene of the murder. However, two points against her should be made. Her letters, 'extravagantly couched' as the police said, probably made a strong emotional impression on the far younger man and led him to hate her husband as well as to love her. Secondly, he knew of the Thompsons' itinerary on the fatal evening of 3 October as he had been told this by Edith the day before. Without her involvement it is unlikely that murder would have occurred. The jury evidently thought so, too.

Agatha Christie refers to the case in four novels, all published in a span of five years (1949-1953). It clearly made an impact on her, albeit nearly three decades later, that she should make so many explicit references to it in such a short timespan but never to mention it before or after.

Firstly, it is referred to in *Crooked House*, when the second wife, Brenda, who is much younger than her wealthy husband, Mr Aristides Leonides, is suspected of conspiring with her lover, Laurence Brown, tutor to the children and a few years younger than Brenda, to murder Leonides. Leonides is poisoned. The family hope that these two are guilty because they deem Brenda to have been a gold digger; she was a waitress with a (possibly invented) hard luck story when she met the elderly widower. A cache of letters is found, as per the real story, and they are arrested for murder. In the same book, Magda, married to Philip Leonides, is an actress in a forthcoming play on the Bywaters and Thompson story.

In *Mrs McGinty's dead*, Superintendent Spence and Poirot are discussing which of a number of female suspects might be guilty of the recent murder of Mrs McGinty, who may have recognised a woman once involved in a murder. Spence says, 'If we hanged Edith Thompson we certainly ought to have hanged Janice Courtland'. In fiction, Mrs Courtland's husband was killed by her younger lover; Mrs Thompson's by her younger lover, Frederick Bywater in Ilford in 1922. Both real and fictional couples had been married for a few years. Much of the evidence against Mrs Thompson came from the letters she wrote to Bywaters in which she fantasised about killing her husband and this was taken to suggest she goaded him to do so or was involved in a conspiracy to murder making her as guilty as Bywaters, though she took no part in the actual killing. The fictional murder takes place at the Courtland home and in reality it was a street stabbing. Spence declares that Janice was a greedy woman and an unpleasant one, manipulating her would-be lover to kill her husband and then abandoning him for a rich man. This is in contrast to the reality where the monetary motive was nowhere to be found and Mrs Thompson, unlike Mrs Courtland, did not get what she desired.

In *A Pocketful of Rye*, Vivian Edward Dubois, golf and tennis partner, as well as lover of the wealthy Mrs Adele Fortescue, worries, after the poisoning by taxine of her husband, Rex, about the letters that he has written to her and what construction the police might put on them as a possible motive. He recalls the case of Mrs Thompson, and this 31 years afterwards. After all, he stands to inherit from her will after she (Adele) is also found to have been poisoned. It transpires he has had no connection with the murder.

Finally, Mr Entwhistle refers to Edith Thompson as a murderer in *After the Funeral*, and that she 'lived in a world of violent unreality', referring to the letters where she wrote about putting ground glass in her husband's food. He clearly does not think that she had done so in reality, but in her fantasy world would have liked to have done so. He does not seem to sympathise with her and unlike in the three earlier books where Christie does not address her guilt, he does label her as a murderer, bracketed along with a number of other well known murderers of the early twentieth century.

It does not seem that Agatha Christie shared the concerns of more recent historians who are indignant about Mrs Thompson being hanged for a crime that she did not physically commit. Both are products of their differing times. There has been a suggestion that she should be given a posthumous pardon and that she was condemned by the morals of the age in which she lived, though historians customarily only sensibly judge the actions of the past by the standards of the day, not those of hindsight. That being said, there were also several contemporaries who were opposed to her execution.

Sources

The National Archives files

Bywaters F. and Thompson, E.; Offence, Murder, DPP1/70,

Murder of Percy Thompson by Edward Bywaters and Edith Thompson, MEPO3/1582

Above left: 1. Madeleine Smith.

Above right: 2. Constance Kent.

Right: 3. Charles Bravo.

Above left: 4. Florence Bravo.

Above right: 5. Adelaide Bartlett.

Left: 6. Jack the Ripper, the Nemesis of Neglect. (Illustration from Punch magazine 1888)

Right: 7.
Grave of Mary Ann Nichols.
(Photograph by Lindsay Siviter)

Below: 8.
Grave of Marie Jeanette Kelly.
(Photograph by Lindsay Siviter)

Left: 9. Lizzie Borden.

Below: 10. Borden house, Fall River.

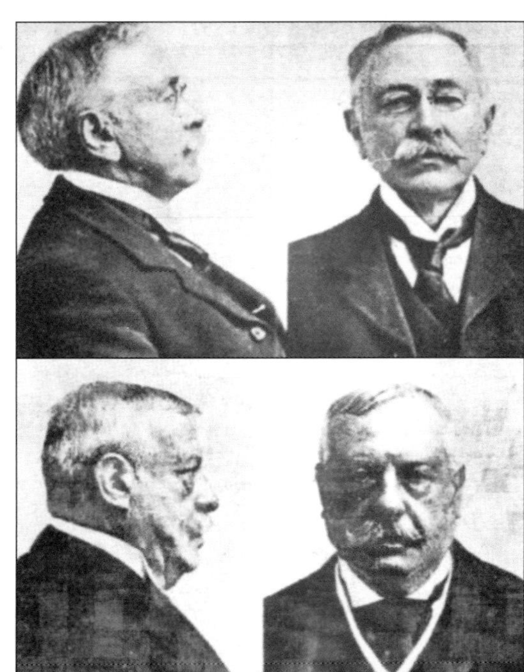

Above left: 11. Neill Cream.

Above right: 12. Adolf Beck (top row) and John Smith, mug shots.

Right: 13. Marguerite Steinheil.

Left: 14. Hawley Harvey Crippen.

Below: 15. Frederick Seddon being sentenced to death.

Bottom:16. Seddon's house at Tollington Park. (Photograph by Jonathan Oates)

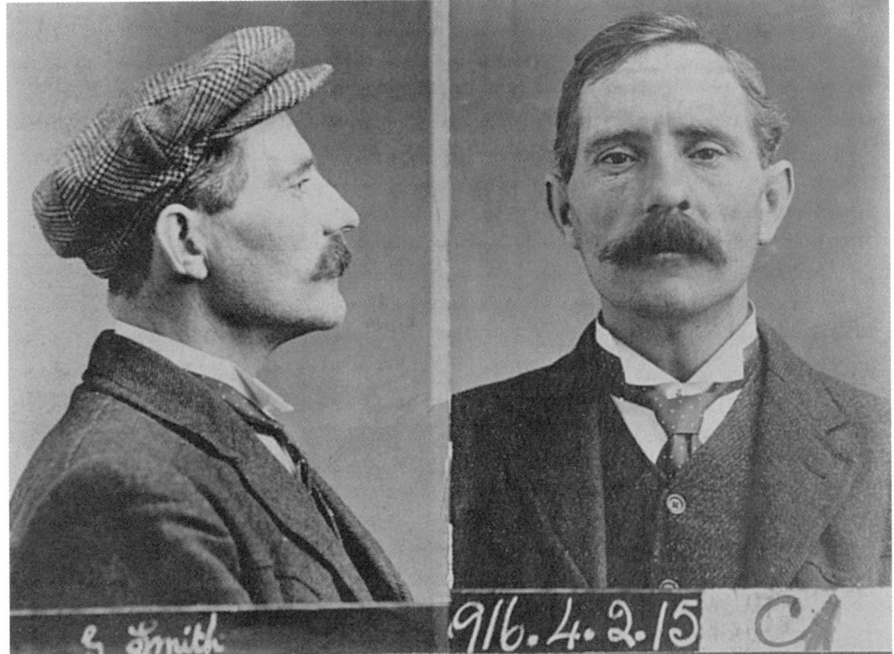

Above: 17. George Joseph Smith.

Right: 18. House in Waterlow (once Bismarck) Road, scene of Smith's last murder. (Photograph by Jonathan Oates)

19. Harold Greenwood (front row, second from left). (Jonathan Oates' collection)

20. Rumsey House, scene of Mrs Greenwood's poisoning. (Jonathan Oates' collection)

Right: 21. Herbert Rowse Armstrong.

Below: 22. Freddie Bywaters, Edith Thompson and Percy Thompson.

Left: 23. Horatio Bottomley.

Below: 24. The Eastbourne bungalow, scene of the murder of Emily Kaye. (Lindsay Siviter's collection)

25. Sir Bernard Spilsbury examining the remains in the garden of the bungalow. (Lindsay Siviter's collection)

26. Gardenholm Linn, known locally as 'Ruxton's Dump'.

27. The Blazing Car mystery: Rouse's burnt-out car.

28. Wolverton Street, Anfield: scene of Julia Wallace's murder.

WANTED

INFORMATION AS TO THE WHEREABOUTS OF

CHAS. A. LINDBERGH, JR.

OF HOPEWELL, N. J.

SON OF COL. CHAS. A. LINDBERGH

World-Famous Aviator

This child was kidnaped from his home in Hopewell, N. J., between 8 and 10 p. m. on Tuesday, March 1, 1932.

DESCRIPTION:

Age, 20 months	Hair, blond, curly
Weight, 27 to 30 lbs.	Eyes, dark blue
Height, 29 inches	Complexion, light

Deep dimple in center of chin
Dressed in one-piece coverall night suit

ADDRESS ALL COMMUNICATIONS TO
COL. H. N. SCHWARZKOPF, TRENTON, N. J., or
COL. CHAS. A. LINDBERGH, HOPEWELL, N. J.

ALL COMMUNICATIONS WILL BE TREATED IN CONFIDENCE

March 11, 1932

COL. H. NORMAN SCHWARZKOPF
Supt. New Jersey State Police, Trenton, N. J.

29. Charles Lindbergh reward poster.

Above left: 30. Bungalow Murder: Emily Kaye's trunk.

Above right: 31. Agatha Christie monument, London. (Photograph by Jonathan Oates)

Left: 32. St. Martin's Theatre with Mousetrap advert. (Photograph by Jonathan Oates)

Right: 33. John George Haigh. (Jonathan Oates' collection)

Below: 34. The Onslow Court Hotel, where Haigh met victim Mrs Durand-Deacon. (Paul Lang's collection)

35. Haigh's London 'acid house'. (Jonathan Oates' collection)

Source: Wikimedia Commons unless otherwise stated.

Chopped Up

Patrick Herbert Mahon (1924), Norman Thorne (1924),
Dr Buck Ruxton (1935), *Dumb Witness (1937),*
Murder is easy (1939), One Two, Buckle my Shoe (1940)

One dilemma facing murderers is what to do with the corpse that they are responsible for. To be caught in its proximity must be avoided if one is to avoid the unpleasant legal consequences. But simple flight is only a realistically safe option if the place where it will be found is not somewhere associated with them, for example a street or park to which anyone can have access. So if someone is killed where the killer lives or works then the finger of suspicion will fall on them, especially if there is a known relationship between killer and victim. But moving bodies unseen is hard.

Three well-known killers in the inter-war years tried to solve this conundrum. The first of these was 'Patrick' Herbert Mahon, born on 22 September 1888 in Liverpool. He had an extensive criminal record by the early 1920s. This is despite being married in 1910 to Jessie, and they had a daughter, Patricia. In his younger days he had been a Sunday school teacher. In 1911, he was employed as a bookkeeper in Liverpool but also stole cheques, for which he was given a caution. In 1912 in Wiltshire, he turned to theft and was given his first custodial sentence. In 1916 he was found guilty of burglary and assault at a house in Sunningdale, attacking Olive Wickens, a servant there, on the head with a hammer and was given five years at the Surrey Assizes.

Despite all this in 1920, his wife took him back and she found him a job as a sales manager at Consols Automatic Aerators at Sunbury on Thames. He began to use the name Patrick instead of Herbert in an attempt to escape his criminal past. They were then living in Twickenham and then nearby in Pagoda Avenue, Richmond. It was in this capacity at work that he met Emily

Beilby Kaye. Miss Kaye had been born in Salford in 1885 and worked as a typist in Lancashire for most of her life. She was described as being hard working, respectable and single. In 1922 she came to London and later took a room in the Green Cross Club at Guilford Street in Bloomsbury. When employed at Robertson, Hill and Co, accountants in the City of London, she met Mahon in July 1923 and fell in love with him, knowing he was married.

In 1924 Emily told friends that she was engaged and was to live with her husband in South Africa. She also gave most of her savings; £300, to Mahon. Mahon was in a dilemma of his own making. He persuaded her that he would marry her. Meanwhile he rented, under the name Mr Waller, a bungalow, 'The Officers' House', Langney Bungalows, Pevensey for two months from 11 April. It was next to the Crumbles, the coastal spot which had been the scene of the vicious murder of Irene Munro in 1920. In April 1924 Emily left her London lodgings and stayed at a hotel in Eastbourne from 7-12 April.

To complicate matters further, Mahon had met Ethel Duncan, aged 32, who lived in nearby Isleworth but in previous years she made her money from various men. They met in Richmond on 10 April. He was a well spoken womaniser and made a habit of such behaviour. Two days later Mahon bought a cook's knife in Victoria Street, London. That same evening he and Emily went to the bungalow. On 14 April she was seen alive for the last time. Two days later he met Ethel again and invited her to the bungalow and she arrived on 18 April, staying there for three days. Ethel later recalled seeing a woman's shoes there and securely locked luggage in another room.

When Mahon was back at his Richmond home, his wife found a left luggage ticket. She contacted ex Inspector John Beard, a private detective, as she suspected her husband of seeing another woman. He went to Waterloo railway station and retrieved the Gladstone bag that Mahon had left there.

This contained a bloodstained knife and scraps of bloody clothing. He called the police and they waited for Mahon to reclaim the bag, arresting him on 2 May. After pretending that the bag had contained dog food, he had to admit that Emily Kaye was dead, but that it was an accident, as she had hit her head when falling down on a coal scuttle after a quarrel on either 15 or 16 April. He made these statements to Chief Inspector Percy Savage. At the bungalow, parts of her body were found in the trunk, a hatbox and elsewhere. A detective said 'the search of the house and the unpacking of the boiled and unboiled portions of her body was a gruesome task, the stench was appalling'.

Mahon explained that between 18 and 27 April he had partially dismembered the body and put it in a trunk and a hatbox (that was the state of play when Ethel arrived). He then claimed he did not know what to do, having been 'so upset and worried' and then was 'wondering how I could dispose of the body'. He eventually did this by burning and boiling parts of it and then throwing some of it out of a train to London and elsewhere. All this was done piecemeal in between travelling up to his Richmond home and work and back. Some of the ashes of the burnt body was taken to a nearby brickyard. The body parts, between 900 and 1,000 of them, were put together by Sir Bernard Spilsbury.

Mahon's story did not add up. He told lies, such as claiming he only bought the knife after Emily's death. The exact cause of Emily's death is unknown as the head was never found, but his story of her falling down was disbelieved because the coal scuttle was not strong enough to have killed anyone. She may have been hit over the head with an axe or hammer or even strangled.

Mahon was put on trial at the Lewes Assizes in July. Sir Henry Curtis Bennett prosecuted and James Dale Cassels defended him. His story was not credible and the physical evidence did not support it. On 19 July he was found guilty of murder and sentenced to death. Following a failed appeal, he was hanged at Wandsworth prison on 3 September. One positive result arising from the case was the establishment of a 'murder bag' which detectives would take with them to a murder scene, containing the tools they needed to protect themselves and to collect evidence. A waxwork of Mahon soon appeared at Madame Tussaud's, near that of Bywaters and Thompson and the murder house became a macabre tourist destination.

In *Murder is Easy*, Mrs Church tells Luke Pinkerton:

> 'You remember the Castor case, sir – and how they found little bits of the poor girl pinned up all over Castor's seaside bungalow. And they've been five or six other poor girls served the same way later'.

The reference to the chopping up and the seaside bungalow are clear references to the Mahon case. However, there is no suggestion that he ever killed anyone else – though the woman he attacked in 1916 could have died had her hair not been extremely thick.

Then there was John Norman Holmes Thorne. He was born on 21 June 1900 in Portsmouth. His father worked in the Admiralty as an engineer but his mother died when he was young. He had no siblings. In 1911 the family moved from Southsea to Kensal Rise, then Harlesden, in north London. In 1914-1915 he briefly attended a grammar school. Then he was apprenticed to an engineering firm before joining the Royal Naval Air Service on 30 April 1918 during the First World War. However, his period of service was over in the following year and he did not see any active combat. Returning to engineering work in Wembley in 1919-1921, he then became unemployed.

In August 1922 he began an entirely new venture, running a chicken farm in Crowborough, Sussex. The farm was two acres and was in a lonely part of the parish. Thorne made himself a number of huts, one for himself and others for the chickens. It was titled The Wesley Farm, doubtless because in north London he had attended a Wesleyan chapel. It was because of this that he had met one Elsie Emily Cameron, an office worker and a couple of years his senior, and a romance began. She would often visit him over the next two years, travelling down from Harlesden to Crowborough. They became engaged. However, Thorne's romantic horizons were not limited to one young woman and he began a romance with Elizabeth Anne Coldicott (1896-1975), a local young woman and a mother's help, in 1924. In this he had a similar problem to Mahon; a man who Thorne despised (both which occurred in the same county in the same year), albeit Thorne was a bachelor.

Elsie was last seen on 5 December 1924. She took a series of public transport from her family home down to Crowborough but never returned. Five days later her father reported her disappearance to the police and he gave them Thorne's address, having already spoken to him but without result. They spoke to Thorne, who as ever was polite, but he told them that he had not seen her. He had not expected her on the date she disappeared but he had a letter from her about her planning to visit on the next day, but she never had. Thorne was anxious about her, so he said and was happy to help if he could. Meanwhile a number of witnesses came forward to say that they had seen a young woman in the vicinity of Thorne's chicken farm on 5 December. There was also local gossip about him and he received an anonymous note which read 'You…Murderer!' and this Thorne found very shocking.

It transpired that Thorne and Elsie had been engaged since December 1922, but Thorne insisted that there had been no sex between them. However, he and Elizabeth were lovers and he preferred her to Elsie. He eventually admitted that Elsie had come to the farm on the evening of 5 December, which had been a surprise for him. She told him that she was pregnant (it was later found that she was not) and that therefore he must marry her as soon as possible. He had to temporarily leave her at the farm at 9.30pm because he had already agreed to meet Elizabeth and her mother.

On 14 January 1925 the police told Thorne that they would search his property. He told them 'I have nothing to fear'. They started to dig, beginning at the entrance to the little farm. Firstly, they found Elsie's suitcase, containing some of her clothes. Thorne was then arrested. Secondly, Elsie's head was found in a tin box under the chicken run. On the next day her severed legs wrapped in sacking and the rest of her body was located, having been buried. Percy Hoskins, crime reporter for *The Daily Express*, wrote 'The police case against him looked overwhelming. It still does [50 years later]'.

He told the police that on his return to the farm, which was about 11.30pm, he found Elsie hanging by the neck from a beam in the ceiling (the hut was about six feet two high). He cut her down. It was obvious that she was dead. He then hacked off her head and her legs, or as he put it, 'I got a hacksaw and sawed off her legs and head by the glow of the fire' and next morning buried the parts of her body in the farm grounds. He also burnt her clothing.

The story was not believed. Thorne was charged with murder and on 10 March at Lewes Assizes he was on trial for his life. Justice Finlay presided, and, as in the Mahon trial, with Sir Henry Curtis-Bennett for the prosecution and James Dale Cassels for the defence. Sir Bernard Spilsbury had carried out the post mortem and found that death had been caused by a blunt instrument to the head. Dr Robert Bronte, for the defence, argued that this was not so, and identified folds in the neck which suggested hanging as stated by Thorne. The defendant was found guilty, however, and on 16 March was sentenced to death. Thorne was hanged at Wandsworth prison on 22 April 1925. He always maintained his innocence, telling his father, who had tried to save his son's life, that 'I am a martyr to Spilsburyism'. A solicitor working for Thorne later wrote that he should have pleaded guilty to manslaughter rather than not guilty to murder and that this would have given the defence more to work on.

It is now fashionable to criticise Spilsbury and his work, as does Andrew Rose in *Lethal Witness* (2007). However, three decades earlier, Hoskins had also raised the issue in this case, writing 'I still have a lingering doubt in my own mind whether this man Thorne should have been hanged'. He concluded the chapter in his memoirs:

> 'One of the pathologists had to be totally wrong, and why might it not have been, just for once, the great Spilsbury? The very fact that so many eminent doctors had been prepared to argue against Sir Bernard casts doubts over the case whenever it is argued by experts to this day.
>
> 'Does it constitute a reasonable doubt as to Thorne's guilt? Or was the evidence against him so damning that any other verdict than guilty was unthinkable?
>
> 'I was in court at the time, and I am still not sure'.

It would seem that Thorne was in a very difficult personal situation, though one of his own makings. His affection for the geographically distant Elsie had given way to his desire for the far nearer Elizabeth. However, he felt unable to tell Elsie of this and she became increasingly desperate for bringing the matter to a head by marriage. He could not or would not give up Elizabeth and so this would have tragic consequences for Elsie. The question is, if Thorne was innocent as he said he was, and had really found her hanging, why should he not call for help but instead do as a guilty man would do and cut her up and bury her in an attempt to conceal the death? He had no previous criminal record, saving an infringement of the bye laws, and was seen as a most respectable young man. His actions were those of a guilty man.

There was a better known case in the next decade. Dr Buck Ruxton's real name was Bakhtyar Rustomji Rantanji Hakim. He had been born in India on 21 May 1899 of French/Indian descent and took a medical degree at Bombay University in 1922. He served in the Indian Medical Service in Basra and Baghdad and then as ship's doctor, where he was known as captain. Travelling to Britain, he studied at Edinburgh University and also worked in London. He lived with a Scottish woman, Isabella Kerr, two years his junior, as man and wife and she took his surname Ruxton. They had met when she was a manageress of a restaurant in Edinburgh and she was already married to a Dutch sailor, one Van Ess.

From 1930 they and their three children (Elizabeth Ava, Diana Ross and William Gladstone) were living at 2 Dalton Square in Lancaster, where he was in practice as a doctor. Also living there was Mary Jane Rogerson, a 19-year-old from Morecambe employed as a nursemaid to the young children since 1932.

Relations between the Ruxtons were not happy. There were reports of arguments, threats and accusations between the two. Dr Ruxton was a jealous man. Sometimes his wife would temporarily leave the family home, only to return shortly. Robert James Edmondson was a young man employed by the council as an assistant solicitor. He became a friend of the Ruxtons in 1934. It seems that the doctor became suspicious of his friendship with his wife and apparently the two stayed briefly in Edinburgh but the young man denied that she visited his bedroom. One of the servants saw the doctor strangling his wife, though not to death and on another occasion pressing a knife to his wife's throat.

Mrs Ruxton and Mary were last seen alive on Saturday 14 September 1935. On the next day Dr Ruxton took his three children by car to Morecambe. He asked a friend, Mrs Ethel Anderson, a dentist's wife, to look after the three. He explained that their mother had gone away for a short holiday. She did so.

Next day the charwoman arrived at the doctor's house. The doctor was the only one there. Mrs Oxley was given specific instructions from him. He had taken up the carpet from the landing on the first floor. He asked her to get rid of the paper underlay and to carefully wash the floor there with hot water. She saw bloodstains on the landing wall and later could smell something noxious. She also thought it was odd that the drawing room and the doctor's surgery were locked.

Others saw unusual activity on the doctor's part. He gave away one of his suits and the recipient later found a bloodstain there. He was seen burning things and neighbours thought the smells were obnoxious. One of the cleaning women fished out an item from the bonfire and on inspection found it was bloody. A nightgown was found likewise stained. The smells were such that the doctor bought disinfectant to remove such odours. On 17 and 19 September, Ruxton drove northwards from Lancaster; on the first instance he knocked down a cyclist in Kendal who made a note of the car.

Ruxton explained to various people, including Edmondson, where his wife was: that is, that she was temporarily on holiday. Others were told that they had gone to Scotland where Mary was to have an operation. He reported the two women to the police as missing persons.

On 29 September a terrible discovery was made by Susan Johnson in a ravine near Moffat, Dumfriesshire. She was looking over a bridge over the Gardenholme Linn, not far from the main road from Scotland to England and saw a bundle with what seemed to be a human arm extending from it. On examination these were found to be parts of human bodies, scattered over the nearby locality. There were some newspaper wrappings attached as well as pieces of clothing. Professor John Glaister, a leading pathologist from Glasgow University, was called in to investigate. He found that there were 70 body parts. Evidence from the two missing women, such as a bunion on one of the feet and that one of them had tonsilitis, matched. The newspaper too, matched that taken by Ruxton. The cause of death in both instances was uncertain. One of the victims had been hit on the back of the head with a blunt instrument but these blows were not fatal. It might have been strangulation because those body parts that were evidence of such would normally have been found had been chopped up. It seemed that the dismemberment was done by a sharp instrument and by a skilled hand who worked in the medical profession. Fingerprints were found in 2 Dalton Square which matched those of the victims. Later when Ruxton's bath was examined, the yellow staining there was also seen as being the remnants of blood.

The doctor was duly arrested on 12 October and charged with murder. He absolutely denied these charges. During the magistrates' court hearings, Ruxton frequently interrupted the witness statements, on one occasion saying 'How can I expect to be silent when I am fighting for my life?' When asked about the quarrels with his wife he did not deny it and said they only lasted two or three hours and she would ask him to buy her new clothes afterwards. He added, though, 'Who loves most chastises most', which is taken from the Bible. He was brought to trial on 2 March 1935 at the Manchester Assizes and had the good luck to be defended by Norman Birkett, who had a string of success in the Mancini and Hearn cases, for example, as we shall see. There were no bloodstains in the doctor's car. He said that Ruxton had explained away the bloodstains on his clothing by saying that he had cut his hand with a tin opener, to which the prosecution countered that the amount of blood found was far greater than would be expected from such an injury. Dr Ruxton admitted marital disharmony, but played it down, 'We could neither live with each other nor without each other'. It was a lengthy trial, lasting eleven days for there was a great deal of forensic evidence to be relayed. However, on this instance, even Birkett's eloquence was insufficient in the weight of the evidence as presented. On 14 March, after the jury discussed it for an hour, the verdict of guilty was given. There was an appeal but it failed. Ruxton was hanged at Manchester prison on 12 May 1936.

It is probable that the Ruxtons argued on that Saturday night, probably just outside the bedroom. He killed her and then had to kill Mary in order to avoid immediate exposure. Once he had taken his children away he could start to try and dispose of the bodies. They were probably dismembered in the surgery and bathroom over the next two or three days and then driven, wrapped up, to Scotland. However, the amount of blood that would have been caused by all the dismemberment – far more so than had been done by Thorne – made his task even more difficult. Burning clothes to eliminate evidence was not wholly successful either and the discovery of the body parts did not take long. Given the history of arguments and threats of violence the motive was clear. Unlike the case with Thorne there is no serious doubt as to Ruxton's guilt.

Both these cases are alluded to in the novel, *One Two, Buckle My Shoe*, and though one is not explicitly named, the contemporary newspaper reader or in more recent years, the knowledgeable true crime historian, should have no problem in identifying what is been referred to. Mrs Sainsbury Seale, a middle-aged single lady and a potentially crucial witness in the shooting of a dentist, disappears from a London hotel and Inspector Japp says to Poirot, 'I suppose you're hinting that she's been murdered now and that we'll find her in a quarry, chopped up in little pieces like Mrs Ruxton?' He adds 'A lonely chicken farm, that's what we want'. Contemporary readers would identify exactly what Japp is referring to in both instances. The Notable British Trials series featured Buck Ruxton though not Norman Thorne, and though there have been two recent books on the Ruxton case, there has not been one on the Norman Thorne murder. In a recent work about Spilsbury, the author took Thorne's side.

Hastings refers to the Ruxton case in *Dumb Witness*. 'Poirot, you don't think she'll turn up in parcels' in reference to a missing woman, and he clearly has the Ruxton case in mind as the dismembered body parts were found wrapped in newspaper. Happily this is not the case in fiction.

In the story there is nothing so dreadful as dismemberment, though when the corpse is found, in a flat in Battersea, her face has been smashed in and this shocks Poirot. The disfiguring of faces occurs in several of Christie's stories, often as a device to conceal the real identity of the victim. Such occurs in *The Mystery of the Blue Train* and much later in *Nemesis*.

Sources

The National Archives files:

Murder of Emily Beilby Kaye by Patrick Herbert Mahon at Pevensey, MEPO3/1605

Murder of Elsie Cameron by Norman Thorne, MEPO3/1610

Jonathan Oates, *The Bungalow Murderer: Patrick and the Killing of Emily Kaye* (forthcoming).

Buck Ruxton, convicted at Manchester, PCOM9/796

Percy Hoskins, *The Sound of Murder* (1972)

Annie Hearn (1930)

Sad Cypress (1940)

This relatively little known case once made national headlines and it revolved around a very strange woman who called herself Annie Hearn. She was born Sarah Ann Everard, known as Annie, in Lincolnshire in 1885 and much of her early life was spent in an unremarkable fashion. Her father, Robert, was a small farmer and gardener and she had seven siblings, all of whom grew to adulthood. They lived in different places in the county. In about 1912 some of the family moved to Hathersage in Derbyshire and it was here that tragedy first struck. Annie's mother, Betsy, died in 1915 and one of her sisters, Grace, in 1917. Apparently two guests (never named) also died. Annie had been employed with her aunt, Mary Anne Everard, working as a cookery teacher in Harrogate, Yorkshire, but had rushed to the family home to tend her ailing kin, though without success.

She continued to act in a caring role, living with her elder sister, Lydia, who was an invalid, for the next decade. It was in 1921 that the two sisters moved to live in Cornwall, possibly for her sister's health. The two took an elderly woman, Priscilla Aunger, into their house in North Hill. In 1926 the three moved to live in part of Trenhorne House in nearby Lewannick, but Priscilla died soon after. Annie, who had called herself Annie Hearn for some years, had her aunt Mary to live with them. This elderly lady died in August 1926 and Lydia died on 24 July 1930, both apparently through natural causes. They were not wealthy and their attempts to make money by taking in lodgers and selling home-made cakes and pastries only met with limited success.

On 18 October 1930, Annie was invited by her good neighbours, William Henry and Alice Maud Thomas, who lived in Trenhorne Farm, to come with them on a drive to the seaside resort of Bude. This middle-aged childless couple were tenant farmers and had been friends with Annie and her late sister, with Thomas often visiting the sisters to bring them a small gift or just to spend time with them. Thomas even lent her the comparatively large sum of £38. At Littlejohns's cafe, a tea shop in Bude, they had tea and cake, and also partook of the salmon sandwiches which Annie had prepared and brought with her.

On the way home, Alice became ill. She was sick and a doctor was called. Food poisoning was suspected. Annie, with her experience of nursing the sick, offered to stay at the farm to help and this was accepted. Over the next few days, Alice's condition worsened. Her mother also came to assist with her daughter. Finally, with worse symptoms, she was admitted to Plymouth Hospital where she died on 4 November. The doctors wondered if she might have died of arsenic poisoning, whose symptoms overlapped with those of food poisoning. Thomas learnt that poison was suspected and when he returned to Lewannick he mentioned this to Annie.

After a post mortem, in which large quantities of arsenic were found, the funeral took place. It was then that Percy Parsons, Alice's brother, learning that his sister had died from eating sandwiches that Annie had prepared on that occasion, spoke to Annie. He said that he suspected her of being responsible. On 10 November, Annie, who had already left Trenhorne Farm following Alice's death, left her home and she posted a note to Thomas suggesting that she was about to commit suicide but that she was innocent of any wrongdoing. She was last seen at Looe, with her abandoned coat on the cliff top. A search took place, but to no avail.

Meanwhile, there was an inquest. Percy Parsons claimed that his brother-in-law and Annie were more than good friends, but this was rumour only. No animosity could be shown as occurring between Thomas and his wife, who had been married for nearly 20 years. Thomas was questioned, as were others employed on the farm or who were family or neighbours. The conclusion was that Alice had died of arsenic poisoning. The question was, who was responsible, could it have been her husband or her friend, Annie? Her flight suggested guilty secrets. Yet the verdict was murder by person or persons unknown. Meanwhile, the doctors who had issued death certificates for Annie's sister and her aunt, began to wonder whether these two women might have been poisoned. The bodies were exhumed and quantities of arsenic, far above that normally expected in a human body, were found in both.

This became a very high profile case. It was widely reported in the national as well as the Cornish press. Reporters came down to the little village of Lewannick in droves. Annie's relatives were interviewed, as well as Thomas. It was also found that Annie Hearn had claimed to have married one Leonard Hearn, a medical student, in 1917, but that this was entirely fictitious. She had even carried around with her a picture of a deceased war hero, pretending that he was Leonard Hearn, who had died a few days after the alleged marriage. No evidence of such a marriage existed. The mystery of Annie Hearn thus deepened. It was uncertain whether she was alive or not, and if she was alive, her whereabouts. A newspaper offered a reward of £500 for her discovery.

It was in January 1931 that Cecil Powell, an architect in Torquay, was suspicious about his new housekeeper, a middle aged widow called Annie Faithful, who had been working in his house since November 1930. He reported this to the police and she was arrested. Annie Faithful was Annie Hearn. On being questioned, she let slip, when talking about Thomas coming over to their house with newspapers, 'That was only a blind'. Annie claimed that she had taken a train from Looe to Torquay on the night of her disappearance, changed her name and applied for the housekeeper post at the Powells' house. She was then charged with the murder, by arsenic, of both her sister Lydia and her friend, Alice. After numerous appearances at the magistrates' courts, she was tried at the June sessions of the Bodmin Assizes. She pleaded not guilty.

The trial began on 15 June 1931 and took a week. The prosecution, led by Herbert du Parcq, showed that Annie had purchased arsenic just before her aunt's death. They brought forward doctors who had seen Lydia and Alice before they died. They explained the symptoms that they had seen. Dr Roche Lynch, the Home Office pathologist, listed the amounts of arsenic in the bodies. However, they were not allowed to use the evidence of her sister's final months of life as revealed in her diary.

The defence, led by Norman Birkett, poured as much doubt as they could on the evidence brought forward by the prosecution. They suggested that there was no motive for these crimes, if indeed that was what they were. It was suggested that the arsenic in the corpse of her sister was caused by the arsenic in the soil seeping into the coffin or during the exhumation. Not said at the trial, was that arsenic would have discoloured the sandwiches and so no one would have touched them and so there could have been no arsenic there. Dr Sydney Smith of Edinburgh University was convinced that this was the case and he acted as adviser to Birkett.

Annie was the sole witness for the defence. She was an intelligent woman and a good witness, replying calmly to the examination and cross examination. She was asked about her claims that she was married and then widowed, but stuck to her guns in believing she was a widow. There was a suspicion that she was attracted to Thomas and that she might have poisoned Alice so she could marry him. The summing up by the defence urged the jury to give the defendant the benefit of the doubt and stressed that there was no real motive for these crimes. She was found not guilty and sold her story to the newspaper who funded her defence. In it she stated her complete innocence, as a caring sister and a good friend to Lydia and to the Thomases. No one else was ever charged with these murders.

After that Annie disappeared, though in 1933 she gave another newspaper a lengthy account of her life story, before, during and after the trial. She changed her name to Margaret Day and by the decade's end was living in Shrewsbury with Bessie Poskitt, another of her sisters. It was there she died in 1948 in complete obscurity. Back in Cornwall, Thomas moved to another farm in the county and eventually remarried. He died in 1949. Again, this death was largely unremarked upon. Neither made any subsequent comments about the mystery in public.

The mystery remained as to who killed Alice Thomas and Lydia Everard. Some contemporaries and subsequent authors have suggested that since Annie was innocent, Thomas was the murderer and that possibly he wanted to marry a neighbour (not Annie), though he never did so. It was pointed out that as a farmer he had products containing arsenic in the house and that he had access to his wife. More recently the pendulum has swung the other way. Several now have suggested that Annie was the killer and had also poisoned her aunt and possibly others before her. It has been revealed that in 1920 Annie was tried for stealing from the house in Worle that she and her sister were residing in, though was found not guilty. On her aunt's death she had received a legacy. The evidence from her sister's diary also points to the fact that in the last year of her life she had all the symptoms of arsenic poisoning and that Annie, in 'caring' for her, was giving her 'special medicine' not prescribed by the doctors. Regarding her aunt, it is curious that she died shortly after Annie's surreptitious purchase of arsenic. It is quite possible that Annie was a serial poisoner akin to Mary Cotton and Amelia Winters in the Victorian era, but with the difference that Annie got away with her crimes.

The motive for the murders probably lies in Annie's psychological makeup. She was a fantasist, as seen with her persistence in her story that she had been married to a man called Hearn. She may well have believed that Thomas' friendship with her was rather more than what it was and that it was only his wife who stood between their marrying. She was unable to differentiate between fantasy and reality and attempted to make the former the latter. In this we are in the realm of speculation, but the evidence for guilt is not hard to find, beginning with her flight after being accused of murder by Parsons and being suspected by Thomas.

Nine years later, Agatha Christie's newly published Hercule Poirot novel was *Sad Cypress.* There is an explicit reference in the book's text to this case and much in the novel is similar to it. Clearly Christie was aware of the real story. In many ways, though, the novel is very different to reality. In fiction, the elderly and rich widow Mrs Laura Welman dies, apparently by natural causes, at her home, Hunterbury, near Maidensford in the south east of England. Her niece, Elinor Carlisle, inherits the estate and so suddenly becomes very wealthy, but her fiancée, Roderick Welman, has fallen for Mary Gerrard, apparently daughter of the lodge keeper but in reality Mrs Welman's illegitimate daughter. The engagement is broken off.

However, the novel then begins to bear a resemblance to reality. Mary dies after eating a lunch of fish paste sandwiches, prepared by Elinor, her rival in love for Roderick. Elinor had gone to Hunterbury to sort through her late aunt's possessions. En route, she visits the local grocers and purchases from Mr Abbott, three tins of various fish paste. Once at the house she makes these into sandwiches and then invites Mary and Nurse Jessie Hopkins to eat them for lunch with her. They eat the sandwiches and drink the tea. Morphine is found in Mary's body and Mrs Welman's corpse is exhumed. Morphine is also found there. Elinor is arrested and charged with murder.

Dr Peter Lord is the local medical practitioner and along with two nurses, attended Mrs Welman prior to her death. He is in love with Elinor and in a bid to save her from the gallows, visits Hercule Poirot. It is then that the two mention the real life case explicitly, in their discussion of the sandwiches. This revolves around the impossibility of the poisoner being able to guarantee that their intended victim will eat the poisoned sandwich. Yet as Poirot observes, this is perfectly easy because it can be put on the plate nearest to the person it is intended for and they will naturally choose that closest to them.

Dr Lord says 'I understand Counsel will make a song and dance about sandwiches, too, saying all three ate them, therefore impossible to ensure that one person should be poisoned. They said that in the Hearne [sic] case, remember?'

Poirot replies:

> 'But actually it is very simple. You make your pile of sandwiches. In one of them is the poison. You hand the plate. In our state of civilization it is a foregone conclusion that the person to whom the plate is offered will take the sandwich which is nearest to them. I presume that Elinor Carlisle handed the plate to Mary Gerrard first?'

Poirot spends much of the novel interviewing all the witnesses and professionals involved in the case, as well as Elinor herself. The case ends with a trial at the Old Bailey. Poirot reveals new evidence which points away from Elinor's guilt and to that of the real poisoner.

There are obvious differences. The novel is focussed around the upper middle class and their servants in a country house in the Home Counties. Large sums of money are involved. A far cry from the remote village in Cornwall populated by working people.

Yet there are other similarities. Firstly, there is the apparent method of murder: poisoned salmon sandwiches. There seems little doubt that in reality this was where the poison lay, prepared hitherto by the poisoner herself.

Secondly, the death of Mrs Welman, passed off initially as natural causes, bears some resemblance to that of Lydia Everard, Annie's sister who died in July 1930. Her death was certified as being one of natural causes and she was buried without any post mortem or any suspicion that there had been foul play. Only, as in fiction, when there is another death in which poison is suspected, is the body exhumed and the real cause of death is known.

However, unlike reality, there is a solution provided by Poirot and no loose ends are left. It is envisaged that justice will be done and there is also a happy romantic ending.

The book has been made into a radio drama starring John Moffat as Poirot for BBC Radio Four in 1992 and was televised in 2003 as part of the long running David Suchet series *Agatha Christie's Poirot*. The TV drama makes no explicit reference to the Hearn case, quite possibly because it would mean nothing to modern viewers, which would not have been the case to many readers of the novel when it was first published.

We could also add that there are a couple of points in Agatha Christie's own life which coincide with this real-life case. Firstly, Annie lived and worked at her aunt's cookery school in Harrogate in the 1900s/1910s. It was at a hotel there where Christie was found in 1926 after her famous disappearance and ironically Annie and her sister were in Harrogate at the same time. Secondly, Annie was found in Torquay in 1931 after her disappearance. This was where Christie was born in 1890 and lived for much of her early years; it is also where her 1929 novel *Peril at End House* is set. Whether Annie was aware of these is unknown, but probably not as she was not known as a reader of detective fiction.

Sources

Mark John Maguire, *They got away with murder II* (2023)
Jonathan Oates, *The Murders of Annie Hearn: The Case which inspired Agatha Christie* (2024)

The Blazing Car Mystery

Alfred Arthur Rouse (1930), *The Body in the Library (1942), After the Funeral (1953)*

Alfred Arthur Rouse's case was once well known and there has been a book published recently on the topic. He was born in Brixton, in south London on 6 April 1894, was working as a warehouseman in 1911 and served as a private in the 2nd battalion of the London Regiment in the First World War. He had volunteered for military service on 8 August 1914 and fought in France, where he was wounded by shrapnel in the head and left leg in 1915. Returned to England, he was discharged on 11 February 1916 with a wound pension, which expired on 14 September 1920. He married Lily May Watkins, a clerk, in 1914 at St. Alban's, but there were no children of this union. From 1927 he was living at 14 Buxted Road, North Finchley, London. He was employed as a travelling salesman.

From June 1929 he was working for W. B. Martin and Co., Ltd., a firm of brace and garter makers in Leicester. His travelling as a salesman took him to London, the south coast and the Midlands. He was paid £4 per week, payable every month, plus travel expenses and a commission on sales. In the summer of 1930 he bought a new car, a two seater Morris Minor M4 1468, paying a deposit of £64 10s and then twelve monthly repayments of £6 14s 9d.

However, his life was a most complex one. Rouse was an attractive man, with 'good looking features, with the slight auburn moustache'. During his trial, women used opera glasses in court to have a better view of him until they were rebuked by the authorities for doing so. In outlook he was described as being cheerful and rational. Despite being married, Rouse was very much a womaniser. He had a number of affairs with young women around the country. There was Helen Campbell, who was a waitress from Edinburgh and much younger than him. She bore him a child in 1921, who died shortly afterwards. They married bigamously in Islington in 1924 and she had another child with him in the next year and who was looked after by Rouse's wife, oddly enough.

Then there was Nellie Tucker, a servant, he had known since about 1925 and whom he promised marriage. She had her first child by him in 1928. Initially he did not pay maintenance until a court order forced him to do so. Yet relations between Rouse and Nellie did not cease and in 1930 she again became pregnant by him. Ivy Jenkins, a coal mine owner's daughter in Wales was another of his women, and was pregnant with his child though she told her family she was married to Rouse. He had other female lovers; once referring to having a 'harem'. He also said 'I am very friendly with several women, but it is an expensive game', as he needed to provide financially for his illegitimate children, as well as making repayments for his car and his mortgage. Certainly money problems were uppermost in his mind in 1930; and he was behind with his payments to the finance company for his car. It was a very tangled web that he had got himself into.

On Wednesday 5 November 1930 Rouse paid a visit to the Central London Maternity Hospital to visit Nellie, who had given birth to a baby daughter only a week previously. He seemed depressed, citing money worries, and left her at eight o'clock that evening. He later gave the police an account of what happened next; and for this we only have his word:

> 'I picked up a man on the Great North Road and he asked me for a lift. He seemed a respectable man and he told me he was going to the Midlands. I gave him a lift this side of St. Alban's. He got in and I drove off. After going some distance I lost my way. A policeman spoke to me about my lights'.

This was about 11.15pm. PC Lilley of the Hertfordshire Constabulary recalled stopping him a mile from Markyate. He thought that Rouse's passenger was 'a man of small stature and an over pale face'. Meanwhile, to use Rouse's words:

> 'I did not know anything about the man and then I thought I saw his hand near my case. I later became sleepy, and my engine began spitting. I pulled up beside the road and I thought I said to him "There is some petrol in the can"'.

Rouse and his passenger were at Hardingstone Lane, in the little village of Hardingstone in Northamptonshire. It was now in the early hours of 6 November and shortly afterwards two young men, William Bailey and Alfred Brown, saw a hatless man. This was Rouse and he drew their attention to a blaze nearby. 'It looks as if someone has had a bonfire'. Had he not met the two then all might have been well for him. He left them and managed to hitch a lift to London, where he briefly saw his wife. The two young men saw the blazing car and contacted the police. The fire was extinguished and they found the charred remains of a man there, slumped in the passenger seat. On discovering the identity of the car's owner, it was initially assumed that Rouse was the victim and his wife was informed. It was first thought to have been a tragic accident, but the police wanted to track down the man who had been seen nearby.

Dr Eric Shaw examined the corpse at Northampton Hospital. Yet the remains were in such a condition that very little could be said with certainty in the way of a description. The height might have been between five feet seven inches and five feet eight inches. The age could not be less than 21 and was probably around 30. He was well built. The clothing that survived had been saturated with petrol. It was a portion of trousers, of brownish or dark lavender colour and of good quality. Part of a shoe was recovered. Anyone who knew a man who was missing from home in the London or Northampton districts from 5 November was asked to come forward. It was found that the man had died from shock and burns so was not dead when he was first in the car.

Later on Thursday 6 November, Rouse took a bus from London to Wales to see Ivy Jenkins but on the next day he read the news about the blazing car mystery. He returned to London and was seen that night in Hammersmith and was arrested by the police. He appeared to be relieved to have been taken, telling them 'I'm glad it's all over…I was responsible and I am glad it is over as I have had no sleep'. Next day he was driven back to Northampton by the police for attendance at the inquest. He was named by the jury as responsible for the murder and so remanded in custody at Bedford Prison.

In contradiction to what he had implied to the police on 7 November, Rouse claimed he was innocent of murder. He claimed that once he stopped the car and the two men got out, he asked the man to fill the car's tank up with petrol from the can:

> 'I wanted to relieve myself. He said "What about a smoke?" and I replied "I have given you all my cigarettes". I then went some distance along the road. I then noticed a big flame and I ran quickly towards the car and tried the door. I could not do so, as the car was a mass of flames. I then began to tremble violently and I did not know what to do. I ran as hard as I could along the road. I felt responsible for what happened. I lost my head. I did not know what to do…I don't know what I have done since'.

It was all a tragic accident stated Rouse; the man had been smoking whilst filling the car with petrol and he and the car caught fire. There is an alternate explanation. A mallet was found near the scene and on examination it was found to have two human hairs attached. The prosecution at the trial hypothesised that Rouse had murdered the stranger by rendering him unconscious with the mallet or killing him with it (there was not enough of the remains to discern which) and then tried to cover up the identity of the man by setting the car on fire. His motive was so that he could start a new life away from his wife and the other women whose children he was responsible for.

Rouse was found guilty at the Northamptonshire Assizes on 31 January 1931 and sentenced to death. Women in the court room sobbed on hearing the news. On appeal, by Sir Patrick Hastings, KC, it was stated that the prosecution should not have been allowed to dwell on his moral character (which had occurred in the Bywaters and Thompson case, of course). This had created prejudice against him from among the jury. He had been convicted on merely prejudice and on grave suspicion only. As is often the case the three appeal judges threw the case out.

Rouse was hanged on 10 March 1931 at Bedford Prison. A likeness of him then appeared in Madam Tussaud's Waxworks. His effects of £102 4s went to his wife.

He later wrote a confession for a newspaper about the murder. He explained, 'I was in a tangle in various ways. There were other difficulties and I was fed up. I wanted to start afresh'. In this, he described his meeting with his victim rather differently than in his first statement. Apparently in this version he had met him previously in a pub, The Sun and Pyramid on Whetstone High Road. The man was a 'down and out' and Rouse had bought him a few drinks. On 5 November Rouse had arranged to meet him after seeing Nellie. On the journey northwards, his passenger dozed off and Rouse 'grasped him by the throat…He just gurgled. I pressed his throat very hard'.

After strangling the man, Rouse claimed:

> 'Then I got out of the car, taking my attache case and the mallet with me. I walked about ten yards in front of my car and opened the [petrol] can, using the mallet to do so. I took the mallet away with one purpose in view. I also poured petrol over the man and loosened the petrol union joint and took the top off the carburettor. I put the petrol can in the back.
>
> 'I ran to the beginning of the petrol trail and put a match to it. The flame rushed to the car which caught fire at once…The fire was very quick and the whole thing was a mass of flames in a few seconds'.

The mystery that remains is the identity of the victim. Rouse claimed that he might have been from a mining district. He was probably a man who had left home and his disappearance had gone unreported. In the 90 or more years since the murder the man's identity is still unknown. The difficulty was that there were no fingerprints or dental records to examine. There have been attempts to match the DNA of people alive now who believe that an ancestor of theirs may have been the man in question but these have been unsuccessful. He was probably a man who had no immediate family or close friends or colleagues who would naturally report him missing. Had Rouse not been apprehended he would have been acknowledged as the victim and that is probably why he chose a man who would not be missed if he disappeared. He claimed to have been inspired by the Alice Kesson case, where a young woman had been killed in July 1930 with her corpse taken to a lonely lane in Surrey and deposited there. Her murderer was never found.

In *The Body in the Library,* the second Miss Marple novel, the body of a young woman is found in the remains of a burnt-out car. This was seen by a labourer who reports the glare of a fire to the police. On investigation they find the remains of a burnt out car in Venn's Quarry. There are 'Traces of a charred body inside'. Superintendent Harper remarks, 'Don't tell me we are going to have a Rouse case now'.

This is a major plot development. One of the suspects for the murder of Ruby Keene, apparently found strangled in the library of Gossington Hall, is George Bartlett, whose Minoan 14 car has gone missing. The burnt out case is a Minoan 14. Initially the corpse in the car is thought by Miss Marple to be that of Pamela Reeves, a Girl Guide who disappeared on the same night as Ruby Keene and that she might have seen something of the murder of Ruby Keene and so was herself murdered.

Harper goes to the scene and 'stood looking at the charred and twisted scrap of metal. A burnt-out car was always a revolting object, even without the additional gruesome burden of a charred and blackened corpse'. The quarry where it is found is a remote spot, only accessible by a cart track, and is itself disused. But for the glow of the fire it might have remained undiscovered for weeks.

Albert Biggs was the man who saw the blaze and at first he wondered if it might be a bonfire, but didn't really think so. He tells a passing policeman. The police photograph the charred body and then the police surgeon investigates. Only part of a foot and shoe remain and he cannot tell if the body is male or female. However, he thought that a later examination of the bones should help. He adds that the shoe is the type as a schoolgirl might wear. Harper then mentions the missing sixteen-year-old girl and Harper sadly concludes that it is probably her.

The surgeon tells Harper that she was probably dead before the car was set on fire because there's no sign that she tried to get out. The corpse was found 'just slumped down on the seat – with the foot sticking out'. She was dead first and then the car was set on fire to try and get rid of the evidence. A sergeant who specialises in car cases tells Harper that petrol was poured over the car and then set alight. He points to some empty petrol cans nearby. Items are picked out of the wreckage and among them are a scorched black leather shoe and a button from a Girl Guide uniform. Harper then has the grim task of breaking the news to the grieving parents.

He learns that Pamela attended a Girl Guide rally on the previous night before going with some friends to Woolworths department store in Danemouth. It was then expected that she would come home by bus. It is later learnt by Miss Marple that Pamela met someone who claimed that he could introduce her into the film industry. Finally it is found that the truth is yet more complex: Ruby was the main victim but Pamela had to be killed so as to create an alibi for the real killers who were motivated by money.

Unlike the real case, no one was seen in the vicinity of the blazing car as Rouse had been. The identity of the corpse was guessed at early on, again unlike reality, though initially erroneously. As in reality part of a shoe was found and as in reality the victim was killed prior to being put in the car. In both cases the culprit is arrested.

Clearly Christie's use of the burning car case was based on the real life one and as noted Rouse is explicitly mentioned. In both cases the central reason for the blazing car is to create the impression that it was someone else whose body was destroyed by fire, because they are unidentifiable. For Rouse this was in order that he could disappear from his very complicated life, rather than to create an alibi for another murder. There was, incidentally, another real life contemporary blazing car mystery when a young woman, Evelyn Foster, was found dying in a car in Northumberland in January 1931 and whose assailant (if such event ever existed) was never found. But clearly this is not what inspired the plot in this novel as Rouse is explicitly mentioned. There was another instance in north London in 1933 when a killer tried to fake his own death by burning a man he had murdered, though no car was involved in this instance. It failed.

As an aside, another aspect of *The Body in the Library* was probably inspired by another real crime of the 1930s. One of the two victims in the novel is a young working-class woman called Ruby Keene. On 11 April 1937 a factory worker in Leighton Buzzard, Bedfordshire, was found strangled with a ligature. Her name was Ruby Keen. Leslie Stone, her ex-boyfriend, who had been with her on the fatal night, was hanged for the murder. However, the real Ruby was killed due to jealousy not money, but similarities exist and it is possible that Christie recalled them when writing her novel a few years later.

Rouse as an individual is referred to by Mr Entwhistle in *After the Funeral* as having 'an incredible fascination for women'. That this was the case is proved by even a cursory examination of Rouse's complex lifestyle. He could act in the way he did because as a travelling salesman he would motor throughout the country at a time when car ownership was limited to those in the middle class. Furthermore, it should be recalled that only a decade or so after the First World War, with the loss of so many able-bodied young men in the fighting, there was a great surplus of women to men and so able bodied healthy men would naturally seem more attractive to women than in pre war years. Any man bent on philandering, whether or not he had 'an incredible fascination for women', was favoured by the sex imbalance brought on by the war. Rouse also told lies in order to impress the young and impressionable young working-class women he met, claiming he had been a major in the war and had attended Eton and Oxford rather than being a private who attended a council school.

Sources

The National Archives file:

Alfred Arthur Rouse, convicted at Northampton, PCOM9/289.
Helena Normanton, *The Trial of Alfred Rouse* (1931)

William Herbert Wallace (1931)

Evil Under the Sun (1941), Sleeping Murder (1976)

Agatha Christie's crime mysteries often contain intricate alibis and narrow timelines, seemingly excluding some suspects. In real life, criminals rarely bother with such ingenious constructions. However, one case that could have been taken straight out from a Christie novel is the murder of Julia Wallace in Liverpool in 1931. After more than 90 years, this strange murder mystery continues to fascinate criminologists and amateur detectives, causing heated discussions over the identity of the killer. The American novelist Raymond Chandler – founder of the hardboiled school of detective fiction – concluded: 'The Wallace case is unbeatable; it will always be unbeatable'.

Fifty-two-year-old William Herbert Wallace lived with his wife Julia at 29 Wolverton Street in Anfield, Liverpool. By profession he was a collections agent with the Prudential Assurance Company. The couple had been married for 16 years, had no children, and lived a somewhat reclusive life. In appearance, Wallace was tall and lean with spectacles and sharp features. He was a reserved, quiet man with few close friends. His spare time was spent on chemistry (he had set up his own small laboratory in the house), chess and reading. Julia was a skilled pianist and William had recently learned how to play the violin, to be able to play duets with her. Neighbours and friends regarded them as a devoted couple; he himself described their marriage as 'perfect'. However, both struggled with health problems: William suffered from renal disease (one of his kidneys had been surgically removed); Julia was often affected by bronchitis.

A curious circumstance that came to light much later was the fact that Julia apparently had misled William about her age. When they married in 1914, she claimed to be 37 but was in fact 53, 17 years older than her husband. It is unknown when William found out about it, but it seems unlikely that he would have remained unaware for any length of time. A nurse who assisted in the home when Wallace was ill with pneumonia in 1923 considered them to be 'a very peculiar couple' who seemed to have a strained relationship. She perceived Wallace as 'a man who appeared to have suffered a keen disappointment in life'. If he entertained hopes of becoming a father when he married, it must indeed have been a great disappointment when he realised that his wife was well past childbearing age.

On the evening of 19 January 1931, a Monday, William Wallace went to a meeting with his chess club at Cottle's City Café in central Liverpool. He had just arrived there and started a game of chess when he was informed that a man had telephoned the café half an hour earlier, asking for him. The man gave his name and address as R.M. Qualtrough, 25 Menlove Gardens East, Mossley Hill. He wanted Wallace to call at his house the next evening, to discuss insurance: Qualtrough's daughter was turning 21 and he wanted to 'do something for her'. Wallace claimed he had never heard of R.M. Qualtrough before; Menlove Gardens, moreover, was located outside his regular district. The chance of a lucrative commission, however, made him decide to go to the meeting.

At 7 o'clock on the evening of Tuesday, 20 January, Wallace took the tram south to meet Mr Qualtrough. It turned out that Menlove Gardens East did not exist; there was a Menlove Gardens North, South and West but no East. Wallace asked several passersby for directions, but no one was able to help him. He also spoke to a constable on his beat and made inquiries at a newsagent's shop, to no avail. After wandering around the Menlove Gardens area for 45 minutes, Wallace returned home. It was now around 8.40pm. Neighbours John and Florence Johnston were on their way out when they encountered Wallace, who said he could not get into his house either at the front or the back. While the neighbours waited, he tried the back door again, which now opened without any problem. As Wallace expressed concern that something might have happened, the Johnstons remained outside while he entered the house. A short while later he came back exclaiming: 'Come and see! She's been killed!'

Julia Wallace lay dead on the carpet in front of the fireplace in the parlour, the back of her head crushed by a blunt instrument of some sort. The autopsy showed that the killer had struck 11-12 blows, one of which had been so violent that it drove part of the skull bone into the brain, causing brain matter and blood to seep out between the bone fragments.

In the kitchen, a cabinet door was on the floor and some coins were found scattered on the floor. Wallace kept his insurance collection money in a box high up on a bookshelf. The box was in place but according to Wallace about £4 was missing. Upstairs, there was slight disorder in a bedroom, but otherwise there were no signs that burglars had searched the house. Money in Julia's purse had been left untouched, as had her wedding ring on her hand and other jewellery.

The police suspected immediately that Julia Wallace had been murdered by her husband. Several circumstances suggested that it was a staged domestic murder. A common occurrence in such cases is that the victim has been exposed to excessive trauma while there usually is minimal damage to property. The killer may have tried to give the appearance of a robbery, but typically nothing of great value has been removed from the scene. The murder weapon is often missing, which was also the case here. It is common for the perpetrator to try to arrange for someone else to be present when the corpse is discovered. Wallace's claim that there was something wrong with the door locks, while the back door suddenly opened when the Johnstons came along, fits that pattern.

The police were able to trace the phone call from 'Qualtrough' to a phone box in Anfield located just a few minutes away from Wallace's residence. Admittedly, the person who took the call at the café was certain it was not Wallace who spoke, but he could probably have distorted his voice. The police theorized that Wallace had placed the phone call on his way to the City Café on Monday night, left a message for himself and then feigned ignorance when he received it. On Tuesday evening he had gone to Menlove Gardens and – despite being a reserved and not particularly talkative man – had spoken to several people about the location of the non-existent address. The intention was to gather as many witnesses as possible to the fact that he was there, and thus unable to have committed the murder.

The time frame for the murder, assuming Wallace was the culprit, was extremely narrow: a milk delivery boy had seen Julia Wallace around 6.40pm; in order to catch the tram, William would have needed to leave the house by 6.49 pm. Was it really possible to carry out the brutal attack, arrange it to look like a burglary, and clean away the blood that surely must have splashed on the killer, all within a space of nine minutes? Wallace's raincoat, which was found tucked beneath the corpse, seemed to provide a solution. The police thought that he had protected himself from blood spatter by either wearing the raincoat or holding it up in front of him as a shield. One rather fanciful theory held that Wallace could have been completely naked under the raincoat to avoid blood spatter on his trousers and shoes.

Even though the evidence against William Wallace was entirely circumstantial and that there was no apparent motive, he was charged with the murder of his wife. At the trial in St George's Hall, Liverpool, in April 1931 he gave evidence on his own behalf and managed well, although he came across as being cold and distant. During the evening of the murder, the police officers had been struck by Wallace's amazing coolness. However, Mrs Johnston had seen him show signs of distress and he himself claimed that he had struggled to keep his composure. Perhaps it was their unfavourable impression of Wallace rather than the evidence as such that made the jury return a verdict of Guilty. In this aspect we can find a parallel with Frederick Seddon, who probably would not have been convicted if he had refrained from giving evidence, revealing himself as a cold and arrogant man.

One month later the Court of Criminal Appeal quashed the verdict on the grounds that 'the case against the Appellant...was not proven with that certainty which is necessary in order to justify a verdict of guilty'. The judge at the original trial, Mr Justice Wright, said in an interview many years later: 'I should say that, broadly speaking, any man with common sense would have said that Wallace's alibi was too good to be true, but that is not an argument you can hang a man on'. Wallace left the courtroom a free man, but he did not enjoy his freedom for very long: two years later, in February 1933, he succumbed to kidney failure.

The case has been the subject of several books and a TV movie: *The Man from the Pru* (1990), starring Jonathan Pryce as Wallace. The debate continues to this day between those who believe in Wallace's innocence and those who regard him as a calculating, cold-blooded killer who went free due to lack of evidence. As an alternative perpetrator, Richard Gordon Parry – a former junior colleague of Wallace's – has been suggested. In one of his statements to the police, Wallace said that Julia would have let Parry into the house, because she knew him. He emphasized that the younger man knew where the insurance collection money was kept. Parry was not overly law-abiding; he had embezzled money from the Prudential, committed thefts from phone booths, tried to steal a car and allegedly on one occasion (five years after the murder) assaulted a young woman. A man who worked in a garage later claimed to have found a bloodstained glove in Parry's car on the night of the murder, when he took his car to the garage for cleaning.

Although at first glance Parry may seem like a more likely perpetrator than Wallace, he evidently was investigated by the police and found to have a solid alibi for the night of the murder. It has been suggested that he may have had an accomplice. Regardless of that, one must ask why – if the motive was robbery – the carefully thought-out plan was to lure only William, not Julia, away from the house. If Parry, acting alone or with an accomplice, was cunning enough to make the Qualtrough phone call, surely he would have figured out a way to get Julia to leave the residence for a short time? Parry knew where the money was kept, he needed only to go inside for a few minutes to empty the cash box. On the other hand: what could Wallace's motive for killing his wife, and in the most brutal way possible, have been? Professor McFall, the pathologist who examined the body at the scene and carried out the autopsy, was of the view that the killer acted 'in a frenzy'. Asked in court by Wallace's barrister for the defence, Roland Oliver, if he thought the killer was insane, McFall replied that he could have been temporarily insane:

> Oliver: 'The fact that a man has been sane for 52 years and has been sane while in custody for the last three months would rather tend to prove he has always been sane, would it not?'
>
> McFall: 'No, not necessarily'.
>
> Oliver: 'Not necessarily?'
>
> McFall: 'No, we know very little about the private lives of people or their thoughts'.

The case remains open.

In *Evil Under the Sun*, a triangle drama with unexpected twists, Agatha Christie makes a reference to Wallace in connection with the murdered woman's husband, Captain Kenneth Marshall, being interrogated by Hercule Poirot and two policemen (Chief Constable Weston and Inspector Colgate). Marshall is described as a very calm and composed, outwardly unaffected man. He answers all questions coolly, sometimes slightly arrogantly. Afterwards, the following dialogue unfolds between the two police officers and Poirot:

Weston said:

> 'Cool customer. Not giving anything away, is he? What do you make of him, Colgate?'

The Inspector shook his head.

> 'It's difficult to tell. He's not the kind that shows anything. That sort makes a bad impression in the witness-box, and yet it's a bit unfair on them really. Sometimes they're as cut up as anything and yet can't show it. That kind of manner made the jury bring in a verdict of Guilty against Wallace. It wasn't the evidence. They just couldn't believe that a man could lose his wife and act so coolly about it'.

William Wallace's cool demeanour at the trial has already been mentioned. The author F.J. Salfeld, who had been present in the courtroom, wrote: 'What probably harmed [Wallace] most at his trial was his extraordinary composure. Like every other observer, I found enigmatic his seeming indifference to his surroundings. Shock? Callousness? Stoicism? Confidence? We shall never know'. The pathologist, Professor McFall, considered William Wallace's behaviour on the evening of 20 January to be 'abnormal... He was too quiet, too collected, for a person whose wife had been killed in that way... He was not nearly so affected as I was myself'.

Agatha Christie probably hits the nail on the head when she has Inspector Colgate explain that the reason Wallace was convicted had nothing to do with the evidence – it was clearly insufficient – but because his apparent lack of emotion seemed repulsive and abnormal. Christie's own opinion regarding Wallace's guilt is more difficult to ascertain, although it seems that she was inclined to give him the benefit of the doubt. However, the reference in *Evil Under the Sun* is not the only one. There is also a mention of Wallace in the posthumously published *Sleeping Murder*. Here we find a young married couple, Giles and Gwenda Reed, discussing whether the solicitor Walter Fane could be capable of committing murder. Gwenda finds it hard to believe because Fane is 'much too quiet and gentle...the kind of person you never really notice'. She adds: 'He's not my idea of a murderer at all' to which Giles replies:

> 'You don't really know of a lot about murderers, though, do you, my sweet?'

> 'What do you mean?'
>
> 'Well – I was thinking about quiet Lizzie Borden – only the jury said she didn't do it. And Wallace, a quiet man whom the jury insisted did kill his wife, though the sentence was quashed on appeal. And Armstrong who everybody said for years was such a kind unassuming fellow. I don't believe murderers are ever a special type'.

Since Wallace is mentioned here in connection with Armstrong (a convicted murderer) and Lizzie Borden (acquitted but apparently guilty), the author seems to indicate that he belonged to the same category as them and probably was guilty.

No plot based on the Wallace murder is to be found among Agatha Christie's novels; however, some of them contain elements that are reminiscent of the famous case. This raises the question of whether the killer of Julia Wallace – be it her husband or someone else – could possibly have been inspired by a Christie novel? In the ten-year period immediately preceding the murder, she had become a widely read and celebrated author, so it is hardly far-fetched to speculate about such a possibility. In her first novel, *The Mysterious Affair at Styles* (1920), the suspected murderer has a watertight alibi, which he initially conceals for strategic reasons. The plan also includes casting suspicion on an innocent person. Here we can find parallels to Wallace's 'too good to be true' alibi and his attempt to send the police in the direction of Richard Gordon Parry.

In *The Murder at the Vicarage* (1930), the first Miss Marple novel, the Rev. Clement receives a telephone call asking him to come to Lower Farm, about two miles away, to attend to a dying man. When the vicar arrives, it turns out that the dying person is in fact in excellent health. Clement returns to the vicarage, where he discovers the body of the murdered Colonel Protheroe. It turns out that the killer – or rather, one of them – has disguised his voice on the phone: 'you remember what a good amateur actor he was' says Miss Marple. (Incidentally, Parry was also an amateur actor).

In *The Murder of Roger Ackroyd* (1926) there is a narrow timetable for the execution of the murder, and a telephone call plays an important role. It appears that Parker, the murdered man's butler, is the one who makes a phone call to inform another person about his master's death. In reality, the killer has assigned someone else to call about a completely unrelated matter; no one but the murderer – who receives the call – knows what is being said. The police manage to trace the call to a phone booth at the railway station. 'But why telephone at all?' asks Colonel Melrose. Poirot replies that there must be a reason. 'But what reason could it be?' Melrose insists. Poirot retorts: 'When we know that we shall know everything. This case is very curious and very interesting.'

It is almost as if Agatha Christie could have predicted the elusive Qualtrough's phone call five years later: just as in the book, it is the key to the mystery. Whoever made the Qualtrough call was certainly also the killer of Julia Wallace.

Sources

Jonathan Goodman, *The Killing of Julia Wallace* (1969)
Roger Wilkes, *Wallace*: *The Final Verdict* (1984)
James Murphy, *The Murder of Julia Wallace* (2001)
John Gannon, *The Killing of Julia Wallace* (2012)
HO 144/17938, HO 144/17939, PCOM 9/293 (accessed at: https://www.williamherbertwallace.com/)

The Lindbergh kidnapping (1932)

Murder on the Orient Express (1934)

At 9 o'clock in the evening of 1 March 1932, aviator Charles Lindbergh – world famous for his nonstop solo flight across the Atlantic five years earlier – was sitting chatting with his wife Anne in the living room of the couple's newly built house in Hopewell, New Jersey. In the upstairs nursery, their first-born son, 20-month-old Charles junior, slept soundly in his crib. Earlier in the evening, Anne and the nanny, Betty Gow, had put him to bed. Since Charles had a cold, he had been given extra warm clothes under the covers. Around 10 o'clock Betty slipped into the nursery to check on the little boy. To her horror, she found the crib empty. A shutter was open, and a white envelope rested on top of a radiator case just below the window. It contained a handwritten note demanding a $50,000 ransom for the return of Charles junior.

So began what came to be known as 'the crime of the century', a tragic kidnapping drama that created huge headlines around the world. Kidnappings were by no means an unknown phenomenon in the American depression era; on the contrary, they were so common that the newspapers often relegated them to minor notices. Usually, kidnappings were carried out by professional criminal gangs, using them as an income opportunity in addition to bootlegging, bank robberies and other illegal activities. But this crime stood apart from the crowd: after all, it was the son of one of America's most celebrated heroes who had been abducted from his home. Ever since his unlikely solo flight between New York and Paris in the single-engine plane Spirit of St. Louis, tall and handsome Charles Lindbergh – now a colonel in the US Army Air Corps Reserve – had been something of a living legend. He was popularly called Lucky Lindy and lived a seemingly carefree life together with his wife Anne Morrow, daughter of one of America's wealthiest men. When curly haired baby Charles junior was born in June 1930, happiness seemed complete. But now, not quite two years later, the idyll had suddenly turned into blackest nightmare.

The police found clumps of soil below the window in the nursery. Outside, two indentations were found in the ground, marks of a ladder that had been leaning against the wall and used by the intruder. The ladder itself – a home-made wooden one, put together by someone who knew his craft – was found 75 feet away, partially broken. It was speculated that the ladder had held the weight of the kidnapper on the way up but became broken when he climbed down with the added weight of the child. The handwritten ransom note was carefully analysed. Although no fingerprints were found, the text provided other clues. The terse message contained several typos which indicated that the writer was a person of foreign – probably German – background.

Colonel Lindbergh's first priority was to get his young son back unharmed as soon as possible. He therefore issued a public appeal to the kidnapper, promising that all agreements between them would be kept confidential. Shortly afterwards, the kidnapper contacted Lindbergh via a letter postmarked in Brooklyn. It was obviously written by the same person who wrote the first message: the same handwriting, the same grammatical errors, and 'signed' with the same sort of symbol. The ransom had now been raised to $70,000. Sometime later, Dr John F. Condon, an eccentric former school principal, offered Lindbergh his services as an intermediary in the negotiations with the kidnapper. His offer was accepted.

On the evening of 12 March 1932, Dr Condon, following instructions from the kidnapper, went to a cemetery in the Bronx, New York. A partially masked man calling himself John addressed Condon in the darkness. They discussed how the delivery of the ransom would be organized, the unknown man promising to send something that could confirm the identity of the abducted child. Condon perceived 'John' as a foreigner but could not make out his face. Four days later, Condon received a baby's sleeping suit, later identified by Lindbergh as belonging to his son. Negotiations with the kidnapper – or kidnappers – continued. On 2 April, Condon handed over $50,000 to 'John', whose face he now got a better glimpse of, in exchange for a receipt and a note stating that Charles junior was aboard the boat Nellie near Martha's Vineyard, Massachusetts. The next morning, Charles

Lindbergh flew along the Atlantic Coast, frantically searching for the boat. It was never found.

In parallel with Condon's and Lindbergh's negotiations with the kidnapper, an extensive police operation was underway. The Bureau of Investigation (later the FBI) assisted the New Jersey police with the investigation. Large sums were promised as a reward to whoever could bring about the safe return of little Charles junior: the Lindbergh family offered $50,000 and the state of New Jersey $25,000. All employees of the Lindbergh family were thoroughly questioned and checked. The police suspected that the kidnapper had acted with help from an insider: how else could he have known that the child would be in the house on this particular Tuesday? Normally, the Lindberghs stayed in Hopewell only on weekends (during the week they stayed with Anne Morrow Lindbergh's parents in Englewood), but because of Charles junior's cold they had chosen to remain a couple of extra days.

On 12 May 1932, more than two months after the kidnapping, a badly decomposed child's body was found by a truck driver near the village of Mount Rose, four and a half miles southeast of the Lindbergh home. Charles Lindbergh and nanny Betty Gow identified the dead child as Charles junior. Anne Morrow Lindbergh, six months pregnant, collapsed at the news. The autopsy showed that the child's skull was crushed. Everything pointed to Charles junior having died shortly after he was abducted, either from a direct blow to the head, or because of the kidnapper dropping him when the ladder broke during the climb down. Bizarrely, newspaper photographers broke into the morgue and took pictures of the baby's remains, selling them for $5 each.

Despite the intensive hunt for Charles junior's killer, the investigation failed to make much progress. After many months, a breakthrough finally was achieved with the tracing of the ransom money. Before the banknotes were handed over to the mysterious John, their serial numbers had been recorded. Pamphlets containing this information were distributed to banks, petrol stations, post offices and various shops in New York. A large part of the ransom had been paid in so-called gold certificates, a special type of currency that could be exchanged into gold coins. Police officers and FBI agents were able to pinpoint an area in New York where several of these gold certificates had been used by a man as payment. In some cases, the recipients remembered what the man in question had looked like and their descriptions matched a phantom image of 'John', produced by an artist in collaboration with Dr Condon.

In September 1934 – two and a half years after the kidnapping – a Manhattan petrol station attendant became suspicious when a customer paid with a $10 gold certificate. The attendant noted the license plate number of the customer's car, a 1930 Dodge, on the certificate. When the banknote was redeemed at the bank, it was discovered that it belonged to the ransom money. Via the car license number, the police were able to track down the person who had paid with the gold certificate: this was 35-year-old German carpenter Bruno Richard Hauptmann, an illegal immigrant with a criminal record in his home country. Hauptmann was arrested in the Bronx on 19 September. At a search of his home, $14,000 of ransom certificates were found hidden in the garage.

Over the following months, the police were strengthened in their belief that they had arrested the right man. Comparisons between Hauptmann's handwriting and the letters from the kidnapper showed striking similarities, both in style as well as in terms of flaws in spelling and grammar. Dr Condon eventually identified Hauptmann as 'John', despite having first failed to pick him out at a line-up. A wood expert was able to show that one of the planks in the kidnapper's ladder matched wood used in the floor of Hauptmann's attic. Police also found a notebook in the German carpenter's home, containing a sketch of a ladder like the one used in the kidnapping. Dr Condon's name and phone number were indistinctly written on the wall of a closet. Finally, Hauptmann had stopped working as a carpenter shortly after the kidnapping in March 1932, spending his time ever since on the stock exchange market. He had also bought furniture and expensive clothes.

The trial of Bruno Hauptmann began on 3 January 1935, in Flemington, New Jersey. It was a huge spectacle with hundreds of newspaper reporters, excited onlookers, and vendors of souvenirs in the form of miniature ladders and alleged locks of Charles junior's hair. The evidence for the prosecution was circumstantial but nevertheless strong. The defence had difficulty challenging the handwriting experts' and wood experts' statements. Hauptmann's explanation for having a large part of the ransom hidden in his home was that he had received it in a sealed box given to him for keeping by a friend, a countryman named Isidor Fisch. This man had returned to Germany, where he – timely enough – died shortly afterwards. When Hauptmann opened the box and saw that it contained several gold certificates, he had decided to spend them, as Fisch owed him money. Few if any believed this improbable story.

On 13 February 1935 the jury returned a verdict of guilty. Hauptmann was sentenced to death. Following several rejected appeals and postponements, he was executed in the electric chair in New Jersey on 3 April 1936, without confessing his guilt. Hauptmann's widow Anna fought for half a century to vindicate her dead husband. She argued that there had been prejudice against him because of his German ethnicity and that evidence had been falsified. For instance, she claimed that the rail of the ladder taken from the attic had been planted by the police. Although she lost a wrongful death suit against the state of New Jersey, her persistent campaign attracted a lot of attention. Journalists and writers showed a renewed interest in the case, many taking the position that Hauptmann had been a victim of corruption and police brutality.

During the 1970s and 80s, several books were published, claiming that Hauptmann had been innocent, for example *The Airman and the Carpenter* by Ludovic Kennedy, known for his earlier books on alleged miscarriages of justice. Some writers put forward a fantastic theory concerning Charles junior's survival: they asserted that the dead baby found in May 1932 was not Lindbergh's son but another child, and that the kidnapped boy survived, grew up and became a salesman of computer supplies. In fact, several people have claimed to be Lindbergh's first-born son. One of them sued the estate of Charles Lindbergh in 1976 to collect his inheritance (he lost the case). Former FBI agent Jim Fisher, who has written two books about the case, does not believe in Hauptmann's innocence. In an article in 1988, he says: 'Notwithstanding all of the books, TV programmes, and legal suits, Hauptmann is as guilty today as he was in 1932 when he kidnapped and killed the son of Mr. and Mrs. Charles Lindbergh'.

On 1 January 1934, Agatha Christie's novel *Murder on the Orient Express* was published. The story of a group of passengers of various nationalities, stranded aboard a luxury train caught in a blizzard – while Hercule Poirot tries to figure out which one of them killed a fellow passenger – quickly became a tremendous success. Not only were readers and critics impressed by the novel's ingenious construction, but they were also fascinated by the obvious parallels to the Lindbergh kidnapping. The murder victim on the train, Mr Ratchett, aka Cassetti, turns out to be an evil man who several years earlier has been the principal instigator of – and escaped scot-free with – the kidnapping of three-year-old Daisy Armstrong in the USA. Her wealthy parents, Colonel John Armstrong, and his wife Sonia, pay a ransom of $200,000 – only to be met by the news that their daughter has been found murdered. Sonia Armstrong, who is pregnant, gives birth to her baby prematurely due to the shock. Both mother and child die, whereupon the devastated husband shoots himself.

In real life, Anne Morrow Lindbergh gave birth to her second child, son Jon, on 16 August 1932, and both mother and child survived the birth. The Lindbergh couple had four more children together, a total of six including the murdered Charles junior. Naturally, Agatha Christie altered many details, yet the similarities between the Armstrong and Lindbergh families are striking. We learn that Colonel John Armstrong was a First World War hero, having received the Victoria Cross for bravery. Charles Lindbergh was too young to serve in the war; however, he had become the hero of a whole nation following his daring solo flight across the Atlantic. Armstrong was half English, half American – Lindbergh was half Swedish, half American. The description of Daisy Armstrong makes the reader recall little Charles junior: 'She was so sweet – so happy – she had such lovely curls'. The blond, curly hair was the most characteristic physical trait of Lindbergh's son.

There are other parallels to the Lindbergh kidnapping in *Murder on the Orient Express.* A French nurserymaid, Susanne Michel, is reminiscent of Violet Sharpe, a young British woman employed by Anne Morrow Lindbergh's mother in Englewood. Interrogated by the police, Violet answered questions evasively and appeared to be extremely nervous. Learning in early June 1932 that yet another interrogation shortly would take place, she panicked and committed suicide by drinking cyanide chloride. The police investigation showed that she had been depressed and worried that her private affairs would figure in the press. There was no indication that Violet had anything to do with the kidnapping.

As Violet Sharpe was a British citizen, much was written about her suicide in British newspapers Christie must have read these articles, including the criticism levelled at the New Jersey police for alleged harshness and persecution of the young woman. Violet's treatment by the New Jersey police even became the subject of questions in the British House of Commons; however, there was nothing to suggest that she had been given 'the third degree' or otherwise treated badly. In *Murder on the Orient Express,* Countess Andrenyi (sister to Sonia Armstrong) tells the story about the unhappy Susanne Michel:

> 'Poor Susanne? Yes, I had forgotten about her. The police questioned her. They were convinced she had something to

> do with it. Perhaps she had – but if so, only innocently. She had, I believe, chatted idly with someone, giving information as to the time of Daisy's outings. The poor thing got terribly wrought up – she thought she was being held responsible.' She shuddered. 'She threw herself out of the window. Oh it was horrible.'

There is one further possible allusion to the Lindbergh case. Antonio Foscarelli, chauffeur to the Armstrongs, tells Poirot that he has been suspected by the New York police of involvement in the kidnapping: 'They could not prove a thing against me – but it was not for want of trying'. Early in the Lindbergh investigation, a Norwegian sailor called Henry 'Red' Johnson – boyfriend of Betty Gow, the nanny – came under suspicion. The police questioned him intensively and even beat him up before concluding that he had nothing whatsoever to do with the crime.

In the creation of some of the other characters aboard the train it seems likely that Christie was inspired by her fellow passengers during a journey with the Orient Express in 1931, an adventurous experience that she described in a letter to her second husband Max Mallowan. In the letter, Christie mentions 'an elderly American lady...a Hungarian Minister and his wife...two Danish lady missionaries...a Director of the Wagons Lits Company...' and others.

Agatha Christie wrote *Murder on the Orient Express* while the hunt for the Lindbergh kidnapper was still ongoing. She assumed – as many did at the time – that the kidnapping was the work of a criminal gang. The villain Cassetti is described as the head of a gang that has conducted kidnappings in the past, killing their victims when the police have come too close. Cassetti is an Italian name, suggesting perhaps the involvement of the Mafia. Hauptmann was a foreigner too, but this seems to be the only similarity between him and Cassetti. There is nothing to indicate that Hauptmann belonged to a gang; most likely he acted alone. Christie's views on the question of Hauptmann's guilt have not been recorded. As far as is known, she never spoke publicly about the matter.

Murder on the Orient Express has been the subject of several films. The first cinema version (1974, directed by Sidney Lumet), with Albert Finney as Poirot, was an award-winning success. Christie herself is said to have been pleased, although she remarked on Finney's moustache. In 2010 there was a TV film with David Suchet as Poirot and in 2017 another cinema version, with Kenneth Branagh in the lead role. Although these movies differ in many respects, they have one thing in common: true to the book, Daisy's killer is portrayed as a thoroughly evil man. In the famous ending, Poirot allows those guilty of Cassetti's murder to walk free. The dead kidnapper may have escaped the law, but justice has finally been served in a different way. In contrast, Bruno Richard Hauptmann was convicted in court of the kidnapping and murder of Charles Lindbergh junior. Has the last word been said on the case? As recently as 2012, it was suggested that Hauptmann did not act alone but had an accomplice, another German, who was the real mastermind behind the kidnapping – and who got away.

Sources

https://famous-trials.com/hauptmann (retrieved 7 December 2023)

Jim Fisher, *The Ghosts of Hopewell: Setting the Record Straight in the Lindbergh* case (1999)

Jim Fisher, The Lindbergh case: how can such a guilty kidnapper be so innocent? In *The Chief of Police* (Nov./Dec. 1988) pp. 99-109.

Ludovic Kennedy, *The Airman and the Carpenter: The Lindbergh Kidnapping and the Framing of Richard Hauptmann* (1985)

Janet Morgan, *Agatha Christie – a biography* (1984)

David Stout, *The Kidnap Years: The Astonishing True History of the Forgotten Kidnapping Epidemic That Shook Depression-Era America* (2020)

Robert Zorn, *Cemetery John: The Undiscovered Mastermind of the Lindbergh Kidnapping* (2012)

Brighton Trunk Murders (1934)

Cards on the Table (1936), Dumb Witness (1937), The Body in the Library (1942), The Horses of Diomedes (in: The Labours of Hercules 1947), 4.50 from Paddington (1957), The Adventure of the Clapham Cook (in: Poirot's early Cases (1974))

The dilemma for a killer who needs to conceal his victim has already been discussed in an earlier chapter. In 1934 there was a brief spate of bodies being deposited at railway stations and elsewhere in trunks (in 1927 the dismembered body of Minnie Bonati had been found in a trunk deposited by John Robinson at Charing Cross railway station; Robinson was found guilty of her murder and hanged). These created problems of identity of both victim and murderer. They were also referenced in a number of subsequent Agatha Christie stories – and had been anticipated by her in an early Poirot story.

In the first instance, on 17 June 1934 there were noxious odours coming from an item of left luggage in the cloakroom of Brighton Central Station. On investigation, a torso of a woman was found in a canvas covered motor case. One day later the legs and feet belonging to an adult female corpse were found in a suitcase at King's Cross Station, in north London. This was also due to the smell. Initially the former was thought, by Brighton's police surgeon, to have been part of a corpse of a middle aged woman. However, Spilsbury identified the legs as coming from the same body as the Brighton torso but the arms and head were never located. He also found that the woman was aged about 25 and was five months pregnant. She was probably between five feet two inches and five feet three inches in height. Care had been taken on the woman's feet in life as they were pedicured. Her toenails were unpainted. There was cooking oil on these limbs. There was no clothing on any of these remains. The Chief Constable of Brighton stated, 'There is absolutely no indication of the identity of the murdered woman. That is very strange'. It was a press sensation, with between 40 and 50 reporters descending on Brighton as Chief Inspector Donaldson of Scotland Yard took charge of the case.

The body parts were wrapped in brown paper and tied with cord. In blue pencil on that in the Brighton trunk was the word Ford. This might be a clue to part of a word; perhaps Stafford or Guildford or it might be part of someone's name. There was also part of two newspapers in the case with the words Home Counties edition on them, so clearly bought in or near London. Other left luggage cases at railway stations were checked but there was no sign of the head and hands.

It was known that the case in question had been deposited at Brighton on 6 June and that at King's Cross on the next day. The procedure was that someone leaving a case would pay threepence and receive a receipt. However, with so many people doing so every day, it was impossible for staff to recall the man who had left these items. It was noted that the left luggage office at Brighton was next to the platform where trains coming from London Victoria would arrive.

Men seen with trunks at railway stations were asked to come forward. In particular there was a man seen with a trunk on 6 June. He came forward and was eliminated from enquiries. Police called at sellers and makers of such cases but to no avail.

The police thought that someone, somewhere must know something. Killing someone and then chopping them up was not a quiet task. There was no evidence of any particular skill at dissection and anyone with a basic knowledge of anatomy could have done it. The body's internal organs were examined by Dr Roche Lynch, but nothing significant was found, despite earlier suspicions of poison.

The woman was never identified, despite the discoveries being widely advertised. Mothers contacted the police with information about missing daughters and some missing women did report themselves to the police. There were no identifying marks on her, no scars or wounds. Without the head or the hands, which could be helpful with fingerprints or dental records, or any possessions, it would be hard to know who this was. These may well have been buried or thrown into the sea or the Thames. She may have had a criminal record, so the hands had to be severed. Families of missing women came forward to see if this was their missing relative, but to no avail. Lists of missing young women were compiled and nurses were asked if they had seen anyone who was pregnant and who might resemble the corpse. It was suggested that she might have come from abroad. She might have been killed by the man who made her pregnant but could not or would not marry her and perhaps she presented him with an ultimatum as in the case of Norman Thorne. Or maybe an abortionist was to blame. Clearly the association between murderer and victim was known to others; hence the need to conceal her identity. The reason for the two trunks was surely that the weight of an adult woman would be too much for one man to carry.

The manufacturers of the trunks were ascertained; the one found in Brighton was made by Mr Sewell in Shepherd's Bush, but the seller could not identify all the buyers of his products. That at King's Cross was made by Messrs Lewis of Leyton. A clue that the woman might have been from Jersey was followed up. There were anonymous letters. The press talked about this being the 'perfect crime' (not so perfect for the victim, of course). This was soon known as the Brighton Trunk Murder One.

There were a number of adjourned inquests on the body in 1934 but the lack of evidence and the fact that the body was unidentified caused delays. The final inquest took place on 20 February 1935. Neither Spilsbury nor Lynch were present, but they had sent written reports. It was inconclusive; there was no evidence as to how death had occurred; no clue as to any natural disease nor to poison. The victim and killer were unknown. An open verdict on the cause of death was thus returned and that has stood.

On 30 October 1934 newspaper articles were published based on the revelations of recently retired Chief Inspector Bowden, much to the ire of some senior officers. The articles were titled 'I know the man'. They claimed that the suggestion was that one William Augustus Offord of 152 Fortress Road, Kentish Town was the murderer. He had once been a suspect as his car had allegedly been seen in Brighton the day the trunk was deposited there, but had since been cleared.

All that could be surmised was that the murder had taken place at the end of May or the very first few days of June. It was thought that it probably occurred within a 50 mile radius of London. The killer was probably not a motorist as a man of average strength could have carried the body parts about in a case on a train quite easily. The victim might have been stabbed or shot with the fatal injury to the neck or head (poison, strangulation, drowning and suffocation being ruled out). Needless to say, no one was ever charged with the murder and there were no serious suspects. Once the luggage had been deposited there was little danger that the crime would be brought home to anyone because of the lack of clues, barring a confession. Whether more advanced forensic science of later decades would have led to an arrest is another question. It seems possible that the murderer and the murder may have been in central London because that would mean a minimum of travelling by train to the places we know the killer visited. Yet busy railway stations are anonymous places and so ideally suited for such.

The second Brighton Trunk murder was discovered in the next month after the first, as the former was still being investigated. On 15 July 1934 a large black trunk containing the corpse of another woman was found in a room in 52 Kemp Street, Brighton, which was 100 yards from the railway station. This time the body was whole and clothed. The woman had been doubled up and had a fractured skull; she might have been killed by a hammer blow. Her name was Violet Saunders. She had been born in Peckham, south London, on 14 May 1892, the daughter of a commercial traveller. In 1919 she married George Saunders, a soldier, in Pontypridd, Wales, where she had been performing in pantomime. They had not had any children and had not seen each other for a long time. She was allegedly partial to drink and drugs. She earned money as a dancer and a prostitute in London and elsewhere, working in a dance act.

It was known that she had been living with a man known as Jack Notyre or Toni Mancini, aged 26 and sometimes employed in cafes. His real name was Cecil Lois England, born on 7 January 1908 in New Cross, south east London, and his father was a lighterman. They had met in a café in Leicester Square, London, in 1933 and went down to Brighton, where they lived at various addresses as man and wife. He lived off her earnings for a time. He then took a job in the Skylark café as a waiter on 5 May 1934. At that time the two were living in three rooms at 44 Park Crescent. She was last seen alive on the afternoon of 10 May.

He later claimed that he had returned home that day to find her dead. As she had died of a fractured skull, he said he felt he could not report this to the police or tell anyone because of his previous petty offences and so would not be believed. He said that he had thought that she was fearful of some man, but she never gave his name and that was why they moved from place to place. Instead he told anyone who asked that she had left him.

Mancini bought a large black trunk from Rowland Wood of the Open market for 7s 6d. Mancini told Wood that he needed it because he was going to France. The two men took the trunk back to number 44. On

14 May, Thomas Capelin, a colleague of Mancini's from the café, helped him take the very heavy trunk to 52 Kemp Street. Mancini explained that it was weighty because of clothes and china therein. Meanwhile, he sold some of the furniture from number 44, telling the buyer, Sam Hall, that he had had a 'bust up' with his 'missus' and she had left him to go to London.

Mancini gave some of Violet's clothes to Florence Attrill, a young waitress at the café. He told her that she had taken a job in Paris, but was unable to fit all her clothes in her case and he had told her that he would send the remainder over, but was not going to do that. He told Dorothy Gordon a similar story and sent a telegram to Violet's sister to say she had left him. To Joyce Golding he said that 'Now she won't follow me about the streets nagging and calling me names'. This has shades of the Crippen case when Crippen told others that his wife had gone overseas and he gave away some of his clothes to Ethel. As Poirot observes in *Murder on the Links*, man, and this includes criminal man, is an unoriginal animal, but what else could be done? Over time, the body in the trunk inevitably began to give off a noxious smell as decomposition set in. Mancini sometimes had people visit him. It became obvious to them that something was wrong and so he said it was because someone had died there or that the landlady had failed to open the house's windows. But this could not go on forever. He left Brighton on 15 July. Just after his departure, he met a young woman who he asked to give him an alibi; that they had been in the flat in Brighton with Violette and some men. Then Mancini and the young woman left and on their return they found Violet dead.

Once the corpse was found and the landlord told the police who the room's recent tenant had been, they searched for Mancini and soon found him. He was arrested in south east London on 17 July, having been found wandering along Eltham Road by two constables in their patrol car. He was then taken to Lee Police station and then to Brighton where he was charged with murder. Evidence was found against him. The new tenant of no. 44 found bloodstains in the cupboard. A hammerhead was found in the rubbish in a cellar in the house. Witnesses came forward to tell the police that Mancini had used threatening language about Violet. George Boxall had heard him say that he had 'knocked his wife about from pillar to post' and that he had 'bashed her'. Mancini also said 'Why knock women about with your hands? You only hurt yourself. Hit 'em with a hammer and slosh 'em out the same as I did'. He had certainly covered up her death.

He was charged with the murder of Violet and was tried at Sussex Assizes in Lewes on 10 December 1934. James Cassels was the barrister for the prosecution and Norman Birkett for the defence. Mancini pleaded not guilty. The trial lasted for five days. Birkett made much of the lack of any motive and as ever, was an eloquent counsel, as in Annie Hearn's case. He said that if Mancini was guilty he could have thrown the hammer off Brighton pier. He also suggested that Violet could have been killed by a client or other man that she may have aggrieved. Mancini denied he had ever threatened Violet and some witnesses said that they got on well together, as Mr and Mrs Watson. The judge told the jury that this was not a court of morals and so they should not be influenced by what they thought about Mancini. Mancini was found not guilty. The police were convinced that he was, and there was no further investigation. He lived for decades longer, and in 1939, as a married man with a daughter, was employed as an Air Ministry clerk, living in Gloucester. He died in 1987.

Yet it seems he was probably guilty of manslaughter or murder. The likely scenario is that the two had an argument at 44 Park Crescent. This may have been over Mancini's flirtations, real or imagined (and he certainly spent time with her after Violet's death) with the teenage waitress Florence Attrill. In the course of the argument, Mancini struck Violet with a hammer and so killed her. He then did all he could to conceal the body, ineffectual though this was. He confessed to the murder to a newspaper, in 1976, later retracting his statement.

There was a similar, but less well-known case in February of the following year, when the legs of a man were found on a train from Hounslow to Waterloo and the torso found in a sack in the river near Brentford. It was that of a middle-aged man this time. But there were no hands or head, as in the first Brighton trunk murder and so no way of identifying the corpse or the killer. Possibly the killer in the crime had copied the methods of the two other murderers. They certainly got away with it.

It is ironic that the second trunk murder actually occurred before the first one and was unsatisfactorily concluded before the first was equally unsatisfactorily brought to an end. There was no connection between the two except that two of the three trunks were found in Brighton. In both cases the murderers got away with their foul deeds; arguably the second was less intelligent than the first who was not even suspected.

There are five references to these cases in Agatha Christie's books. Mr Shaitana, in *Cards on the Table*, referring to a hypothetical private

Black Museum, scoffs that one of the exhibits could be the 'cup used by the Brighton murderer'. Quite what this is a reference to is unknown as there is no mention of a cup playing any part in the objects associated with these crimes. This book was set in 1936 so the Brighton Trunk murders would have been very much in the collective memory of the majority of contemporary readers. Shaitana is dismissive of the importance of these physical artefacts and claims that the interesting exhibits are the killers themselves.

Hastings refers to the case (and that of Dr Ruxton) in *Dumb Witness* when a female character goes missing. 'Poirot, you don't think she'll turn up in parcels or dismembered in a trunk?' Here he refers to the 'first' trunk murder but is thankfully wrong in his supposition.

That the murders were unsolved is attested in *The Body in the Library* by Miss Marple, who is discussing the murder of a young woman found in Colonel Bantry's library in Gossington Hall. She says 'there's a great possibility of this crime being the kind of crime that never does get solved. Like the Brighton trunk murders'. Happily for the Bantrys the miscreants are caught and the innocent saved.

In 'The Horses of Diomedes' in *The Labours of Hercules*, a character asks, 'perhaps Anthony Hawker is the Brighton Trunk murderer?' Hawker is apparently a drug dealer and so perhaps is assumed to be capable of anything, though it turns out he is actually an addict who is being framed by others. It is interesting that his Christian name mirrors that of the chief suspect, Tony Mancini and perhaps this is Christie's suggestion that he was indeed guilty of Violet's murder. Or probably not, as noted above.

In *4.50 from Paddington*, written over two decades later, Mrs McGillicuddy witnesses a murder of an initially unknown woman on a train and tells Miss Marple, 'You read about bodies being put in trunks… but no one travels with trunks nowadays'. No trunk is used in this story, with the victim being thrown off the train and concealed elsewhere.

There is, however, another trunk murder in an Agatha Christie story which is not inspired by any of these real cases because it was first published a decade prior to them. In 1924 'The Adventure of the Clapham Cook', appeared and was later to be found in the short story collection *Poirot's Early Cases*. The story seems a petty case of a disappearing domestic servant but it transpires that something far more serious is afoot. An old trunk belonging to the said servant also vanishes from her employer's home, adding to the mystery.

The servant was decoyed away so another resident of the house could use her trunk to store the corpse of a bank employee that he has killed in that house on that day, when the other occupants were absent. He does so to cover up a major theft from the said bank by directing suspicion towards the other man. The trunk is sent to Glasgow railway station, where it is opened. The killer is identified by Poirot and apprehended before he can flee the country. This story was also the first to be broadcast, in 1989, of the long running TV series *Agatha Christie's Poirot*, starring David Suchet. Whether this story inspired any of the real crimes is a moot point. Unlike the Brighton cases, though, the victim is male.

Sources

The National Archives files:
Evening News and *Daily Mail* reports in the crimes, DPP2/237.
Leakage of information to press about case, MEPO3/735,
Acquittal of Tony Mancini of murder, MEPO3/1692

Spies

The Cambridge Five (1934-1951), Klaus Fuchs (1950), The Portland spy ring (1960), *Destination Unknown (1954), The Clocks (1963), Passenger to Frankfurt (1970)*

In several of Agatha Christie's novels, espionage is an important component of the plot, sometimes even the main theme. The topic of spies, and the activities of British intelligence, were obviously areas of interest to her. *The Secret Adversary* (1922), *They Came to Baghdad* (1951), and her wartime novel *N or M?* (1941), dealing with the danger of the enemy within, are some examples. Direct references to real life spies are, however, rare. In *Passenger to Frankfurt* – an extravagant story of a global mass movement led by an Aryan superman – there is a reference to three notorious British spies. Sir James Kleek reflects, 'Extraordinary, how we can breed them, how we trust them, tell 'em our secrets, let them know what we're doing, go on saying: "If there's one person I'm absolutely sure of it's – oh, Mclean, or Burgess, or Philby, or any of the lot".' Additionally, the novel's hero, Sir Stafford Nye, in conversation with a colleague asks, 'Who do they think I am – another Philby, something of that kind?'

Donald Mclean, Guy Burgess, and Kim Philby were at the centre of a much-publicized spy scandal involving a group of Cambridge educated men (referred to as the Cambridge Five) who held top jobs within the British Foreign Office and intelligence, at the same time passing large amounts of state secrets to the Soviets. Because they belonged to a privileged elite and thus were above suspicion, they were able to operate over a long time, from before the Second World War and into the Cold War era. The unwillingness of the British establishment to believe that such men could be capable of treason explains why they escaped detection. This is what Kleek refers to in the quote above. The documents betrayed to the Soviets contained highly classified information on the development of nuclear weapons, the formation of NATO, the Venona decryption project, and the Korean war. The affair seriously undermined the confidence in British intelligence and had a negative effect on Britain's special relationship with the United States.

None of the spies was ever brought to justice. The three mentioned in *Passenger to Frankfurt* defected to the Soviet Union while two others – Anthony Blunt and John Cairncross – were given immunity from prosecution. The latter two had been working at Bletchley Park, the centre for codebreaking during the Second World War, providing the Russians with decoded German messages. Incidentally, Agatha Christie herself was briefly investigated by MI5 because she named a character in *N or M?* 'Major Bletchley'. It was feared that Christie could have been given inside information by someone working at Bletchley Park (she and her husband Max Mallowan were, in fact, close friends of Professor Knox, one of the codebreakers). Everyone was relieved when she explained that she had named 'one of my least lovable characters' after the town of Bletchley, where she had once been stuck during a train journey.

Two other Agatha Christie novels contain elements showing the author to be familiar with contemporary espionage affairs. In *The Clocks*, the narrator Colin Lamb – an MI5 agent – is investigating a spy network with roots at the naval station of Portlebury. A man named Larkin used to work there, having access to highly sensitive documents that he photographed and passed on to a foreign intelligence service. When the novel starts, Larkin has already been arrested. Colin Lamb discusses the case with his friend, Inspector Dick Hardcastle, who wants to know Larkin's motive for betraying his country. Was he a political idealist? No, it was only for money, says Lamb, adding that Larkin 'splashed it about'.

Lamb feels that Larkin is merely a henchman, 'he just did as he was told'. There are other, more cunning, individuals involved whose identities are still unknown. At the end of the novel, he finally discovers the missing link, a highly respectable, elderly lady – Miss Pebmarsh – who uses Braille books (for blind people) to convey secret information. In contrast to Larkin, she is not in it for the money but for a political cause. A third person, Mr Ramsay, has functioned as a courier – he has managed to defect behind the Iron Curtain.

Readers of *The Clocks* in 1963 probably had no problems associating the fictional espionage plot with the so-called Portland spy ring, exposed three years earlier. There is a clue already in the fictional name Portlebury, sharing its first five letters with Portland. A clerk named Harry Houghton, employed at the Admiralty Underwater Weapons Establishment (AUWE) on the Isle of Portland was recruited by the Soviets to photograph thousands of sensitive documents dealing with submarine technology. Houghton had a drinking problem and was chronically short of money, which seems to have been the main reason for his actions. Like the fictional Larkin, he spent his money liberally. Others involved in the Portland spy ring were Houghton's girlfriend Ethel Gee, a KGB agent who went by the name of Gordon Lonsdale, and an American couple, Helen and Peter Kroger (real names: Lona and Morris Cohen).

Houghton and Gee passed the secret information to Lonsdale, who handed it on to the Krogers. They were fanatical communists who had fled their native country when the Venona decryption project began to expose Russian spies in the United States. In 1954 they turned up in Ruislip, on the outer fringes of west London, pretending to be New Zealanders. Peter Kroger established an antiquarian book shop in the Strand. Some of the sensitive naval documentation received by the Krogers was passed on to Moscow via radio, some was converted to microdots that were inserted into the spines of books sent from the shop overseas. This appears to be the inspiration for Miss Pebmarsh's use of the Braille microdot system to transfer secret information in *The Clocks*.

In 1960, the Portland spy ring was exposed. All five were arrested in January 1961, put on trial in March, and sentenced to long prison terms. None of them served their full time, however, Lonsdale and the Krogers were released in spy swaps between Britain and the Soviet Union in 1964 and 1969, respectively; Houghton and Gee were set free in 1970. In 1965 Lonsdale published his autobiography *Spy*, written with the help of a 'colleague' – none other than the master-spy Kim Philby, who had defected to the Soviets the year before. Incidentally, Agatha Christie was a favourite author of the latter.

Destination Unknown is another Christie novel that bears the stamp of contemporary espionage events. Written during the Cold War, it contains many references to anti-communism, bombs, secret scientific research, and political defections. At the centre of the story is the riddle of vanishing young scientists, brought to an inaccessible but luxurious prison. This theme seems to have been inspired by the famous Manhattan project: a large group of scientists working secretly in remote Los Alamos during the Second

World War, developing the atomic bomb. While none of the characters in the novel can be said to be based on specific individuals, the readers at the time of publication no doubt associated *Destination Unknown* with the Italian physicist Bruno Pontecorvo, who defected to the Soviet Union in 1950, and the German-born atomic spy Klaus Fuchs. The latter worked at Los Alamos, sending important technical information to the Russians. After the war he went to the United Kingdom, where he was exposed, tried, and convicted in 1950. Sentenced to 14 years imprisonment, he obtained an early release in 1959 and emigrated to East Germany.

Sources

Sally and Tony Hope, *Agatha Christie: plots, clues and misdirections* (2023)
Janet Morgan, *Agatha Christie, a biography* (1984)
Trevor Barnes, *Dead doubles: the extraordinary worldwide hunt for one of the cold war's most notorious spy rings* (2020)
Jonathan Oates, *Foul deeds and suspicious deaths around Uxbridge* (2008)

Dorothea Waddingham (1935)

After the Funeral (1953)

This is one of the least known true crime cases in this book and there is only one full length study of it and that published very recently. Given recent concerns about murderous nurses killing their patients such a book was long overdue. Joseph Baguley worked variously as a labourer for the council and by at least 1901 was a self employed boot maker. He was married to one Louisa, born in 1847, in about 1883 and they had a daughter, Ada Louisa, born in Nottingham in about 1884. She was an only child and never seems to have worked due to her physical health problems, but was attractive enough to have a longstanding fiancé. They lived in a house Carnarvon Cottage, on the Main Road of Burton Joyce in Nottinghamshire, from at least 1901. Baguley acquired eight small cottages, one of which the three of them lived in and the others he rented out. He died on 4 April 1929. The terms of his will were that his widow was to inherit the furniture and household effects and a life interest in the income from the cottages and his daughter to have the eight cottages, but if she died first, they went to her mother.

Neither woman was in good health and though they lived by themselves in the cottage for a few years after Joseph's death, by early 1935 it was thought that they must move. The 87-year-old Mrs Baguley was 'somewhat feeble, her heart was not very strong and she was getting very frail'. It was said of her daughter, now aged 50, 'she had a long record of ill health for a very long time – many years. She was pretty helpless, she was a woman of about 16 stones weight and had been more or less a cripple for very many years. She could not walk'.

Miss Blagg, of the County Nursing Association, seeing their helpless condition, in December 1934, thought that what they needed was to be cared for in a nursing home. There was one newly opened at 32 Devon Drive, Sherwood, in Nottingham, run by Dorothea Nancy Waddingham and

Ronald Joseph Sullivan (born in 1894). They rented the property. It had been established in July 1934 titled 'Nursing Home for the Aged: Medical Surgical and Chronic Cases'. Miss Blagg saw Sullivan and he said they could take them and that his 'sister' never refused any patient. They settled there on 5 January 1935, paying £3 per week for their board and lodging. The alternative was a poor law institution in Basford and this was not desired by the Baguleys.

If the Baguleys and their friends had known more about the nursing home's keeper, who had no medical or nursing qualifications and only a limited experience of the work, they would have been more wary. Dorothea had been born in Ilkeston, Derbyshire, on 23 July 1901, as Ann Waddingham Chandler. She was born out of wedlock and took her mother's name as her surname. She left home in 1920 after an argument with her parents and was employed as a probationer nurse at Burton on Trent Poor Law Institution on 9 July 1923, but was ordered to resign on 10 December 1924 because she had claimed on starting that she was married (she was not) and because her work was deemed unsatisfactory.

She married Thomas Willoughby Leech on 25 February 1925 at Burton on Trent Registry Office. They had three children: Maurice Edwin, Eric Alan and Dorothea May. She, as Dorothy Leech, also had an extensive criminal record, with five convictions from 1925-1931. She was bound over for obtaining two dresses by fraud (1925), fined for taking poor law relief for two years under false pretences (1927), given three years probation for trying to get £500 credit by fraud (1929), then three months in prison and hard labour for the theft of a lady's gold watch (1930) and two months likewise for trying to gain money by use of a forged post office savings book (1931). She and her husband lived at Greasley in Derbyshire from 1925-1928, leaving with rent unpaid and then at West Bridgeford, Nottinghamshire and other addresses and seem not to have done any honest work. Rent and debts to tradesmen went unpaid (hence the frequent changes of addresses). Leech died on 20 July 1933.

Dorothea then met Sullivan and they lived together as Mr and Mrs Joseph Sullivan, firstly at 22 Bingham Road, Nottingham in 1933-1934 and left without paying £10 rent. More creditably, Sullivan had served in the army in the First World War and was awarded the Military Medal for saving an officer's life. Sullivan's job at the nursing home they established was to make the fires, help prepare the meals, write letters for patients and move patients about, often wheeling Ada's wheelchair. He did not involve himself in medication. He was married but had separated from his wife and he and Dorothea had two children together: Ronald John and Margaret, both taking his surname, although he and Dorothea were not married.

The care was thought to be good. Alice Northmore claimed 'Waddingham was doing all she could for Mrs Baguley'. Another observer noted 'The Baguleys were perfectly happy and comfortable'. There certainly does not seem to have been any known complaints from the two women. However, there may have been unspoken control over two vulnerable women who had limited care options.

The Baguleys had not long been in the home when Mr Alcock, sub manager of the Netherfield branch of the Midland Bank, where the two women had their accounts, visited them. He later said 'When he went they both appeared quite happy and quite comfortable' (Miss Blagg, visiting on 16 January concurred with this). Dorothea told him that when they arrived they seemed quite poor, but she found that this was not so. She also found that the work they entailed was much harder than she first thought, given the women's physical needs, and that £3 per week was insufficient for all the work involved. She therefore asked Alcock if he could use his influence with them to come to a settlement where they gave all their assets to her in return for being looked after at the home for life. He disagreed with the proposal.

Similarly, the Baguleys' cousin, Lawrence Frederick Baguley, who visited in January and February, recalled Dorothea talking to him about being unhappy with the payments. Lawrence suggested he ask them if they could possibly pay her more per week. Dorothea disagreed with the idea and proposed the arrangement she had already suggested to Alcock.

Sullivan arranged to meet John Lane, the solicitor who had drawn up Baguley's will and knew his widow and daughter professionally. They met on 23 March 1935. He told Lane that Ada wished to settle her property on him and Dorothea. Lane went with him to the nursing home and met the two. Miss Baguley was happy to go ahead with it but Lane advised her not to. Sullivan called on Lane again on 7 April and a week later he went to the nursing home again. Lane protested about the proposal but Sullivan said that Ada insisted.

In the meantime, Sullivan and Ada went to the bank and emptied her account of just over £70. Ada also wrote to Lane to ask for her savings pass book and conversion bonds, totalling about £162. Furthermore, when the Baguleys' relatives tried to visit them they were told that the two were absent from the home and did not want to see them. Ada also wrote to Lawrence to say that her mother was very unwell.

Finally on 4 May Lane went to the nursing home in order to draw up Ada's will. Neither Waddingham nor Sullivan were then present. It was witnessed by Lane and a man unfortunately called Mr Daft. It left all Ada's property, worth about £1,600, to be divided between Dorothea and Sullivan. The will was executed on 7 May.

Five days later, Louisa died, and the death certificate, made up by Dr George Manfield, stated that this was due to cardiac muscular degeneration, and she was buried at Caunton churchyard two days later. The death of such an elderly lady would have caused no one any great surprise, and she had been bedridden for the last ten days anyway, and there was no post mortem or investigation into her death. Her will was proved and her £23 17s 6d went to Sullivan. This was mere chicken feed. The bulk of the Baguley money lay with Ada and she seemed to live comfortably and was well looked after in the next few months. Dr Jacob visited her six times and rather less so, so did Dr Manfield. She made no complaints to them.

Mrs Briggs, a family friend, visited Ada in August and early September. She seemed 'quite bright' and happy, though later Dorothea claimed the woman was very ill. On 10 September, she saw Ada in the afternoon. She had been taken out into the garden. Everything seemed normal and the conversation concerned the last 30 years, the time that they had known each other. Meanwhile, Dorothea told Mrs Briggs that Ada had maggots and that she suffered from incontinence. Mrs Briggs left at about 4pm.

Next day Ada was appearing increasingly unwell and so Dorothea called for Dr Manfield at 8.45 am. He was out on a call and did not arrive until at least noon, by which time Ada had been dead for two hours. Dorothea stated that on the previous day she had taken Ada back inside the house and had fed her a substantial meal. She had then given her medicine, before taking her to her room. She had looked in on her during the night and at first she seemed well. Just after 2am on 11 September she seemed unwell.

On that same day Sullivan took a letter that he had written, though allegedly dictated by Ada, to George Musson, a local undertaker. It expressed the now deceased's desire to be cremated, then relatively unusual. Sullivan wanted this to happen in two days' time. Musson explained that two doctors' permission was needed, not just that of Dr Manfield. It also needed to be signed by a magistrate, which Sullivan was unaware of. The process was delayed and this became indefinite.

There had been a post mortem on the day after the death and then there was an inquest on 16 September. The cause of death had been originally stated by Dr Manfield, based on what Dorothea told him, as cerebral haemorrhage. This was now thought to be incorrect as morphia was found in the deceased. It was also known that on 27 August and 2 September Dr Mansfield had given Dorothea a total of ten morphine tablets. She at first denied giving Ada morphine, but later said that she had on Dr Manfield's instructions, though he denied this. Dorothea claimed that Ada had appreciated the care she had received at the home and that she had been fond of Ada. The inquest was adjourned. On 30 September, her mother's body was exhumed and Dr Roche Lynch undertook the examination. Ten to twelve grains of morphine were found in the body, easily enough to kill her. This was now looking like a potential double murder. A further tragedy occurred at the month's end when Frederick Gilbert, who had been engaged to marry Ada, shot himself. By now, Dorothea was heavily pregnant and gave birth for the fifth time at the end of October.

An adjourned inquest and magistrates' court hearings in January 1936 led to many pleadings and interventions from Dorothea. When a relative of the deceased gave evidence, she shouted, 'It's a lie. Don't tell lies'. When Dr Lynch told of his findings, she said, 'It is a lie. It is not right. It is not true. He knows it'. When the inquest jury found against her she said 'The jury did not have an open mind'. She and Sullivan were arrested on 31 January.

The trial took place as part of the Nottingham Assizes on 24 February. Dorothea and Sullivan were jointly charged with the murder of Ada Baguley. Both pleaded not guilty. The judge was Justice Goddard. Unusually, Norman Birkett led the case for the prosecution (he had successfully defended Annie Hearn in 1931 and Mancini in 1934). He asked whether there was any doubt that Ada died of morphine poisoning and whether there was any question of Dr Manfield supplying such tablets to Dorothea (a single tablet could be fatal). Mr J. Eales, for the defence argued that medical men had made mistakes and that the Baguleys had been well looked after there. Nor had Dorothea tried to conceal the fact that their wills benefitted her. The judge asked the jury to consider whether the morphia had been administered to relieve pain or whether to cause death. They took two hours to return with a verdict; clearly this was no clear-cut case.

On 27 February, Sullivan was found not guilty – there was no suggestion that he administered anything to anyone. Dorothea, though, was found guilty with a recommendation for mercy. Dorothea told the court, 'I am innocent'. There was an appeal, on the grounds that the judge did not tell the jury that this could have been a case of manslaughter with the accused having merely incompetently given too much morphine, but it was turned down on 30 March. She wrote letters from her cell to state her innocence, even claiming on 8 April that she was pregnant (she was not). She wrote, 'Tell my children of my death and that I am innocent – and never forget that'.

Dorothea was hanged at Winston Green Prison in Birmingham at 9am on 16 April 1936. Mrs Van der Elst, a staunch opponent of capital punishment protested, as did others. In 2020 there was a TV investigation as to whether Dorothea should have been hanged and the programme upheld the verdict despite representations from her descendants. Sullivan's future is unknown; after being found not guilty he was freed and said that Dorothea was innocent too. He may have subsequently changed his name or gone overseas. He may have been involved in caring for the children. Yet he may have been an accomplice, as Dorothea's lover. Could he really have known and suspected nothing? He certainly pressed for a cremation in the case of Ada and had this happened then all evidence of the poison would have been removed. He was also involved in various of the earlier financial transactions. Possibly he was acting under Dorothea's direction (had the gender roles been reversed this would certainly have been thought probable) but this was the 1930s and he was an older man and a decorated army veteran, so would he have meekly deferred to a younger woman? It is possible, and we know little about their personal relations, but unlikely. He seems to have been an accessory to murder.

There is the possibility, never explored, that other patients may have died before their time in the nursing home. These were Louie Kemp on 26 February 1935, who was recorded as dying from Parkinson's disease, aged 68. She was found to have been given doses of heroin in the last two months of her life, but there was no post mortem. Elizabeth and Jane Harwood had been similarly treated in December 1934.

Nurse Waddingham as she was known seems to have been a cold and calculating murderess of a type occasionally found in the 'caring' professions. She had a record of theft and fraud already, and when faced with the opportunity of making money dishonestly from very vulnerable victims who had assets she could take, she gave into temptation. Almost as soon as the Baguleys arrived she was attempting to have them sign their property over to her and she talked to anyone who might influence them in order to bring this about. As it was, it was less than four months after the Baguleys' arrival that a legal agreement had been drawn up in her favour. Then it was only a matter of time before she snuffed out the two women in her power. In Sullivan she seems to have found a willing accomplice.

Mr Entwhistle in *After the Funeral* notes, in a survey of murderers that he has read about, that Dorothea Waddingham 'had put her elderly patients out of the way with business like efficiency'. As a brief summary this is fine, but it does suggest that her killing was rather more extensive than perhaps it was, not that this is to lessen her crimes against the defenceless in her power.

Such institutions do not feature much in Agatha Christie's books. A nursing home, Sunny Ridge, is the scene of an early chapter in *By the Pricking of My Thumbs*, the penultimate of the five Tommy and Tuppence Beresford stories, published in 1968. The middle aged couple visit an elderly relative, Aunt Ada (whether this is conscious irony as regards Miss Ada Baguley is another question), in a nursing home where something seems to be wrong. One of the other elderly residents, one Mrs Lancaster, asks them 'Was it your poor child? There behind the fireplace', which is a phrase uttered in both *The Pale Horse* and *Sleeping Murder* but here it is no irrelevant cameo. A few weeks later, Aunt Ada dies of natural causes and when her relations visit they also find that Mrs Lancaster has been taken from the home by a Mrs Johnson. Tuppence tries to track her down but to no avail.

There are numerous nurses in some of Christie's works, such as in 'The Lernaean Hydra' in *The Labours of Hercules*. Then there is nurse Jessie Hopkins in *Sad Cypress*, finally there is the narrator, Amy Leatheran in *Murder in Mesopotamia,* for example. Then there is Nurse Copling in The Blue Geranium in *The Thirteen Problems*.

Sources

The National Archives files:

Criminal Cases; Dorothea Waddingham, HO144/20186-20187.
Dorothea Waddingham: convicted and sentenced to death, PCOM9/797

Reginald Gough (1945)

The Mousetrap (1952)

One of the most disturbing cases which led to the inspiration for an Agatha Christie story was that which was revealed in early 1945. It deals with the maltreatment and death of children and so is particularly harrowing to read. Yet because of it Christie's greatest theatrical production resulted (following a short story published only in America). The reader may well find parts of the following narrative difficult to read.

Dennis and Terrence O'Neill were two brothers who, together with their six siblings, were taken into care by Newport Council. They had been born on 2 March 1931 and 1934 to working class parents, Thomas and Mabel. They lived in a house on Commercial Road, Newport, Monmouthshire. However, on 30 May 1940 after an order by the juvenile court, they were taken into care by Newport Council because of the abuse they had suffered at their parents' hands. They went through several foster parents in the next four years. The boys were certainly a handful, even by Terrence's later admittance. For a time they were fostered in Leominster and were to go to one Mrs Pickering of Minsterley, but she could only take two children. In any case the siblings were broken up.

They were sent, a month apart, in the summer of 1944 by Newport Education Committee to Bank Farm, Hope Valley, Ministerley, Shropshire. The people there were Reginald Gough, born in 1914 and his wife, Esther, born in 1916 and who had been married in February 1942. As a lad he had apparently enjoyed dissecting live frogs in front of schoolgirls he wanted to 'impress'. He had previously been in a fair ground, employed as a prize fighter. He then worked as a farm labourer where he did perfectly well.

Esther was employed in domestic service prior to the war. She was then in the WAAF before being invalided out. The marriage had not been entirely happy and Gough was violent towards his wife. They separated in

July 1942 and she asked for a separation order on the grounds of cruelty. She later returned to live with him after the probation service intervened. It was later stated that he had one conviction for assault. If this had been known it seems dreadful that the couple were entrusted with two children (they had none of their own).

The council's school attendance officer who took Dennis to the farm saw nothing wrong, with the boy's intended room being clean and tidy and that seemed good enough to him. Dennis was a fit and healthy boy then. Gough signed paperwork to state he would take care of them and was given almost £2 per week to pay their living costs.

Conditions at the farm for the boys were terrible in many ways. Hard work, beatings and scant food were not unknown among some of those evacuated from London into rural communities during the Second World War. But what happened here was extreme in its nature.

Terrence said that they were ill fed; three pieces of bread and butter and tea and that was all each day. When he and his brother made raids into the pantry for additional food they were often caught and beaten. They were so hungry that they would crawl to the cattle and suck their teats. Dennis was once whacked for taking a bite from a turnip. The post mortem examination on his brother showed that his diet had been wholly inadequate. Dennis weighed four and half stones on death which was a stone and a half underweight. He was thin and wasted. There was no fat under his skin.

Being beaten was commonplace. Sometimes they would receive 100 strokes of a stick, though if the Goughs were tired the boys only received ten at one time. Apart from food raids, these beatings were for taking too long working with the farm's horses, not cleaning the cow house properly, getting their clothes dirty and it was a rare day that neither were punished. Terence later stated, 'Mr Gough stripped Dennis in the kitchen, took him into the back kitchen, told him to get onto the pig bench, tied a rope across his back and fastened him down with it. Then he started hitting him on the top part of the back with a stick and Dennis cried and shouted'. They had to tell Gough at the end of the day what they had done wrong and he would then beat them accordingly. The boys were often locked up in a dark place in the kitchen. Apparently he would also read scripture to the boys and insisted they said their prayers.

The only fun the boys ever had was at school. Dennis recalled that they had to wash in cold water in the farmyard, even during winter time. Terrence later said that he and his brother did misbehave, fighting each other with fists, allowing two calves to die and also abusing chickens at the farm.

Yet when a council clerk visited the farm on 20 December 1944, both boys replied that they were happy, though they were in the presence of the Goughs. However, she was suspicious that there was no affection between the Goughs and the boys, and Dennis seemed ill and frightened. The clerk was planning to recommend their removal and did so on 22 December. By then it may have been too late and nothing was done. It should be noted that the boys attended a nearby school and yet nothing was picked up on.

Matters came to a head on 9 January 1945. This was when Dennis died. On the previous day he had been beaten. On the next day all the household was late to rise. Terrence was up at 9am for breakfast but Dennis was not. Later that morning they found Dennis leaning on the stairs, naked. He was taken back to bed, but Reginald saw nothing to worry about and went about work on the farm. Mrs Gough later said 'He seemed ill, but we did not really know whether he was ill or shamming'. Later that day Mrs Gough began to worry when she saw that Dennis was immobile. She went to a neighbour's house to telephone for a doctor. Dr Holloway Davies of Ministerley arrived and found Dennis had been dead for between four and six hours. In the meantime, Terrence had been told by Mrs Gough that he must tell that the marks on Dennis were caused by himself thumping his brother. The doctor had seen slum conditions in Birmingham but he thought that those at the farm were far worse; the boys' room was cold and dirty and the bedding was far from adequate. He called the police and the Goughs were arrested.

Gough claimed that the boys had been well until early January He claimed that Dennis had always been a weakling. He said that the boy refused his offer of seeking medical attention. His wife told that Terrence was telling lies about the two of them. He was rushed to hospital.

Dr Andrew Rhodes, a pathologist, said that the cause of Dennis' death was the assault which had caused chest injuries, Dennis being so emaciated and weak in his general health. There was malnutrition and chronic sepsis. His feet were ulcerated and so would have been painful to have walked on. There was an inquest at Pontesbury, Shropshire, on 5 February. The public was outraged with large crowds gathered outside the court house and mounted police were needed to keep order.

Gough was charged with manslaughter and neglect, and his wife with being an accessory. Both pleaded not guilty. They were tried at Stafford

Assizes, beginning on 16 March 1945. Terrence was the chief witness for the prosecution as he was the only one who had actually seen what had happened and was prepared to speak about it. He spoke for three and a half hours and was often in tears. Gough stressed that he was lenient and moderate and that the boys were troublesome and needed disciplining occasionally. They were only beaten once a week, so he said. He had played football and indoor games with them, his wife had given them proper meals and Christmas presents. He was not guilty of the charge. His defence barrister stated 'The boys were a pair of little demons…They were wicked and naughty. They were capable of doing each other grave injury'. The prosecution did not claim that the boys were angels but that what the Goughs had done was beyond the pale.

However, on 19 March the jury only needed 23 minutes to decide their verdict and Gough was found guilty of manslaughter, with the judge stating 'you killed, partly by slow and partly by swift means, a boy whom you knew to be in your power' and sentenced him to six years in prison with hard labour; extended to ten after a public outcry. His wife was deemed to have been unable to deal out such severe beatings. But this did not mean that she was necessarily not guilty of child neglect and she was found guilty of that but not guilty of manslaughter and so was sentenced to six months in prison. Justice Wrottesley said at the trial's end that she was deemed to have 'shown a beastly cruelty….your behaviour has, I think, rightly shocked the world and shocked England'.

The councils who put this tragedy – unwittingly – into motion were also censured. They had failed in their duty of care by having no one visit the boys between 23 August and 20 December. There had been no medical inspection of them and nor had the schools officer paid a visit. Wartime conditions had not helped, with a dearth of suitable accommodation, many children being deprived of parental care and a lack of available staff given the competing war demands. Even so, the authorities had failed the children. MPs asked for a public enquiry and the Home Secretary ordered a KC to investigate. Public sympathy for Terrence was profound.

Gough appealed against his sentence, but to no avail. He later complained about its length and the alleged ill treatment he had received in various prisons. Terrence later wrote an autobiography to tell his story. He was unaware of the Agatha Christie play being based in part on his experiences but went to see it and was quite pleased by what he saw. It is not clear what happened to the Goughs; they may well have changed their identities given the hate directed against them. Terrence was still alive in 2015 and the Goughs must have died by then.

Agatha Christie felt strongly about the case and it forms the backstory to *The Mousetrap* which is London's longest running stage play, at St. Martin's Theatre, just off London's Shaftesbury Avenue. In turn it is based on a radio play of 1947 titled *Three Blind Mice* and a subsequent short story, (only ever published in the USA; in 1950). The play was given a new name (taken from *Hamlet*) because of an earlier West End play which had the same name as the short story. It began its theatre run in 1952, only stopping during the covid lockdown of 2020-2021.

The story is set at Monkswell Manor, Berkshire, converted as a guest house run by newlyweds Giles and Mollie Ralston, who know little about each other, having married in haste. The time is a few years after the end of the Second World War. Five guests (a middle-aged Italian, a soldier, two women and a young man) come to stay. The place becomes snowed in and so impossible to leave, and much later the telephone wire is cut. The police ring to say that Detective Sergeant Trotter, will be arriving and he does so, on skis and he then investigates the mystery of who killed Mrs Boyle, one of the guests. The background of the murdered woman is soon revealed, for she was one of the magistrates who made the order for three children to be sent to be fostered with the Lyons. In previous conversation she admitted this but denied all responsibility for what happened to them. She is a cold hearted and self-righteous woman. There is little concern about her.

The harrowing narrative based on the O'Neill case forms the back story to the play. Maureen Lyon and her husband were responsible for the maltreatment of three foster children, the Corrigans. The youngest died. Both Lyons were imprisoned. Mr Lyon died in prison and Maureen was later released. She has been strangled at the play's outset and a notice next to her reads 'This is the First' and gives the address of Monkswell Manor.

The police believe that the oldest of the three children would be a young man in his early 20s now. Following the death of Mrs Boyle, the young male guest, one Christopher Wren, seems the most likely suspect, because he could be the surviving foster brother, out to revenge his dead sibling. Trotter says that this is not necessarily so, because there was a sister, now a young woman, and a father, who was in the army. This implicates Mollie and the two older male guests. It transpires that Mollie was the schoolteacher of the three unfortunate children and that was why she was evasive when questioned earlier. Apparently one of the children wrote to her and she failed to act; but only because she was ill and never received the letter. She is the intended third victim.

To say any more would be the act of a spoilsport and a cad, but the reader can be assured that justice prevails, and the killer is identified. Theatre goers are then urged not to reveal the conclusion. As is often the case with Christie, various characters are not who they appear to be and true identities are revealed at the end, not just that of the killer.

There are obvious similarities between reality and fiction. In reality there were two brothers who were fostered out by a council; in the play there are, for plot purposes, three children. In both cases one of the children dies. The play and story spares the reader/audience the grim details (it is not meant to be that realistic). The back story is very similar, generally speaking, but we are only told about it, not shown it, and the two guilty principals do not feature in the play as characters.

The fate of the guilty is rather different. Gough spent a few years in prison but was released; he did not die in gaol as per his fictional depiction in the story. His wife was released after a few months and was not murdered as in fiction. Terrence later said he would never have done any violence to the Goughs if he had met them as an adult. Those in the local authority were not the targets of someone seeking revenge – or justice. Clearly Christie saw the agents of the council as culpable as the foster parents and this mirrored the opinion of many contemporaries who saw them as blameworthy too.

However, the real events at the farm make a strong background to the story. Theatre goers in 1952 would have been well aware of the shocking case of seven years previously but most in the audience for decades since will be completely unaware of it. Curiously, in her autobiography, the author refers to Dennis O'Neill as Daniel O'Neill, a pardonable slip.

Sources

The National Archives file, Reginald Gough, convicted at Stafford Assizes, HO45/23827

John George Haigh (1944-1949)

One Two, Buckle my Shoe (1940), Ordeal by Innocence (1958), The Mirror Crack'd from Side to Side (1962)

Haigh was one of the most infamous of the post war murderers in Britain. His crimes were perhaps anticipated in the first of these three novels, then referred to both implicitly and explicitly in two later ones.

On Friday 18 February 1949, Mrs Henrietta Helena Olivia Robarts Durand-Deacon, the widow of a solicitor, took leave of her home for the last few years, the Onslow Court Hotel on Queen's Gate, South Kensington. She was a wealthy woman with just over £36,000 to her name. She had made arrangements with a fellow guest, Haigh, who stated that he was an engineer with a workshop in Leopold Road, Crawley and wondered if the old lady might be interested in his project to make false fingernails.

Mrs Durand-Deacon never returned to the hotel and on the next day a friend began to become worried. Courteous as ever, Haigh offered to take her to Chelsea Police Station to report her missing. They did so and a police investigation into the missing woman began. It was soon found that Haigh had a criminal record for fraud and theft dating back to 1934. When questioned, he agreed he had arranged to meet the missing lady on the day of her disappearance but that she never turned up.

The police investigated his workshop in Crawley and received information from shops which had bought valuables belonging to the missing woman. Brought in for questioning again, part of Haigh's next statement read as follows: that after shooting Mrs Durand-Deacon dead in the workshop at Crawley, and taking anything worth selling from her corpse,

> 'I put her in a forty-five gallon tank. I then filled the tank up with sulphuric acid, by means of a stirrup pump from a carboy. I then left it to react. I should have said that in between having

> her in the tank and pumping in the acid I went round to the Ancient Prior's for a cup of tea…On Monday I returned to Crawley to find the reaction almost complete, but a piece of fat and bone was still floating in the sludge. I emptied the sludge off with a bucket and tipped it on the ground opposite the shed'.

Although the term acid bath murderer was employed by the press, it is worth noting that Haigh actually put his victims into a specially coated acid resistant steel drum, not a bath. Wearing a gas mask and other protective clothing he then put their clothed corpses into the drum and then inserted the acid. Dissolution often took a couple of days – not a couple of minutes as per a Bulldog Drummond book. He would then pour the sludge away into the rubbish outside the shed and it would continue to dissolve. Apparently, Haigh came up with the idea when he was in Lincoln prison during the Second World War.

Haigh went on to confess that he had killed five other people between 1944-1948 and destroyed their bodies in the same manner. He had been motivated by money in all cases. In the most recent case he had a negative bank balance and owed money to both the hotel and to various bookmakers. He was desperate for money. He was already on good terms with Mrs Durand-Deacon as they had lived in the same hotel for years and he was a polite, intelligent and charming young man who was able to inveigle his way into Mrs Durand-Deacon's trust.

Haigh thought that if there was no body, then the police could not prove that there had been a murder. *Corpus delicti* was a phrase that he had read and he interpreted it literally. He may have been inspired by a similar case a few years previously. In France, one Georges Alexandre Sarrett, a swindler, dissolved his two victims (an accomplice and his mistress) in sulphuric acid. This occurred in 1925 but he was not arrested until 1931 when another accomplice confessed her knowledge and Sarrett was guillotined in 1934. Like Haigh fifteen years later, Sarrett was known in the British press as 'the acid bath murderer'. Popular thrillers also used the device of an acid bath, as in the 1920 novel *Bulldog Drummond* when a corpse is destroyed in minutes.

Yet even though Haigh's idea that where there is no body no one can be accused of murder, is untrue, pathologist Dr Keith Simpson found enough of the remains of Mrs Durand-Deacon to prove it was her. In particular he found her false teeth and these were identified by the dead woman's dental records. So the sulphuric acid that Haigh used and thought was omnipotent did not destroy everything.

Haigh attempted to show that he was insane and told the police that the murders, where he benefitted financially, were in reality due to his need to drink human blood. Some newspapers referred to him as being a vampire. This was a ploy to escape the gallows. It failed and on 10 August 1949 Haigh was hanged at Wandsworth Prison.

An example of a fictional crime foreshadowing this real life one can be found in *One Two, Buckle my Shoe*. Japp and Poirot are discussing the disappearance of Miss Mabelle Sainsbury Seale. She has been living in a hotel in South Kensington (as per Mrs Durand-Deacon) and the detectives need to talk to her because she was one of the patients who saw a dentist, Mr Morley, shortly before he was shot. No one seems to have seen her after her departure yet she cannot have vanished into thin air. Japp wonders if she might have been dissolved in acid (her disfigured corpse is later found in a house in Battersea).

There is a reference to Haigh in *Ordeal by Innocence* (1958). Before he murdered anyone he had a record of theft and swindles. In this book reference is made to 'Like Harmon…Long record behind him of… swindled money, frauds on elderly women and finally he does one woman in, pickles her in acid, gets pleased with himself and starts making a habit of it'. Haigh's first victim, in 1944, was his apparent friend Donald MacSwan, not a woman, but even so, the parallel is striking.

Haigh is referred to explicitly in *Mirror Crack'd*, 'and that man, Haigh, who pickled them all in acid, they said he couldn't have been more charming'. Not everyone found Haigh to be especially pleasant; a journalist who went to tea with him thought not, but the majority seem to have found him so, including Mrs Durand-Deacon and his other victims.

Sources

Lord Dunboyne, *The Trial of John George Haigh* (1950)

Jonathan Oates, *John George Haigh the acid bath murderer: Portrait of a serial killer and his victims* (2014)

The Great Train Robbery (1963)

At Bertram's Hotel (1965)

Unusually, this was neither a murder nor a crime that occurred in the distant past, but one that was a major item of news in 1963-1964. Perhaps the best known robbery in British history (and until the 1980s, the biggest in terms of value) was the theft which took place in 1963 and has been immortalized and mythologised in film, TV, memoirs of participants and histories. On Wednesday 7 August 1963 the Travelling Post Office diesel train was travelling from Glasgow to London Euston. It left Glasgow at 6.50pm and was expected to make the 401 mile journey by 3.59am on Thursday 8 August. It made seven stops en route to collect mail from various railway stations. It also collected used banknotes; £5, £1 and 10 shilling notes, from bank branches for deposit at their bank headquarters in the City of London.

On this occasion they totalled almost £2.6 million, in 636 packets. These were held in the second of the train carriages, known as the High Value Packages. Unfortunately the train in question was unguarded. There was no communication between carriages or with the outside world. There were no police on board and the doors to the HVP were flimsy. It was a sitting duck to any criminal gang.

At 3am when the train was travelling through Buckinghamshire on the last part of its journey, the signals at Sears Crossing told the train's driver, 57 year old Jack Mills, to stop the train. He did so. The fireman, David Whitby, left the train to go to the telephone box. The wires had been cut and he was approached by three hooded men, who ordered him to stay silent as they bundled him to the ground. Other robbers went to immobilize Mills. He was struck on the head with bars and additionally hit his head when he was knocked over. He was then forced to drive the train a little further to Bridego Bridge.

The assailants then went to the second carriage to take the money. They broke into the carriage and attacked the postal workers there. Seizing the mail bags they transferred them to the three vehicles they had arrived in. They then drove away. It was now 3.30 am. The police were not on the site until nearly an hour later.

The sixteen robbers went back to the place that they were in the process of buying: Leathersdale Farm, near Oakley, about half an hour's drive away. No one knew where they were and they were now rich beyond their dreams. The sixteen men were all from working class backgrounds in London. So far, the plan had worked perfectly.

It was now about to unravel at an alarming speed as the robbers made a very serious blunder. The press took up the story on Friday 9 August. The robbers were aware of this and panicked, believing the police knew rather more than they did. That evening they left the farmhouse. More importantly they left behind a mass of forensic evidence, despite some attempts to burn it.

On Tuesday 13 August, two policemen, hearing about unusual activity near the farm in recent days, decided to investigate. They found a great deal of abandoned equipment. Most significant of all were several of the mailbags taken from the train, with very little of the money still there. Over the next few days fingerprinting yielded much information and given that the thieves all had criminal records, the majority could be identified very quickly. They later claimed that they had arranged for someone to destroy all the evidence but were let down.

Allied to this, the police sought informants who could supply information about the thieves and arrests began to be made. Indeed, in a matter of weeks the majority of the gang had been arrested. Only three evaded capture. The trial of those caught took place at Aylesbury at the Buckinghamshire Assizes in the following year. It was the longest criminal trial to date, and no wonder, with the number of defendants and the seriousness of the crime. On 16 April 1964 the verdict was given: guilty, and 307 years imprisonment in total was given out, with seven men receiving 30 years each (more than most murderers received). These were later reduced on appeal.

Two of the thieves escaped from Wandsworth Prison in 1966, but one was recaptured and two more were arrested and sentenced between 1968-1969. Ronnie Biggs, who had escaped from prison in 1966, and was never one of the leading thieves, became the most well known. He fled to South America and despite attempts of the police to take him, he remained there until 2001 when health problems forced him to return and then served eight years in prison, by which time all his companions had already been long released, some were dead and many had written their memoirs.

The robbery had been a failure. The majority of the criminals spent years in prison, save for Biggs and even he spent some years behind bars as an old man.

Questions remained however. Much of the money was never recovered. There was a question over whether the thieves were given information by a member of postal staff who knew the train schedule and that it would be carrying a more than usual amount of money. Was there a criminal mastermind behind the robbery?

It is noteworthy that the Great Train Robbers are also occasionally called the Bank Robbers; both in real life (by Mary Bell, the murderess) and in Agatha Christie's novel, *Nemesis*. This may seem odd, as they stole from a train. But given that the thieves were taking money that had been in banks, perhaps it is not so absurd a term.

Christie's novel, *At Bertram's Hotel,* was written only two years after the robbery and seems to have been influenced by it. In this novel, Miss Marple spends a holiday at a London hotel she recalled from her youth. It seems to retain its Edwardian values in the middle of the 1960s, 'too good to be true' and the modernisations are all discreetly hidden away.

At the same time there have been a series of major robberies throughout England, by an organised gang who seem to have a member who looks like a prominent and respectable establishment figure, such as a judge in one case and he is often seen at or near the scene of the robbery. These include bank robberies. During Christie's stay at the hotel, there is a train robbery, where the Irish mail train (travelling between London Euston and Holyhead and then onto Dublin and vice versa) is robbed and a substantial sum is taken.

In the book, the Irish mail train is travelling through the night when the guard sees a red signal light ahead. The train begins to slow down and stop. Then six men enter the mail coach from the embankment, joined by another six on the train itself. Two men wear balaclava helmets and stand with coshes. The train crew are bound and gagged. Mailbags are thrown out to be removed to the robbers' den. Newspaper placards declare 'BIG TRAIN ROBBERY. IRISH MAIL ATTACKED BY BANDITS.' In real life the train was stopped by tampering with signals, with a glove of one of them being put over the green light and so halting the train. The driver was indeed coshed; other crew members were also attacked, though they were not bound and gagged, but were told to stay where they were and not to raise the alarm because gang members would be staying behind to keep watch on them. This is a lie that is commonly used by thieves and is never truthful; criminals want to flee from the scene as soon as possible but say otherwise in order to terrify the victims into immobility.

The real life thieves did wear balaclavas and carried pick axe handles to deal with the opposition they might face. None, though, were on the train already in advance of their raid as in fiction. It was certainly a major news story and caught the headlines on the day after the crime, which as noted helped panic the gang into their major blunder.

In the story, the police suspect that there might be links between these robberies, the gang and the hotel. It is eventually found that the hotel is a front for the gang's activities. Loot is stored there and distributed by phoney guests. One of the prominent guests, and a very flamboyant figure, is the gang's leader and they die in a car crash whilst trying to escape and it is presumed the others are rounded up as the hotel's days are at an end.

There are similarities and differences with the Great Train Robbery. The scale and audacity of the crime is similar. But the Great Train Robbery was a one off crime; if it had been successful there would be no more need for any more such heists. The men were brought together for one single raid and there was no clear leader, though sometimes Bruce Reynolds is seen as such. They had never all worked together before but some knew one or more of the others hitherto. They were motivated by money whereas the leader of the fictional gang does so for the thrill of it. No women were prominent in the real life gang, whereas their leader in fiction is female.

Readers would probably have made the connection between such daring robberies on such a scale and the recent Great Train Robbery (a term used by the press and probably copying the title of the 1900s film of the same name). The old fashioned image of the hotel is in stark contrast to the modernity of the crimes which it conceals.

The novel also features a murder, rather late in the narrative, but it is unrelated to the robbery plot. Although the train robbers in reality were violent they were not murderous and no guns were used. The fictional robbers were fairly non-violent as far as is known.

The other link is that in real life Roy John James (1935-1997) was one of the robbers. He was also a racing car driver, having bought a Brabham BT6 with his share of an earlier robbery in which he was the getaway driver.

He had won the junior formula race at Oulton Park in early 1963 and had all the makings of a successful competitor, despite a criminal record for thefts. After the train robbery he spent 12 years in prison and then resumed driving, albeit briefly. In the fictional story one of the gang is Ladislaus Malinowski, a racing driver in his 30s, which is probably not coincidental. In the story he is also the lover of two of the female characters, and provides the motive for murder.

However, there was a robbery on the Irish Mail Train on 20 February 1963 and this is very little known in contrast with the Great Train Robbery of August 1963. Whether Agatha Christie was aware of this earlier robbery is unknown, but it is worth referring to. In this instance the train was held up between Watford and Hemel Hempstead. It was 9.30pm and train staff saw seven or eight masked men rifling through the mail bags in the guard's van and there was a fight. Mr Owen, the guard had already been tied up. One of the two dining car attendants who disrupted the robbers, a Mr Thomas, was injured. Another member of railway staff pulled the communication cord to stop the train.

However, the robbers were able to flee, jumping off the train after the emergency cord was pulled bringing it to a halt. However, very little was stolen; although 27 bags were interfered with, only 17 registered items were missing. Police found abandoned nylon masks near Boxmoor station. A man was questioned at Hemel Hempstead police station about the robbery in the following month, but nothing seems to have come of it. No one was ever charged with these assaults and thefts.

Sources

Andrew Cook, *The Great Train Robbery: The Inside Story* (2013)

Nick Russell-Pavier and Stewart Richards, *The Great Train Robbery: Crime of the Century* (2012)

Something wicked this way comes

Ian Brady and Myra Hindley (1963-1965), Mary Bell (1968), *By the Pricking of My Thumbs (1968), Hallowe'en party (1969), Nemesis (1971)*

The Agatha Christie stories have been criticised by some for being 'cosy' and 'genteel' fantasies, far removed from real world crime and policing. In part this is because the TV dramatizations are set in the aspic of the more civilised, if poorer, 1930s and 1950s. Yet this is not a criticism that can be attached to some of her later works. There is a real sense of evil in these books just cited. This is doubtless the author's response to reality, an increasingly violent and disturbed world spawned by the promiscuity and permissiveness of the 1960s which unleashed unintentional horrors (the abolition of capital punishment in this decade would, it was naively hoped, bring about a more civilised society). This is not to say that the author's works before then had been entirely free from such; in *Dead Man's Folly* (1956) a teenage girl is strangled, in 1952 and 1953 an elderly woman's head is caved in by a chopper and there is a child who murders in *Crooked House* (1949). Neither of the cases about to be discussed are mentioned explicitly in these novels but we would contend that they are informed by them. Christie could have chosen to retreat to the apparently safer world of the past but chose not to and to confront the increasingly disturbing contemporary world.

These cases both involved child murder (not unknown before the 1960s), but both went far further than that. The first concerned a young couple, Ian Brady and Myra Hindley. He was born in Glasgow in 1938 and had an obsession with the Nazis, hated God and admired extremist philosophy. He had a record of petty crime and low level manual and clerical jobs. All this he shared with his younger girlfriend, who was besotted with him and was employed in an office. They were known as the Moors Murderers after they killed four children and one youth (two female and three male) for sexual and sadistic pleasure between July 1963 and October 1965, in and around Manchester.

The first three victims were taken by car or van to Saddleworth Moor to be abused, killed and buried. Pauline Reade, aged 16, knew Myra, as the latter's sister was a schoolfriend of hers. On 12 July, 1963 Pauline was on her way to a dance, when she accepted a lift in Myra's car, never to be seen alive again. John Kilbride, aged 12, was the next unfortunate child, taken at a market on Ashton under Lyme on 23 November 1963. Then there was Keith Bennett, also aged 12, on his way to Longsight to visit his grandmother on 16 June 1964. Ten-year-old Lesley Ann Downey was kidnapped from a fairground in Ancoats on 26 December 1964 and killed. Unlike the first three children, she was killed at the home of Hindley and Brady. The bodies of these four were buried on Saddleworth Moor but Keith's body has never been found. All four were stabbed to death by Ian Brady. Finally, Edward Evans, an apprentice aged 17, was given a lift from Manchester Central Railway Station on 6 October 1965 to be killed with an axe at Brady and Hindley's house in Hattersley but this time there was a witness – Myra's terrified brother-in-law, David Smith, who went to the police and the two were arrested.

It was only then that the full scale of their depravity was revealed and that the missing children had all been murdered. What made these crimes even worse was that the children had been assaulted and tortured and the sadistic Brady recorded Lesley's piteous pleas on tape. Jurors at their trial were forced to listen to such, lasting as it does, 16 minutes. Even reading it on a page is very difficult to say the least. It was also seen as even more heinous in that a young woman was involved in the crimes; although Brady did the killing they could not have been kidnapped without her as she was a driver and he was not. She was perhaps the most hated woman in Britain.

The pair were found guilty at Chester Assizes in April and May 1966 and sentenced to life imprisonment, capital punishment having been suspended for five years in 1965 (and permanently abolished in 1969). They never revealed where all the bodies were buried despite parents' pleas for them to do so so that Christian burials be given. Both Hindley and Brady died in prison (2002 and 2017), despite her attempts to be released on the grounds that she had been sufficiently rehabilitated. It is a very well known case and has been the subject of several books and dramatizations.

Three years later there was the equally disturbing case of Mary Bell in Newcastle upon Tyne. Mary Flora Bell was born in 1957 and by 1968 was living with her mother and stepfather at 70 Whitehouse Road in Scotswood, a deprived part of Newcastle. Next door lived 13-year-old Norma Bell (no relation). The girls often went about together. In May of that year they attacked three other children. One was a boy aged three. Later, on 25 May, four-year-old Martin Brown was found dead outside some derelict houses on Margaret's Road in the district. There was no apparent cause of death but on the next day a nearby day nursery was broken into and found scribbled in note books were the phrases 'We did murder Martain brown' and 'We murdered Martain Go Brown'. Norma and Mary were suspected of having broken in.

On 31 July of that year, like Martin Brown and most other local young children, Brian Howe, aged three, was playing outside the home, unsupervised by adults or anyone else. He went missing that afternoon. In the evening his body was found near Scotswood Road. He had been strangled. The evidence was that another child was responsible. Mary and Norma Bell were eventually arrested and charged with the murders. Both blamed the other. It was Mary who was found guilty at Newcastle Assizes of double manslaughter (not murder because of diminished responsibility) and sentenced to life imprisonment. Norma was acquitted. Mary was sent to a boys' approved school in Lancashire and then to a women's prison and was released in 1980 and was given a new identity. At the time of writing, she is still alive. That a child could murder other children was deemed beyond the pale, though Harold Jones had done likewise in Abertillery four decades earlier.

As far removed from the genteel world of Miss Marple as can be imagined, you might think. Yet in two novels published in the late 1960s, *By the Pricking of my Thumbs* and *Hallowe'en Party*, multiple child murder features for the first time and the inspiration for such may well have been the Moors case and that of Mary Bell. In the latter novel, as Ariadne Oliver states 'children do queer things sometimes. I mean there are queer children about…and then they go about and do something like this'. The suspicion is that the killings may be the work of teenagers (they turn out not to be).

Two children are murdered in *Hallowe'en Party,* both by drowning. These are thirteen-year-old Joyce Reynolds (drowned in an apple bobbing tub at a party in a house) and later, Leopold, her younger brother (drowned in a stream). A third child is targeted but saved at the last minute. Though the motive in all these cases is to prevent disclosures about past crimes rather than anything resembling the Moors crimes, it is significant that children are involved as they do not play a major role in any of Christie's books previously, except for *Crooked House*. It is not the kind of crime that she would have written about in the apparently more peaceful 1920s and 1930s.

The prevalence of violent crime committed by or to children is commented on several times throughout the book. Mrs Oliver says, of Joyce, the first victim, who is aged 13, that she is 'rather mature, perhaps. Lumpy'.

Poirot replies, 'Well developed? You mean sexy looking?'

'Yes, that is what I mean. But I don't think that was the kind of crime it was – I mean that would have made it more simple, wouldn't it?

Poirot replies to Mrs Oliver thus: 'It is the kind of crime…of which one reads every day in the paper. A girl who is attacked, a school child who is assaulted – yes every day'. He later muses 'It was not unknown in the present age for children to commit crimes, quite young children. Children of seven, or nine and so on and it was often difficult to know how to dispose of these natural young criminals'.

Superintendent Spence states 'There doesn't seem to have been any evidence of any sexual assault or anything of that kind, which would be the first thing one looks for. Plenty of that sort of thing in every small town or village'. Dr Ferguson agrees, 'Mind you, doing in a child isn't anything to be startled about nowadays. I've been called out to look at too many murdered children in the last seven to ten years – far too many'.

References to a' sexually disturbed personality' and that there was 'no evidence of sexual assault' are very contemporary terms. There is mention twice of children getting into someone's car and never seen alive again and this chimes in with the Moors murders.

As to the perpetrators, Dr Ferguson tells Poirot, 'The reason's in the killer's mind. His disturbed mind or his evil mind or his kinky mind. Any kind of mind you like to call him…Take your man or boy. He wants to kill someone. Not at all unusual. Over in Medchester we had a case of that. Came to light after about six or seven years. Boy of thirteen. Wanted to kill someone, so he killed a child of nine, pinched a car, drove it seven or eight miles into a copse, burned her there…he may have gone on doing it. Probably did. Found he liked killing people'. His comments certainly align with the motivation of Ian Brady whose reasoning was internal to him, as opposed to any conventional and rational reason such a greed or revenge. As to the reasons for such crimes, 'Broken homes. Negligent and unsuitable parents' are blamed and that was exactly what was said, broadly speaking, about Mary Bell. Maybe the author had her in mind when she has a female character say 'I knew a little girl once. Seven years old. Killed her little brother and sister – twins they were – five or six months old. Beautiful little creature she was, too. Rotten on the inside'. This occurred in Yorkshire.

In *By the Pricking of my Thumbs*, we learn that 20 years ago, so in the late 1940s, there were 'Child Murders' in a particular rural locality. A little girl of nine failed to return home from school one day and was later found strangled in the woods: 'Makes me shiver to think about it', says Mrs Copleigh. Three weeks later, at another location but within the same district, another child was found dead, easily done by the same hand if the killer had a car. 'And then there were others. Not for a month or two sometimes. And then there'd be another one'.

It is later stated that at least three children have been killed, but not how many nor who the children were (or even the sex of most of them), nor their age. Apparently the killings took place 'Over six months it was, nearly a year. Then the whole thing stopped...he must have gone away. Gone away altogether'. The killer was never caught and an outraged local tells Tuppence Beresford, 'Maniac I suppose it must have been, it's awful, that there should be men like that. They ought to be shot. They ought to be strangled themselves. And I'd do it to them for one...Any man who kills children and assaults them. What's the good putting them in loony bins and living soft. And then and sooner or later they let them out again, say they're cured and send them home.' This could also be a reference to the John Thomas Straffen case in the 1950s when double child murderer Straffen was sent to Broadmoor, escaped and killed again before being incarcerated in a number of conventional prisons (where he died in 2007).

It is also assumed that the police suspect who the culprit is but have not the evidence to proceed. There is the possibility that the killer has been provided with an alibi by family or friends and the police are unable to break that. The killer is described as someone who lives within a 20 mile radius of the murders. Amos Perry – 'a bit queer, you know, simple minded' – is a suspect, as is Sir Philip Starke, a wealthy man, married but childless. He is noted as being fond of children, giving them parties, giving children sweets or money but an 'odd man' and no longer living locally.

The killer turns out to be a woman. After an abortion as a teenager she is unable to have children. She is later struck with religious mania, believing that she is told by voices to go out and kill children because they are without sin and would never know it and the innocents are then sent to Heaven to join the child she lost. These she refers to as sacrifices, to atone for her murder as she describes the abortion. She is married and her wealthy husband takes her abroad and then relates how his wife has died, whereas she has not. When she first meets Tuppence early in the story she says 'Was it your poor child?' thinking she was a mother of one of the victims. The idea about religious mania being a motive for murder may originate from theories about the motivation behind the Jack the Ripper murders of 1888.

In *Nemesis,* the last Miss Marple novel to be written, two teenage girls have been murdered, possibly by Michael Rafiel, son of millionaire Jason Rafiel. He was to marry the young Verity Hunt, but she disappeared just before the marriage and he is described as 'a wicked devil' who has in the past been charged with assault and rape. it was thought he had killed her. Six months later the body of a teenage girl is found in a quarry 30 miles away, strangled and with her head beaten in, but the corpse is identified as Verity by one of her guardians, Miss Clotilde Bradbury-Scott, with whom she lived. Another young woman, Nora Broad, from a working-class background, has also disappeared, and it is feared, has been killed as well, as she was last seen taking a lift in a car. Miss Marple later says, 'Not a very nice business' and later sums up her thoughts, 'I don't like that sort of thing…I do not like evil beings who do evil things'.

Nemesis is not obviously directly linked to the Moors Murders or to those of Mary Bell, but can be seen in the same milieu of increasingly vicious crime amongst the young. One point of interest is Miss Marple's dismissal of 'excuses' for such behaviour, for instance an unhappy childhood or bad environments. Here Agatha Christie clearly holds a more conservative view than Gitta Sereny, who in her book about Mary Bell cites at length the girl's troubled domestic life with her far from caring mother as a key factor behind her crimes.

Several characters in *Hallowe'en Party* refer to crimes committed by and against the young, and by the mentally ill as being on the increase compared with the past. There is no statistical evidence given and whether this is the commonplace harking back to a golden age that never was is another question. It is also worth noting that in none of these fictional crimes there is a sexual motive, but it is a red herring that the author uses to conceal the true culprits. The reader may fall for such a deception device because Christie is using themes taken from contemporary true crimes that readers at the time would have been fully aware of. Finally, we should remember one of the lines from the prologue of *Passenger to Frankfurt* (1970), of depressing elements of the times, one being 'Children missing and children's murdered bodies found not far from their homes'.

Sources

Gitta Sereny, *The Case of Mary Bell* (1973)
David Kynaston, *A Northern Wind: Britain, 1962-1965* (2023)

Murders and murderers anticipated

John Reginald Christie (1943-1953), Graham Young (1971), Roland Roussel (1977), *The Thumb Mark of St. Peter (in: The Thirteen Problems, 1932), The ABC Murders (1936), The Pale Horse (1961))*

There are several real-life crimes which were inadvertently and coincidentally foreshadowed in some of Agatha Christie's books.

One of these is the apparent killer in the *ABC Murders*. This is Alexander Bonaparte Cust, an unemployed clerk. He is a veteran of the First World War, a bachelor, fairly well educated but a seeming nonentity. Living on the edge of poverty and unemployment he leads a precarious social and economic existence. This is why he is so attractive to the real murderer who uses him as his dupe. The reader is led to believe that this very insignificant man is committing murders in order to prove to himself and the world that he is a man who lives up to the ridiculous Christian names given to him. Psychologically this is plausible and the lives of later real-life serial killers often reveal them to be men of little interest or notability and that is perhaps part of the reason that they kill in order to elevate themselves.

It seems to the authors that this man, in some ways, resembles John Reginald Halliday Christie of 10 Rillington Place, one of the most notorious murderers of the post war era. Christie had served in the First World War as a signaller attached to the Nottinghamshire and Derbyshire Regiment. He had been wounded at Mont Kammel in 1918 during the final German offensive on the Western Front. Christie was given a small war pension, but he exaggerated his injuries, claiming he had been blinded and had lost his voice. The former is not supported by medical records and the latter is also dubious. Yet he had a 'good character' whilst in the army and later claimed he was well thought of as a soldier.

Christie had many different jobs over the next few decades of his life. He was in the RAF, the War Reserve Constabulary and worked as a postman, a lorry driver and a cinema foreman. As he was fairly well educated for a man of his background and intelligent with an IQ of 128, he also took a number of clerical jobs. When he met his wife in 1920 he was employed as a clerk. He was a ledger clerk again in the Post Office after the Second World War and from 1950-1952 did likewise in the British Road Services.

Cust is also employed as a clerk. And like John Reginald Christie he seems to have taken pride in his war service. Cust later tells Poirot, 'I enjoyed the war – what I had of it, that was. I was as good as anyone else'. As with Christie, he was wounded and then discharged. The similarity between the two men extends to their appearance, both having rather nondescript personalities. Christie was smartly dressed, earning as a clerk about £400 a year, but lived in what were almost slum dwellings in Notting Hill. He did not make much of an impression on others. 'The sort of man you don't look twice at on the bus' he said modestly of himself. Compare this with how a witness describes Cust, 'He had glasses, I think – and a shabby overcoat. He wasn't the sort of man you'd notice'.

As a boy John Reginald Christie had felt very inferior to his fellow lads, especially where the opposite sex was concerned. and he had a fear and hatred of women. Yet, as with Cust, some women did find him an object of sympathy (Cust's landlady's daughter, Lily Marbury, has some sympathy for him and rings him to let him know that the police are after him, it will be remembered). Mary O'Neill later said of Christie 'He spoke well and seemed to be very generous. He always seemed kind and gentle and rather sad and I felt sorry for him'. Lilly Taylor likewise remarked 'I felt sorry for him after the other trouble [there had been a double murder at the same house] and it always seemed as if he wanted to stop and speak to people. He was always very polite'.

John Reginald Christie, unlike Cust, had a lengthy criminal record. In 1921 in his native Halifax, he was found guilty of theft whilst a postman and in 1923 he took money under false pretences. In London in 1924 he stole a bicycle and money and in 1929 attacked the woman he was living with. Four years later he stole a car belonging to his employers. These are the crimes that we know about in these two decades.

Worse was to come. In 1943 he committed his first murder, strangling Ruth Fuerst at his home and burying her corpse in the back garden; in the next year he did likewise to Muriel Eady. Although the disappearances were reported there was no effective investigation during wartime and Christie got away with two murders. His motive was sexual in both cases and in the second case he used gas to render his victim unconscious prior to killing her.

In 1952 he killed his wife, Ethel, almost certainly so that he could lure other women back to his rooms. In the first three months of 1953 he killed Kathleen Maloney, Rita Elizabeth Nelson and Hectorina MacLennan. As with Muriel, he used gas to render them unconscious, assaulted them and then strangled them. His wife's body was put under the floorboards; the others in an alcove in the kitchen, before being papered over. He invited others to his lair but claimed no more victims.

Christie, running out of money, left the house and then his crimes were discovered by other tenants. He was arrested on 31 March near Putney Bridge and charged with the murder of his wife. Standing trial at the Old Bailey he pleaded guilty but insane. The jury found him guilty but sane. He was executed at Pentonville Prison on 15 July 1953. This pathetic end is not dissimilar to Cust's, who leaves his lodgings and soon runs out of money, finally handing himself over to the police.

Finally, we might observe the name of the doctor in *The Hollow* (1946); John Christow. John Reginald Christie liked to pretend that he had either been training as a doctor or had been one. In reality he knew and practised First Aid.

It has been recently suggested by Carla Valentine that there was 'an uncanny parody of the methods of Agatha Christie's ABC Killer' in Rochester, New York State in 1971-1973. Three girls were killed; Carmen Colon in Churchville, Michelle Maenza in Macedon and Wanda Walkowicz in Webster. In the novel, Alice Ascher is killed in Andover, Betty Barnard in Bexhill and Sir Carmichael Clarke in Churston. However, as Carla Valentine says, there's no evidence these and similar crimes were inspired by the novel.

The most famous example of an Agatha Christie novel foreshadowing a real-life murder is probably *The Pale Horse*. In this highly original and intriguing story, several unrelated deaths occur, apparently from natural causes. Although there is talk about the deaths being due in some mysterious way to witchcraft and a 'death wish', they are the work of a murderous gang who are being paid to kill people. The method is to ascertain what products – cosmetics, food, drink – the intended victim uses and then to insert poison into these items. The poison in question is thallium, a tasteless and water-soluble compound causing multi-organ toxicity. Symptoms of thallium poisoning are often nonspecific, such as fever, gastrointestinal disturbances, and skin hyperesthesia, mimicking natural disease. The most characteristic sign is alopecia (loss of hair).

The narrator in *The Pale Horse*, Mark Easterbrook, tells Chief Inspector Lejeune:

> 'I read an article on thallium poisoning when I was in America. A lot of workers in a factory died one after the other. Their deaths were put down to astonishingly varied causes'.

Eerily enough, this is exactly what happened in 1971 – ten years after the publication of *The Pale Horse* – when several employees at a firm manufacturing photographic equipment in Bovingdon, Hertfordshire, fell ill. One man developed neurological signs and died, death being attributed to the Guillain-Barré syndrome (a form of polyneuropathy). Two others lost their hair and were severely ill but survived. Finally, yet another man died, being paralysed and blind at the end. The firm conducted an investigation, which initially focused on an infectious agent – 'the Bovingdon bug' – as the cause of the mysterious illness. After a while, suspicions arose against a newly employed storeman, 24-year-old Graham Young. He had displayed an unusual knowledge of poisons and been very keen to hear how his sick colleagues were doing.

The head of the firm contacted the police and Young was arrested. A search of his lodgings revealed toxicology books, bottles containing various poisons – chief among them thallium and antimony – and a diary in which he had recorded the results of his 'experiments'. The victims were referred to by their initials. A typical entry read: 'I have administered a fatal dose of the special compound to F and anticipate a report on his progress on Monday 1 November… F is now seriously ill…It is better that he should die…If he lives it could be inconvenient. Too many health authorities are becoming involved for me to press the matter further'.

Interrogated by the police, Young calmly talked like a scientist about the effects of poisons. He claimed that the diary consisted of notes he was preparing for a novel but eventually admitted to having poisoned eight people within the space of less than a year. When the astonished police officers asked about his motive he replied: 'I suppose I had ceased to see them as people – or, more correctly, a part of me had. They became guinea pigs.' After a ten-day long trial at St Albans Crown Court, Graham Young was found guilty on two charges of murder and sentenced to life imprisonment on 29 June 1972.

This was not the whole story, however. After the jury delivered its verdict, Young's barrister revealed that this was not the first time his client had been convicted of poisoning people. From a young age, Graham had been fascinated by poisons, reading everything he could get hold of about toxicology and famous poisoners. In 1961, at the age of 13, he managed to acquire antimony and thallium from chemists, pretending to be older and in need of the poisons for chemical experiments. He then started to poison members of his own family as well as a school friend. His father, although seriously ill, survived. Graham's stepmother died in 1962, her death attributed to complications of a prolapsed disc. Many years later, he confessed to having killed her with a lethal dose of thallium.

On trial at the Old Bailey in July 1962 – by now 14 years old – Graham Young pleaded guilty to three counts of poisoning and was sentenced to be detained at Broadmoor. In early 1971 he was released by the Home Office, upon the recommendation of psychiatrist Edgar Udwin, who considered that 'profound changes' had taken place inside the mind of his patient, and that Young was 'no longer a danger to others'. After Young's second conviction in 1972, this sad misjudgement led to a review of the procedures for releasing offenders from psychiatric hospitals.

The Pale Horse came to attention during Young's second trial when it was mentioned that Dr Hugh Johnson – a forensic pathologist consulted by the police – had recognized the symptoms of Young's final victim as being similar to those described in the novel (which he had just read) and had told police that thallium could have been used. There was some criticism against Agatha Christie in the press, however, for having highlighted thallium and possibly inspired Young to use this deadly poison. He himself denied ever having read the book and – considering his lifelong obsession with toxicology and poisons – it seems unlikely that he would have needed inspiration from a crime novel. On a positive note, *The Pale Horse* is said to have saved two lives after readers recognised the symptoms of thallium poisoning from the description in the book.

Another interesting parallel between *The Pale Horse* – or, rather, the inspiration for it – and real-life poisoner Graham Young is provided by Agatha Christie in her autobiography. She tells the story of how she worked as a hospital dispenser during the First World War and had as a supervisor a certain Mr P. Despite having a 'cherubic appearance' he struck Christie as 'possibly rather a dangerous man'. He was in the habit of carrying in his pocket a lump of curare, explaining to his puzzled pupil that it made him feel powerful. Agatha Christie could never forget Mr P and his curare and many decades later modelled one of the characters in *The Pale Horse* after him. Graham Young, when arrested the first time as a teenager, was found to carry a small vial of antimony in his shirt. After it had been taken away, he told a psychiatrist: 'I miss my antimony. I miss the power it gives me'.

The Pale Horse resurfaced in another poisoning case nearly 30 years after the Graham Young affair. This time the place was Florida, USA, where a chemist and member of the high-IQ club Mensa called George Trepal was sentenced to death in 1991 for having poisoned his neighbour, waitress Peggy Carr, with thallium. His method was to insert the poison into Coca-Cola bottles, which is reminiscent of the way thallium is put into household products in *The Pale Horse*. Indeed, a copy of the novel was found in Trepal's house, although it could not be proved that he had been inspired by it.

In 1977, Agatha Christie's short story 'The Thumb Mark of St. Peter', from *The Thirteen Problems* (1932), allegedly inspired a bizarre murder by poisoning in France. On Christmas Eve, 80-year-old Maxime Massiron and his wife in Créances, Normandy, toasted each other with a glass of red wine. Minutes later both collapsed. Maxime died and his wife was in a coma for more than a week, doctors attributing their illness to food poisoning. A few days later, their son-in-law and another man visited the apartment and found the wine bottle still on the table. Helping themselves to some wine both men fell unconscious to the floor. Fortunately, both survived.

Police were called in and the remains of the wine analysed, revealing it had been laced with large amounts of atropine, an alkaloid derived from belladonna (deadly nightshade). Commonly used in eye drops to dilate the pupil, atropine acts as an antagonist to the receptors of acetylcholine. If ingested or injected in toxic doses, atropine can cause circulatory collapse, coma and death. The poisoned wine bottle was quickly traced to 58-year-old Roland Roussel, a nephew of the Massirons. He admitted to having added atropine from an eye drop solution to the bottle, which he afterwards had presented as a gift to his uncle and aunt. The intention was not to poison the Massirons, however, but a friend of theirs, a woman who often came for a visit and usually had a glass of wine (the Massirons themselves drank alcohol only on special occasions).

Roussel told the police that he was convinced that this unnamed woman had caused the death of his mother by poisoning, and thus had decided to let her taste her own medicine. Unfortunately, his uncle and aunt became innocent victims. A search of Roussel's apartment revealed a copy of *The Thirteen Problems*, with some passages underlined in 'The Thumb Mark of St. Peter'. This is a Miss Marple story, involving the murder of a man by atropine poisoning. It turns out that the murderer, a close relative, has added atropine eye drops to the victim's water glass. A French police spokesman reportedly declared, 'I'm not saying Roussel was inspired by the book, but we found it in his apartment with the relevant passages on poison underlined'.

Sources

F. Tennyson-Jesse, *The Trials of Evans and Christie* (1957)
Jonathan Oates, *John Christie of Rillington Place: Biography of a serial killer* (2012)
Carla Valentine, *Murder isn't Easy: The forensics of Agatha Christie* (2021)
Anthony Holden, *The St Albans poisoner* (second edition 1995)
Winifred Young, *Obsessive poisoner – the strange story of Graham Young* (1973)

Afterword

The reader is now more informed about the true crimes and real-life criminals that are referred to in Agatha's books. Certainly, the authors are. Of Christie's works, at least 53 (well over half) allude either explicitly or implicitly to real crime. There is a great diversity in the number of times that some criminals have been referenced, with one mentioned a dozen times and some only once, and a few several times. Crippen, for instance, has most references, with a dozen. Then there is Major Armstrong with ten. Lizzie Borden is mentioned in seven stories. The Brighton Trunk murders are referred to on five occasions. George Joseph Smith and Bywaters and Thompson have four references each. About half the criminals are only mentioned once or twice. Some are mentioned by their real name and some, such as Katie Whistance and Harold Greenwood by a pseudonym.

What was it about these oft mentioned criminals which made Christie refer to them over and over again? As has been said, George Orwell referred to Crippen, Armstrong, Smith and Bywaters and Thompson in his handful of classic criminals, so she was not alone in acknowledging their significance. All four were covered in the Notable British Trials series. Even now, they are not forgotten, with new books on all of these being produced this century; in some case more than one. Whereas, to date Katie Whistance and, perhaps more surprisingly, the Brighton Trunk murders have never been studied in any detail.

There are also times where these are just references, as with Mr Entwistle thinking of a number of criminals in *After the Funeral*. In other books part of the plot resembles real murderous activities; such as the plate of fish paste sandwiches in *Sad Cypress* mirroring the Annie Hearn murders of a decade previously. The back story to *Mrs McGinty's Dead* is clearly informed by Crippen's story. *A Caribbean Mystery* is strongly based on George Joseph Smith's crimes. *Murder on the Orient Express* uses a real crime as its backcloth, as does *The Mousetrap*.

Comparisons are sometimes made between real criminals and those in the stories; Kenneth Marshall in *Evil Under the Sun*, or rather his cool demeanour, is likened to that of Herbert Wallace in 1931. Crippen and Armstrong are sometimes compared to suspects because of their apparently meek and polite personalities.

Why some real criminals are referred to by other names is unclear. Why Patrick Mahon is called Castor in *Murder is Easy* fifteen years after his execution, and Haigh likewise in *Ordeal by Innocence* a decade after his demise is a mystery. References to Greenwood had to be guarded as he was found not guilty and so perhaps was thought still to be alive when references to him were made in the fiction.

Although the books refer to many of the most well known cases of the Victorian period to the 1960s, some are excluded. The murderesses such as Katie Webster in 1879, Florence Maybrick in 1889, the serial poisoners Amelia Winters and Mary Ann Cotton nor baby farmer Amelia Dyer in the same period and the doctors Palmer and Pritchard do not make an appearance in any obvious shape or form. However, save for *And then there were none* and perhaps *Murder is Easy*, the murders in her books often 'only' number one or two.

It may seem odd that Jack the Ripper is spoken of in but two books, given the preponderance of the Ripper 'industry' in recent decades. Yet this was not the case in Christie's lifetime and nor do his ghastly deeds have much resonance in her more 'civilised' and logical crimes. Serial killers in reality are rare indeed and so Christie's fiction resembles reality more than modern fiction in which the serial killer is very frequent indeed.

Christie's knowledge and interest in true crime is in part because she lived through many of these criminals being reported in the press in her lifetime as an adult, which she would have read about at the time. Newspapers covered notable trials in detail in the early to mid twentieth century in a way inconceivable now. She never wrote any true crime books per se, however.

Her thinking on these crimes and criminals is in accordance with how most thought of them at the time. Recent views about the possible innocence of Crippen and Armstrong are not to be found here, but the idea expressed by her that Ethel le Neve was not wholly innocent in the murder of her rival is perhaps more commonplace now than it was.

Christie's approach to crime was conservative; she has Poirot state, 'I do not approve of murder', yet in one case where formal law is powerless, he does just that, and in another the killer suggests that he condones such a second time. In another story she has Miss Marple regret the passing of capital punishment. In her autobiography and in *Ordeal by Innocence*, she emphasises that it is the innocent who matter, not the guilty and that the latter need to be kept away from the former.

The world of the Christie canon is fictional, but its background is not. As part of this, the real criminal world is often referenced and at time even used in the plot or its backstory. If this book has shone an explanatory light on these true crime cases then it has achieved its aim.

Acknowledgements

The authors would like to thank several people for helping with the creation of this book. Lindsay Siviter read through several chapters in the book and gave suggestions for improvements; she also lent several pictures from her collection to be used herein. Paul Lang allowed the authors use of one of his postcards. John Gauss read some of the book and helped improve the language and grammar. More anonymously, archivists and librarians from the National Archives and the British Library provided many of the primary sources needed for this book.

List of Illustrations

Source: Wikimedia Commons unless otherwise stated.

Appendix

True crime references in Agatha Christie's stories

Agatha Christie novels, short stories and plays containing true crime references (year refers to publication date of first UK edition; for plays, opening night)	**Real life crime/criminal (year refers to date of crime, * = indirect reference)**
The Mysterious Affair at Styles (1920)	*Frederick Henry Seddon (1911)**
Murder on the Links (1923)	*Marguerite Steinheil (1908)* *Brides in the Bath (1912-1914)*
The Man in the Brown Suit (1924)	*Dr Hawley Harvey Crippen (1910)*
The Murder of Roger Ackroyd (1926)	*Dr Hawley Harvey Crippen (1910)*
The Mystery of the Blue Train (1928)	*Dr Hawley Harvey Crippen (1910)*
Partners in Crime (1929)	*Major Herbert Rowse Armstrong (1921)**
The Murder at the Vicarage (1930)	*Dr Hawley Harvey Crippen (1910)*
Peril at End House (1932)	*Major Herbert Rowse Armstrong (1921)**
The Thirteen Problems (1932)	*Harold Greenwood (1919)** *Roland Roussel (1977)**
Lord Edgware Dies (1933)	*Elizabeth Canning (1753)*
Murder on the Orient Express (1934)	*The Lindbergh kidnapping (1932)*
The Listerdale Mystery (1934)	*Brides in the Bath (1912-1914)**

Agatha Christie novels, short stories and plays containing true crime references (year refers to publication date of first UK edition; for plays, opening night)	**Real life crime/criminal (year refers to date of crime, * = indirect reference)**
Death in the Clouds (1935)	*The Stavisky affair (1934)*
Three Act Tragedy (1935)	*Dr Hawley Harvey Crippen (1910)* *Major Herbert Rowse Armstrong (1921)**
The ABC Murders (1936)	*Jack the Ripper (1888)* *John Reginald Christie (1943-1953)**
Cards on the Table (1936)	*Brighton Trunk Murders (1934)*
Dumb Witness (1937)	*Brighton Trunk Murders (1934)** *Dr Buck Ruxton (1935)**
And Then There Were None (1939)	*Lizzie Borden (1892)*
Murder is Easy (1939)	*Major Herbert Rowse Armstrong (1921)** *Patrick Herbert Mahon (1924)**
One, Two, Buckle my Shoe (1940)	*Norman Thorne (1924)** *Dr Buck Ruxton (1935)** *John George Haigh (1944-1949)**
Sad Cypress (1940)	*Annie Hearn (1930)*
Evil Under the Sun (1941)	*William Herbert Wallace (1931)*
The Body in the Library (1942)	*The Blazing Car Mystery (1930)* *Brighton Trunk Murders (1934)* *Ruby Keen (1937)*
Five Little Pigs (1942)	*Dr Hawley Harvey Crippen (1910)*
The Moving Finger (1943)	*Lizzie Borden (1892)*
The Labours of Hercules (1947)	*Dr Hawley Harvey Crippen (1910)* *Harold Greenwood (1919)** *Major Herbert Rowse Armstrong (1921)* *Brighton Trunk Murders (1934)*
Crooked House (1949)	*Constance Kent (1860)* *Bywaters and Thompson (1922)*
A Murder is Announced (1950)	*Harold Greenwood (1919)**
They Came to Baghdad (1951)	*Horatio Bottomley (1922)*
They Do It with Mirrors (1952)	*Major Herbert Rowse Armstrong (1921)**

Agatha Christie novels, short stories and plays containing true crime references (year refers to publication date of first UK edition; for plays, opening night)	**Real life crime/criminal (year refers to date of crime, * = indirect reference)**
Mrs McGinty's Dead (1952)	*Dr Hawley Harvey Crippen (1910)* *Katie Whistance (1920)** *Bywaters and Thompson (1922)*
The Mousetrap (play) (1952)	*Reginald Gough (1945)**
After the Funeral (1953)	*Lizzie Borden (1892)* *Frederick Henry Seddon (1911)* *Brides in the Bath (1912-1914)* *Major Herbert Rowse Armstrong (1921)* *Bywaters and Thompson (1922)* *The Blazing Car Mystery (1930)* *Dorothea Waddingham (1935)*
A Pocketful of Rye (1953)	*Bywaters and Thompson (1922)*
Witness for the Prosecution (play) (1954)	*Adolf Beck (1896, 1904)*
Destination Unknown (1954)	*Klaus Fuchs (1950)*
4.50 from Paddington (1957)	*Brighton Trunk Murders (1934)**
Ordeal by Innocence (1958)	*Charles Bravo (1876)* *Lizzie Borden (1892)* *John George Haigh (1944-1949)**
Cat Among the Pigeons (1959)	*Jack the Ripper (1888)* *Dr Thomas Neill Cream (1891-1892)*
The Pale Horse (1961)	*Madeleine Smith (1857)* *Graham Young (1971)**
The Mirror Crack'd from Side to Side (1962)	*Dr Hawley Harvey Crippen (1910)* *John George Haigh (1944-1949)**
The Clocks (1963)	*Constance Kent (1860)* *Charles Bravo (1876)* *Adelaide Bartlett (1886)* *Lizzie Borden (1892)* *Portland spy ring (1960)*
A Caribbean Mystery (1964)	*Brides in the Bath (1912-1914)*

Agatha Christie novels, short stories and plays containing true crime references (year refers to publication date of first UK edition; for plays, opening night)	**Real life crime/criminal (year refers to date of crime, * = indirect reference)**
At Bertram's Hotel (1965)	*Major Herbert Rowse Armstrong (1921)** *The Great Train Robbery (1963)*
Third Girl (1966)	*The Tichborne claimant (1874)* *Dr Hawley Harvey Crippen (1910)*
By the Pricking of My Thumbs (1968)	*Major Herbert Rowse Armstrong (1921)* *Moors Murderers (1963-1965)** *Mary Bell (1968)**
Hallowe'en Party (1969)	*Moors Murderers (1963-1965)** *Mary Bell (1968)**
Passenger to Frankfurt (1970)	*Cambridge five spies (1934-1951)*
Nemesis (1971)	*Moors Murderers (1963-1965)** *Mary Bell (1968)**
Elephants Can Remember (1972)	*Charles Bravo (1876)* *Lizzie Borden (1892)*
Poirot's Early Cases (1974)	*Harold Greenwood (1919)* *Major Herbert Rowse Armstrong (1921)** *Brighton Trunk Murders (1934)**
Sleeping Murder (1976)	*Madeleine Smith (1857)* *Lizzie Borden (1892)* *Dr Hawley Harvey Crippen (1910)* *Major Herbert Rowse Armstrong (1921)* *William Herbert Wallace (1931)*
Miss Marple's Final Cases (1979)	*Dr Hawley Harvey Crippen (1910)*

Index